Dedicated to my father, Santosh Saha, and mother, Ranu Saha
and
my husband, Subhash Bagui
and
my sons, Sumon and Sudip
and
my brother, Pradeep, and niece, Priyashi
S.B.

To my wife, Brenda,
and
my children: Beryl, Rich, Gen, and Mary Jo
R.E.

Learning SQL:
A Step by Step
Guide Using Access®

SIKHA BAGUI AND RICHARD EARP

PEAR
Addison
Wesley

Boston San Francisco New York
London Toronto Sydney Tokyo Singapore Madrid
Mexico City Munich Paris Cape Town Hong Kong Montreal

Senior Acquisitions Editor	Maite Suarez-Rivas
Executive Editor	Susan Hartman Sullivan
Project Editor	Katherine Harutunian
Executive Marketing Manager	Michael Hirsch
Production Supervisor	Marilyn Lloyd
Project Management	Argosy Publishing
Composition and Art	Argosy Publishing
Proofreader	Kim Cofer
Cover Design	Gina Hagen Kolenda
Cover Image	From the RF Artville CD, The Big Idea, Rob Colvin
Prepress and Manufacturing	Caroline Fell

Access the latest information about Addison-Wesley titles from our World Wide Web site: *http://www.aw.com/cs*

Many of the designations used by manufacturers and sellers to distinguish their products are claimed as trademarks. Where those designations appear in this book, and Addison-Wesley was aware of a trademark claim, the designations have been printed in initial caps or all caps.

The programs and applications presented in this book have been included for their instructional value. They have been tested with care, but are not guaranteed for any particular purpose. The publisher does not offer any warranties or representations, not does it accept any liabilities with respect to the programs or applications.

Library of Congress Cataloging-in-Publication Data

Bagui, Sikha, 1964-

Learning SQL : a step by step guide using Access / Sikha Bagui and Richard Earp.

p. cm.

ISBN 0-321-11904-5

1. SQL (Computer program language) 2. Microsoft Access. 3. Database Management. I. Earp, Richard, 1940- II. Title.

QA76.73.S67E28 2003

005.75'65—dc21

2002043791

ISBN 0-321-11904-5

1 2 3 4 5 6 7 8 9 10-DOC-060504

Contents

Preface

Recent years have seen a dramatic increase in the use of SQL to manage databases. Given this technological climate, the computer industry needs application developers who can write SQL code efficiently. However, despite this need, very few books are available that employ a step-by-step systematic approach to learning SQL. Most SQL books on the market today discuss several SQL concepts, but these discussions are scattered throughout the book, making it very difficult for the beginner to grasp the concepts. These books generally are written for people who already understand SQL. Furthermore, even though Microsoft Access is one of the most widely used implementations of SQL on the market, few of the numerous books written about the menu-oriented features and other aspects of Access even mention the SQL features of Access.

This situation has generated a need for a concise book on Access/SQL programming for beginners, tied in with database principles and concepts. This book hopes to meet that need. It starts by presenting the simplest Access SQL concepts and slowly moves into more complex query development and SQL. Each chapter includes numerous examples that readers, if they wish, can run using Access. Each chapter ends with a series of exercises that reinforce and build on the chapter material. In presenting these exercises, it is our hope that readers will improve their proficiency with SQL. In writing this book, we have kept database principles and concepts and the novice reader in mind.

SQL and Access

SQL is an abbreviation for SEQUEL (Structured English Query Language) and was originally an IBM product. Since the 1970s, when SEQUEL was introduced, it has become the de facto standard "language" for accessing and working with relational databases. SQL is not really a language as much as it is a database query tool. This book will focus on SQL using Microsoft Access. Although Microsoft Access is readily available to Windows users today, the idea of learning SQL, using Microsoft Access has largely been overlooked, despite the fact that it provides a good platform on which to learn SQL. Second only to Oracle, Access is the most widely used SQL product in business and industry. Whereas Oracle is mainly used to manage large databases, Access is mainly used for personal database applications and for smaller business applications.

SQL allows you to define a relational database and to create tables (in this sense, SQL is a Data Definition Language [DDL]). SQL also allows you to tell Access which information you want to select, insert, update, or delete. SQL provides a way to modify the database definition (using DDL); it also allows you to query the relational database in a flexible way as well as change the data (that is, perform data manipulation). This means SQL, in this sense, is also a Data Manipulation Language [DML]).

Audience and Coverage

This book is written for Microsoft Access users on the Windows operating system. This book can be used in introductory database courses in which students also learn database theory. It can also be used in a course just on SQL, as a stand-alone text, to learn SQL. For this latter scenario, we included Chapter 0, which provides the basic database background needed to begin SQL.

This book consists of 12 chapters. Chapter 0 introduces some of the database terms that will be used throughout the book and shows how and why the relational database model fits into the database world of today. Chapter 1 shows the user, in a step-by-step manner, how to get started with SQL in Access. Chapter 2 introduces the user to very basic SQL table manipulations like selecting rows and columns. Chapter 3 shows the user how to create and populate tables using SQL. In Chapter 4 the user is introduced to the join operation and working with more than one table at once. In this chapter, the user is also shown how joins really work, and different types of joins are also discussed. Chapter 5 covers several basic Access SQL numeric and string functions and manipulations, with lots of examples of the different numeric and string functions. Chapter 6 gets further into query development by discussing derived structures like views, inline views, temporary tables, and so on. Chapter 7 discusses different set operations and how to perform different set operations that Access does not explicitly have. Chapter 8 gets into an explanation of what subqueries are and shows the user how joins compare with subqueries. Chapter 9 covers aggregation (an expansion of what was started in Chapter 5) and the GROUP BY. Chapter 10 offers an in-depth discussion on correlated subqueries by walking the user through the steps of a correlated subquery and shows the user how correlated subqueries compare with uncorrelated subqueries. Chapter 11 shows the user how to create indexes and constraints that can be placed on tables using SQL. As we mentioned earlier, we have included a set of review questions and exercises at the end of every chapter, which test the material in the respective chapters and incorporate a review of previous chapters.

Appendix 1 lays out the `student.mdb` tables and other tables that have been used throughout the book. In addition, we have provided the Glossary of Terms and the Glossary of Important Commands and Functions for your reference. Finally, the Index of Important Commands and Functions has been provided for easy reference.

We do not cover data dictionary concepts in this book because Access does not have a data dictionary. Instead, Access presents much of its data dictionary information through its GUI, coverage of which is not within the scope of this book.

Overall, although this book does not discuss advanced features such as performance tuning issues or advanced SQL, it is an ideal way for a beginning Access SQL programmer to get an overview of what SQL in Access entails. It certainly can be considered a starting point for what Access SQL (and SQL on the whole) has to offer.

Supplements

The exercises at the end of each chapter are drawn from databases that we created and that can be downloaded from the Addison-Wesley site for this book (`www.aw.com/cssupport`) and from `www.cs.uwf.edu/~sbagui` or `www.cs.uwf.edu/~rearp`. The download instructions are also available at these Web sites.

In addition, solutions are available exclusively to qualified instructors only. Please contact your local sales representative or send email to `aw.cse@awl.com` for access information.

Acknowledgements

Our thanks are due to our editors, Maite Suarez-Rivas and Katherine Harutunian, and all other Addison-Wesley support staff and project managers, for all their support in making this project successful.

We are also indebted to our reviewers, who have taken their time and effort to meticulously review this work and make helpful comments and suggestions: Deborah Barreau, University of North Carolina; Michael R. Bartolacci, Penn State University, Berks Lehigh Valley College; Larry Corman, Fort Lewis College; Daniel Duricy, Miami University (Oxford, Ohio); Constance A. Knapp, Pace University; Kim Tracy, North Central College and Lucent Technologies; and Gregory L. Smith, Kansas State University.

Finally we would like to thank Dr. John and Patrice Cavanaugh, President, University of West Florida, Dr. Parks Dimsdale, Vice President, University of West Florida, Dr. Wes Little, Dean, College of Arts and Sciences, University of West Florida, Dr. Ed Rodgers, Chairman, Department of Computer Science, University of West Florida, and several others for their constant encouragement and inspiration.

The Software Engineering Process and Relational Databases

Topics covered in this chapter

This chapter is provided for those students who wish to study SQL and database topics but feel that they lack sufficient computer experience. This chapter is not intended to replace a course about databases; a theoretical database course is often taught concurrently with a study of the material in this book.

    The chapter begins with some preliminary definitions and a short history of databases, followed by a description of how and why the relational database model fits into the database world of today. We then delve into a more detailed description of relational databases and normal forms. Finally, we provide a brief explanation of software engineering. Some knowledge of how software (SQL "programs," if you will) might be developed is useful in understanding why we suggest using some formats and conventions in this book.

What Is a Database?

Data—facts about something—must be stored in some fashion in order for it to be useful (that is, in order for it to be found). A *database* is a collection of associated or related data. For example, the collection of all the information in a doctor's office could be referred to as a "medical office database"; all data in this database would refer to information that is pertinent to the operation of a medical office.

Before the age of computers, databases were kept on paper (medical databases were kept in doctors' offices, personnel databases were kept in employment offices, and so on). However, databases have migrated from paper to magnetic media over the past 40 years or so, and current databases are usually stored on magnetic disks.

Regardless of the format (paper or electronic), information stored in databases is organized into files. A *file* is a collection of data about one subject. A medical office database might well have files other than patient data, such as a pharmaceutical file, employee files, and so on. Individual data is stored in *records* within files. For example, Mr. Smith's medical *records* would be located in his doctor's patient *files*. Individual items in Mr. Smith's records would include his name, address, and so on. Information such as name and address is referred to as a *field* or *attribute*. Thus, databases contain files, files contain records, and records contain fields (attributes).

Database Models

A conceptual way of thinking about data in a database is called a *logical model*. With a logical model, we *conceptualize* how data might be organized. The way that data is actually laid out on the disk—that is, where each bit is located—is called a *physical model*.

Over the past 30 years or so, three different logical database models have evolved:

• the hierarchical model

• the network model

• the relational model

These models represent ways of logically perceiving the arrangement of data in databases. The hierarchical and network models can infer some knowledge of how the physical model operates, whereas the relational model virtually ignores the physical model. We will now give a little insight into each of logical models to see how and why the relational model has evolved into the dominant logical model.

The Hierarchical Model and Structural Constraints

The idea in a *hierarchical model* is that all data is logically arranged in a hierarchical fashion (also known as a *parent-child relationship*). Suppose that you work for a company that has an employee database. Further, suppose that this database contains files about employees and files about the dependents of employees. Some employees have dependents; some do not. For those employees who have dependents, there must be a reference in those employees' records to the location of corresponding dependent records in the dependent file.

If an employee has dependents, you can think of that employee as being the "parent" of the dependent. Thus, every dependent *would have* one employee-parent and every employee *could have* one or more dependent-children. (Please note that the "parent" and "child" inference is not necessarily meant to be a personal relationship; "child" and "parent" are not meant to be taken literally.) The connection of the employee to a dependent and vice versa is called a *relationship.* Figure 0.1 illustrates the hierarchical model.

In all logical models, all relationships between records have what are called *structural constraints*, which indicate how many of one type of record are related to another (also called *cardinality*) and whether one type of record must have such a relationship (also called *participation* or *optionality*).

For example, suppose that an employee *may* have *one or more* dependents, and all dependents in a database *must* be related to *one and only one* employee. We would term the cardinality of this relationship of employee to dependent as *one to many,* or 1:M. Further, since we say that

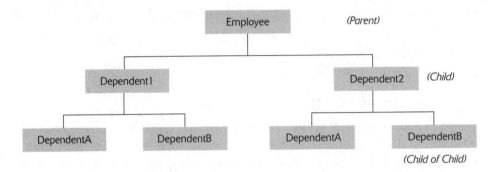

FIGURE 0.1 Hierarchical Model

an employee may (or may not) have dependents, the participation constraint of the relationship from the employee side is *partial* or *optional*. Because a dependent must be associated with one employee, the participation from the dependent side is *full* or *mandatory*. Note that the words "one or more" and "one and only one" indicate cardinality. The words "may" and "must" indicate optionality or participation.

In a hierarchical model, the cardinality of relationships is always either one-to-one (1:1) or one-to-many (1:M) (as shown in Figures 0.2 and 0.3, respectively). The most common relationship in a hierarchical model is 1:M. In our example, a 1:M relationship means that one employee may have many dependents ("many" meaning one or more). Further, the 1:M employee-to-dependent relationship implies that each dependent has one and only one employee-parent.

Less common, but allowable in hierarchical models, is the 1:1 relationship shown in Figure 0.2. In our employee example, a 1:1 relationship would imply that one employee might have one designated dependent and a dependent would be related to only one employee. This relationship might infer a "next-of-kin" designation, for example.

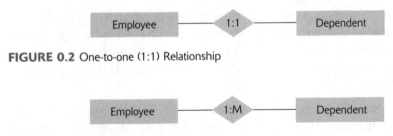

FIGURE 0.2 One-to-one (1:1) Relationship

FIGURE 0.3 One-to-many (1:M) Relationship

Other Cardinalities and the Network Model

A many-to-one (M:1) relationship between employee and dependent would imply that a dependent might have multiple parents (multiple employees who "claimed" a particular dependent). But, because the relationship is M:1, it would infer that an employee could have at most one dependent. The M:1 relationship is not allowed in hierarchical logical models and is used in the network model.

The very common many-to-many (M:N) relationship, shown in Figure 0.4, is not allowed in hierarchical database models either. The difference between the hierarchical and network models is that M:1 and M:N relationships are allowed in the network model but not in the hierarchical models.

> While M usually stands for "many," M:N is used more often than M:M to stand for many-to-many because it's important not to infer that the values for M and N need be equal; in fact, they usually are not.

The Physical Implementation of Hierarchical and Network Models

Before the advent of computers, hierarchical and network databases were implemented by choosing some way of *physically* connecting the parent and child records. Suppose that an employee, Mr. Smith, has three children, Sally, Ann, and Tom. If we think back to paper records, we might visualize that in the dependent file, there could be a Sally Smith record, an Ann Smith record, and a Tom Smith record. Suppose we put the dependent records in a filing cabinet and put the notation in Mr. Smith's record that his dependents are Sally (file drawer 1, record 2), Ann (file drawer 3, record 12), and Tom (file drawer 2, record 13). Here, we are using a system to "point to" the dependent records from Mr. Smith's employee record. This scheme is called a ***multiple-child pointer scheme***.

On a disk, one has little choice but to "point to" physical locations for the dependent records. There are multiple ways to implement pointing schemes in the hierarchical and network models. For example, in addition to using a disk address, a *different* way to implement the employee-dependent relationship would be to have an employee record point to a disk location for the first occurrence of a dependent record. That dependent record would in turn point to the disk location of the next dependent, and so on. In this example, Mr. Smith would point to Sally, Sally

FIGURE 0.4 Many-to-many (M:N) Relationship

would point to Ann, and Ann would point to Tom. This is called a **linked list of child-records**, or, in older database books, a **chain** of records, because they can be thought of as record-links that are chained together.

The multiple-child pointer scheme and the linked list of child-records are two of many ways of implementing physical record connections in hierarchical and network databases. The hierarchical model, with its 1:1 and 1:M restrictions, permit relatively simple record-pointing schemes. The network model requires more complex pointing schemes, but the end result is that, in both cases, records are physically linked via disk addresses.

The hierarchical and network models have two major drawbacks:

• The choice of the way in which the files are physically linked impacts the way underlying database software is developed and hence impacts database performance both positively and negatively.

• The more complex the way in which the pointing scheme is implemented, the less flexible the database becomes. Although many grandiose pointing schemes were developed in the 1970s, the more extravagant the schemes were, the more likely they would include "bad links." As records are updated, inserted, or deleted, all links must be maintained. The more complicated the system, the more danger there is for dead links (that is, corrupted links or lost addresses).

Contemporary Databases: The Relational Model

Dr. Edgar F. Codd introduced the **relational model** around 1970 (Codd, 1970b). The relational model is based on the idea that if you ignore the way data files are connected and arrange your data into simple two-dimensional, unordered tables, then you can develop an algebra for queries and focus on the data as data, not as a physical realization of a logical model.

Before we delve into the details of the relational model, however, it's important that you understand some changes in terminology as databases evolved from file systems to relational databases. As you may know, current terminology refers to an *entity* as something we record information about. For example, we record information (data, facts) about employees; hence, an employee is an entity. Whereas we used to refer to the *employee file*, we now refer to the set of employee entities, or an *employee entity set*. Likewise, employee records (now called *entities*) contain employee information fields (now called *attributes*) of the employee entity. The reason for using the terms *entity set, entity,* and *attribute* instead of *file, record,* and *field,* respectively, is to disconnect the idea of a physical file, record, and field from the logical notion of these things.

The relational model is truly logical in that one is no longer concerned with how data is physically stored. Rather, files (called *entity sets* in the relational model) are simply unordered, two-dimensional tables of simple data values (or sets of rows). Necessarily, there are rules that govern the way these tables "store" data. The first rule is that the *data itself must be atomic*—that is, not broken down into component parts. The tables of data are called **relations,** and because the data is stored in tables, each table has columns (which represent the attributes) and rows (which represent the instances of each entity). A collection of tables is referred to as a **relational database.** Table 0.1 shows an example of an Employee relation (a table with data in it).

Table 0.1: Example of an Employee Table

Employee		
name	address	project#
Smith	123 4th St.	101
Smith	123 4th St.	102
Jones	5 Oak Dr.	101

Employee is a table (that is, a relation) and name, address, and project# are attributes (that is, column names). The rows, such as <Smith, 123 4th St, 102>, represent an employee entity occurrence (data about a person named Smith, Smith's address, and the project number that Smith is working on). In relational databases, *the ordering of the rows in the table is not defined.* The rows are considered a set of rows, and sets do not have to have an order. Also, because rows are sets, *no duplicate rows are allowed* in a strict relational database. Rows are either *in* the set or they or not, but *where* they are in the set is irrelevant. Thus, Table 0.2 is equivalent to Table 0.1.

Table 0.2: A Re-ordered Employee **Table**

	Employee	
name	address	project#
Smith	123 4th St.	102
Jones	5 Oak Dr.	101
Smith	123 4th St.	101

Obviously, databases contain more data than is illustrated in this Employee table. To arrive at a workable way of deciding which pieces of data go into which tables and to arrange the tables so that Codd's relational algebra would work, Codd proposed something he referred to as **normal forms** (Codd, 1970a; Codd, 1970c; Codd, 1971). He originally defined three normal forms: the first, second, and third normal forms. We'll look at each of these next, in turn.

The First Normal Form

The **first normal form (1NF)** requires that data in tables be atomic and be arranged in a two-dimensional layout. Atomicity implies that there be no column containing repeating groups. A *repeating group* refers to columns that may contain multiple occurrences of data. A repeating group is an example of non-atomic data and violates the definition of a relational table. A problem with putting data in tables with repeating groups is that the table cannot be easily indexed or arranged in such a way that data in the repeating group can easily be found. Put another way, data in repeating groups cannot be found without searching each row individually.

An example of a table *not* in 1NF is where there is an employee entity with attributes (fields) name, address, and dependent name, as follows:

```
Employee (name, address, {dependent name}),
```

Here, {dependent name} implies that the attribute is repeated, with rows containing data as follows:

```
Smith, 123 4th St., {John, Mary, Paul, Sally}
Jones, 5 Oak Dr., {Mary, Frank, Bob}
Adams, 33 Dog Ave., {Alice, Alicia, Mary}
```

What do you do if you want to store data about employees and their dependents? Before tackling the problem of dealing with non-1NF data, it is helpful to understand the concept of a key. A *key* in a table is an attribute or group of attributes that identifies a row—a unique handle whereby one can find information in a table. Since relational database theory disallows totally duplicate rows, the entire contents of a row could be considered a key. However, often there is an attribute that will suffice as a key by itself. In Table 0.2, the key could be the employee's last name. For example, if you wanted information about Jones, you would access Jones's row. Clearly, if there were two Joneses, you would have to come up with a better key, such as using name and address together as the key or adding an employee number for a single-attribute unique key.

To resolve the non-1NF problem (and other NF problems that you will encounter), databases must be *normalized*. The normalization process involves splitting tables into two or more tables (a process called *decomposition*). Data can be reunited from decomposed tables with a relational operation called a *join*. We will illustrate the normalization process by first solving the non-1NF problem. To resolve the non-1NF problem, we do the following.

Non-1NF to First Normal Form (1NF): The repeating group is moved to a new table with the key of the table from which it came.

We will assume that the last name of the employee is the key in this version of Employee.

```
Non-1NF:
Smith, 123 4th St., {John, Mary, Paul, Sally}
Jones, 5 Oak Dr., {Mary, Frank, Bob}
Adams, 33 Dog Ave., {Alice, Alicia, Mary}
```

is decomposed into 1NF tables with no repeating groups, as shown in Table 0.3a and Table 0.3b.

Table 0.3a: Employee Table in 1NF

Employee1	
name	address
Smith	123 4th St
Jones	5 Oak Dr
Adams	33 Dog Ave

Table 0.3b: Dependent Table in 1NF

Dependent	
dependentName	employeeName
John	Smith
Mary	Smith
Paul	Smith
Sally	Smith
Mary	Jones
Frank	Jones
Alice	Adams
Alicia	Adams
Mary	Adams

In Table 0.3a, name is the key of Employee1—it uniquely identifies the rows. We would call name, as used here, a primary key. A *primary key* is the key that we choose to uniquely identify a row (tuple). In Table 0.3b, the primary key is a combination (concatenation) of dependentName and employeeName. Neither the dependentName nor the employeeName is unique in Table 0.3b, and hence both attributes are required to uniquely identify a row in the table. The employeeName in Table 0.3b is called a *foreign key* because it references a primary key: name in Table 0.3a. Note that the following original data

```
Non-1NF:
Smith, 123 4th St., {John, Mary, Paul, Sally}
Jones, 5 Oak Dr., {Mary, Frank, Bob}
Adams, 33 Dog Ave., {Alice, Alicia, Mary}
```

could be reconstructed by combining all the rows in Table 0.3a with the corresponding rows in Table 0.3b where the names are equal. The combination of tables based on the equality of some attribute is called an *equijoin* in a relational database.

The Second Normal Form

The *second normal form (2NF)* requires that data in tables depend on the whole key of the table. The key can be called a *defining attribute*. The idea of dependency is usually called a *functional dependency,* which means that if you know a value for some defining attribute, you will always have only one value for the dependent attribute. If, for example, a table contains a Social Security number (a defining attribute), you would expect that only one value for name (a dependent attribute) would exist for that particular Social Security number. (In other words, name depends on the Social Security number; or, put another way, the Social Security number defines name.) Keys are always defining attributes, but defining attributes may not necessarily be keys, as we shall see.

If a table has a key that consists of more than one attribute, it is said to have a **compound key.** If a data item depends on only part of a compound key, it is said to be a **partial dependency.** Partial dependencies are not allowed in the 2NF. Consider, for example, a table called Employee2 with attributes name, job, salary, and address:

```
Employee2(name, job, salary, address)
```

Further suppose that it takes a combination of the name and job fields (which can also be shown as name + job) to identify a salary field, but the address field depends only on the name field. In other words, salary depends on name + job, but address depends only on name. Name + job, a **concatenated key,** then, is the primary key of this table. *Dependence* infers that if you know the name, this will identify the person's address in this data. We would say that the dependence of address on name is a *partial dependency* because name is only part of the primary key of the table. Table 0.4 shows some sample data for the Employee2 table.

Table 0.4a: A Non-2NF Table

Employee2			
name	job	salary	address
Smith	Welder	14.75	123 4th St.
Smith	Programmer	24.50	123 4th St.
Smith	Waiter	7.50	123 4th St.
Jones	Programmer	26.50	5 Oak Dr.
Jones	Bricklayer	34.50	5 Oak Dr.
Adams	Analyst	28.50	33 Dog Ave.

Can you see the problem developing here? The address is repeated for each occurrence of a name. This repetition is called **redundancy** and leads to anomalies. An **anomaly** means that there is a restriction on doing something due to the arrangement of the data. Three types of anomalies exist: insertion anomalies, deletion anomalies, and update anomalies. The key of this table is name + job. This is clear because neither attribute will, by itself, identify information in a particular row—both the name and job fields are needed to identify a salary. (Try to answer the question, "What is Smith's salary?" without saying what the job is.) However, address depends only on the name, not the job. This is an example of a partial dependency because address depends on only part of the key of this table.

An example of an insertion anomaly would be a situation in which you want to insert a person into Table 0.4a but the person to be inserted is not, as yet, assigned a job. You cannot make this insertion because a value would have to be known for the job attribute. A further rule of a relational database is that no part of the primary key of a relation may be a null or have an unknown value (this is known as the *entity-integrity constraint*). What's wrong with null values in keys? If a null were allowed in a key, the key would have a non-unique value and hence would not be a key at all.

An example of an update anomaly would be a situation in which one of the employees changed their address. Suppose the person named Smith had a change of address. You would have to change three rows to accommodate this one change.

An example of a delete anomaly would be a situation in which Adams quits, so Adams' row is deleted; however, the information that the analyst pay is $28.50 is also lost. Therefore, a delete anomaly deletes more than is desired. How do we decompose a non-2NF table to fix these problems? We have to make the non-2NF table a 2NF table, as described next.

Non-2NF to 2NF: To make a non-2NF table a 2NF table, the partial dependency has to be removed to a new table. The attributes or fields that are fully dependent on the primary key (the primary key here being name + job) are put together with the primary key (as shown in Table 0.5a). The salary is dependent on both parts of the primary key (name and job), so the salary is placed with the name and job fields in Table 0.5a.

Table 0.5a: Employee Salary Table

name	EmployeeSalary job	salary
Smith	Welder	14.75
Smith	Programmer	24.50
Smith	Waiter	7.50
Jones	Programmer	26.50
Jones	Bricklayer	34.50
Adams	Analyst	28.50

Then, the fields that are not fully dependent on the primary key are placed with the part of the primary key that they are dependent on. In this case, the address field (which is only dependent on part of the primary key) is placed with name (the part of the primary key that address is dependent on). This is shown in Table 0.5b.

Table 0.5b: Employee Information Table

name	EmployeeInformation address
Smith	123 4th St.
Jones	5 Oak Dr.
Adams	33 Dog Ave.

Hence the non-2NF table, Table 0.4a, is decomposed to the 2NF tables, Tables 0.5a and 0.5b.

The key of the EmployeeSalary table (Table 0.5a) is as before—the name and the job taken together. The key of the EmployeeInformation table (Table 0.5b) is just the name. Note that the "other" non-key attributes in both tables now depend on the key (and only on the key). Also, note the removal of unnecessary redundancy and the ending of possible anomalies. For practice, try adding, deleting, and updating rows and note that the anomalies are gone.

The Third Normal Form

The *third normal form (3NF)* requires that data in tables depend on the primary key of the table. 2NF problems only appear when there is a con-catenated key to begin with; 3NF problems do not require a concatenated key. 3NF problems occur when some non-key data item is more properly identified by something other than the key of the table. A classic example of non-3NF relation could be shown by the `Employee3` table, which has the attributes `name`, `address`, `project#`, and `project-location`.

```
Employee3(name, address, project#, project-location)
```

In `Employee3`, we will assume that the `name` field is the primary key. Suppose that `project-location` in `Employee3` means the location from which a project is controlled, and is defined by the `project#`. Some sam-ple data shown in Table 0.6 will illustrate the problem with this table.

Table 0.6: A Non-3NF Table

Employee3			
name	address	project#	project Location
Smith	123 4th St.	101	Memphis
Smith	123 4th St.	102	Mobile
Jones	5 Oak Dr.	101	Memphis

Note the redundancy in Table 0.6. Project 101 is controlled from Memphis, but every time a person is recorded as working on project 101, the fact that they work on a project that is controlled from Memphis is recorded again. The same anomalies—insert, update, and delete—are also present in this table. You cannot add a `project#`–`project-location` unless you have a `name`. (Remember that `name` cannot be null, because it is the key of that table.) If you deleted Smith's working on project 102 in the preceding table, the "102, Mobile" information is also deleted. Suppose project 101's control is moved to Tuscaloosa? How many changes would this require?

The `name, project#, project-location` situation is called a *transitive dependency*. It is called *transitive* because `name` defines `project#`, and `project#` defines `project-location`. This transitive dependency is relieved by decomposing into 3NF as follows.

Non-3NF to 3NF: To make a non-3NF table into a 3NF table, transitive dependency has to be removed to a new table. Thus, Table 0.6 is decomposed into two tables, Table 0.7a and 0.7b.

Table 0.7a: Employee Table in 3NF

| | Employee3a | |
name	address	project#
Smith	123 4th St.	101
Smith	123 4th St.	102
Jones	5 Oak Dr.	101

Table 0.7b: Project Table in 3NF

| | Project |
project#	project location
101	Memphis
102	Mobile
101	Memphis

Again, observe the removal of the transitive dependency and the anomaly problem.

Before leaving the topic of normal forms, note that there are other cases of non-normality that are beyond the scope of this brief overview. These other cases are not common, and a "good" relational database may be thought of as one that is in the 3NF. One such unusual form is called the Boyce-Codd Normal Form (BCNF), which is stricter than 3NF since every relation in BCNF is also in 3NF.

The BCNF

In the previous 3NF example, we had a dependency where the defining attribute was not the key of the table (project# defined project-location). In fact, neither project# nor project-location were involved with the key. In BCNF, every determinant (a determinant is one or more attributes that functionally determine another attribute or attributes) is a candidate key. For example, consider Table 0.8a, which is not in BCNF:

Table 0.8a: Band Practice Table Not in BCNF

Band Practice		
Player	Instrument	Teacher
Chloe	Clarinet	Fred
Beryl	Flute	David
Kaitlyn	Drums	Christina
Chloe	Flute	David
Lindsey	Flute	Michele

Here, we define the key of the relation as Player + Instrument. Note that neither field uniquely identifies a row. So Teacher is identified by Player + Instrument, but in this database, Teacher defines the Instrument that the teacher teaches, but not vice versa. If you know the Teacher, you know the instrument. We therefore have a situation in which Player+Instrument is the key and defines Teacher, but Teacher defines an attribute that is part of the key. This relation is in 3NF, but is said to be "not in the BCNF." This is a transitive dependency, but it is a special kind of transitive dependency because it involves the key of the relation.

Note that you have redundancy in that "David teaches the Flute" is repeated. Further note the anomalies, because you cannot put the fact that David teaches the Flute in the database by itself without a pupil. If Lindsey is deleted, then the fact that Michele teaches the Flute is also deleted.

The BCNF may be resolved by decomposing, but there will be a price. We decompose the non-BCNF table, Table 0.8a, into two tables in BCNF, Table 0.8b and Table 0.8c. In Table 0.8b, Teacher is the key (since Teacher defines the instrument), and in Table 0.8c, both Player and Teacher form a composite key. Note the absence of anomalies in the decomposed version (Tables 0.8b and 0.8c):

Table 0.8b: Teacher Table in BCNF

Instrument	Teacher
Clarinet	Fred
Flute	David
Drums	Christina
Flute	Michele

Table 0.8c: Player Table in BCNF

Player	Teacher
Chloe	Fred
Beryl	David
Kaitlyn	Christina
Chloe	David
Lindsey	Michele

The anomalies disappear, but the price is that we lost the ability to query the database directly on `Player + Instrument`. We can, of course, manipulate the database to allow such a query, but it would involve combining the decomposed tables back into the original one. The choice to normalize to the BCNF when you already have a 3NF situation may be dependent more on the queries you intend to formulate than on "living with" the anomalies that may be present.

Relational Database Summary

In summary, there are rules that define a relational database. All data is laid out in two-dimensional tables. The tables have no sense of ordering of rows, and no rows are duplicated. In fact, the tables are often called "sets of rows." All data is atomic. A primary key is a chosen unique row-identifier; if you want information from a row in a table, you get it by the primary key value. The primary key may be all the attributes in the relation, but usually a more minimal set of attributes can be found to uniquely identify a row. The 3NF means that the data in a relation depends only on the primary key of the relation. Data in 3NF is assumed to be in the 1NF and 2NF. Data that is decomposed into the 3NF will avoid most redundancy and anomaly problems. The Boyce-Codd Normal Form (BCNF) is a special case of a transitive dependency in which the database designer has to choose between removing all anomalies and the convenience of query writing.

What Is the Software Engineering Process?

As a further bit of orientation to the material contained in this book, we wish to present some insight into how software is developed. The term *software engineering* refers to a process of specifying, designing, writing, delivering, maintaining, and, finally, retiring software. Many excellent references on the topic of software engineering (including Norman, 1996, and Schach, 1999) are available to the interested reader.

A basic idea in software engineering is that to build software correctly, a series of standardized steps or phases are required. The steps ensure that a process of thinking precedes action. That is, thinking through "what is needed" precedes "what is written." One common version of presenting the thinking-before-acting scenario is referred to as a *waterfall model*, described in Schach (1999) as phases that flow from one another in one direction without retracing.

Software production is like a life-cycle process—it is created, used, and eventually retired. The "players" in the software development life cycle may be placed into two camps, often referred to as the *user* and the *analyst*. Software is designed by the *analyst* for the *user*.

There is no general agreement among software engineers as to the exact number of phases in the waterfall software development model. Models vary depending on the interest of the author in one part or another in the process. A very brief description of the software process goes like this:

Step 1 (or Phase 1). *Requirements*: Find out what the user wants/needs.

Step 2. *Specification*: Write out the user wants/needs as precisely as possible.

Step 3. *Designed*: Meet the specification from Step 2.

Step 4. *Development*: Write the software.

Step 5. *Implementation*: Turn the software over to the user.

Step 6. *Maintenance*: Support software until it is retired.

In most software engineering models, some feedback loops are allowed. For example, when completing Step 2, the analyst can go back to Step 1 if he or she does not understand the user's requirements.

For SQL users, the software process involves accessing data from a database. A database is a collection of facts stored on some medium—normally a magnetic disk. Often the question in SQL is "What does some user want to know"? This question is called a *query* in a database because it is a question directed at the information contained in the database.

What does software engineering have to do with writing queries? In the normal business world, the person who writes SQL queries is often not the person who wants to know something. Imagine a supervisor telling a SQL programmer to find the names of all the customers who spent over $1,000 this month. The SQL programmer has to design a query for this request, which requires addressing issues similar to those in the software engineering process:

• Does the SQL programmer understand the nature of the question? (Step 1: requirements)

• Did the SQL programmer provide feedback to the supervisor and verify what he or she thinks the question is? (Step 2: specification)

• What kind of query will the SQL programmer decide upon? (Step 3: design)

• After the query is written, is it efficient? (Step 4: development)

• Does the query answer the original question? Is the execution of the query ready for turning over the result to the supervisor? (Step 5: implementation)

• What if the supervisor now wants to change the amount in the query or the month or the format of the names? (Step 6: maintenance)

Thus, queries should be written so that other people can immediately understand what the writer intended. Most of the money spent on software is on maintenance. Maintenance is a very time-consuming and expensive part of the software process—particularly if the software engineering process has not been done well. Maintenance involves correcting hidden software faults as well as enhancing the functionality of the software.

One of the goals of this text is to teach you not only how to write queries, but how to write them so that other SQL programmers will know that you understood the requirements and so that your queries are open to maintenance. We also have tried to suggest ways to audit your query results. As with other programming, computers only do what you tell them to do. If you ask for garbage, you will get garbage. If your query is not correctly formed, SQL may give you an answer, but the answer may not be correct or make sense. You must ask yourself, does the query really answer the question that was originally asked? Will other SQL programmers understand my query?

REFERENCES

Codd, E. F. (1970a). "Notes on a Data Sublanguage," IBM internal memo (January 19, 1970).

Codd, E. F. (1970b). "A Relational Model of Data for Large Shared Data Banks," *CACM 13*, No. 6 (June, 1970).

Codd, E. F. (1970c). "The Second and Third Normal Forms for the Relational Model," IBM technical memo (October 6, 1970).

Codd, E. F. (1971). "A Data Base Sublanguage Founded on the Relational Calculus," IBM Research Report RJ893 (July 26, 1971).

Norman, R. J. (1996). *Object-Oriented Systems Analysis and Design.* Upper Saddle River, NJ: Prentice Hall.

Schach, S. R. (1999). *Classical and Object Oriented Software Engineering.* New York: WCG McGraw-Hill.

Getting Started with SQL in Access

Topics covered in this chapter

In this chapter, we will introduce some very basic concepts about using Structured Query Language, or SQL (pronounced "sequel"), in Access, including how to get into SQL in Access, type in a query, edit, execute, and save a query. We will also explore how to view table designs, data in the tables, delete tables or queries, and print from SQL in Access.

The database that we will use throughout this book is called `student.mdb`. This database can be downloaded from `www.cs.uwf.edu/~sbagui` or `www.cs.uwf.edu/~rearp` (the download instructions are also available at these web sites). You need to copy this database into the directory that you wish to use for your Access work.

Opening the student.mdb Database

Once you start Access, select the **Open an existing file** radio button, as shown in Figure 1.1, and then click the **OK** button.

In the **Open** dialog box that appears, from the **Look in** drop-down list, select the directory in which you have stored your student.mdb file (as shown in Figure 1.2), and then double-click student.mdb (or highlight student.mdb and then click the **Open** button).

When you open the database, you see an **Objects** list on the left side of the screen that includes the various categories of objects that are available. When you select a category from the **Objects** list, each object you may choose from within the selected category is listed on the right. We are interested in the **Queries** category, so select it, as shown in Figure 1.3.

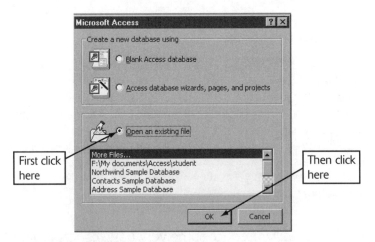

FIGURE 1.1 Opening an Existing Database

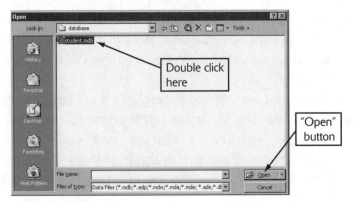

FIGURE 1.2 Opening the student.mdb Database

FIGURE 1.3 Opening the student.mdb Database

Getting into SQL in Access

Queries in SQL in Access have to be typed in the SQL view screen. There is no option to go directly to the SQL view screen in Access. To get to the SQL view screen, we have to go through **Design View**. After you have selected **Queries**, select **Create query in Design view** on the right and then click **New** to open the **New Query** window, as shown in Figure 1.4.

In the **New Query** window, select **Design View**, and then click **OK**.

Next, the **Show Table** dialog box opens, shown in Figure 1.5. Click **Close**.

Click the **SQL** button in the upper-left corner (below the **File** menu) of the main Microsoft Access window, as shown in Figure 1.6. (Alternatively, you can open the **View** menu and select **SQL View**.)

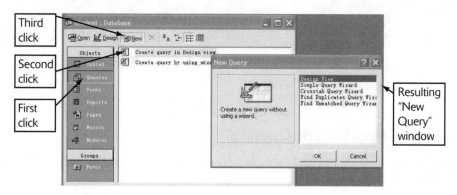

FIGURE 1.4 The New Query Dialog Box

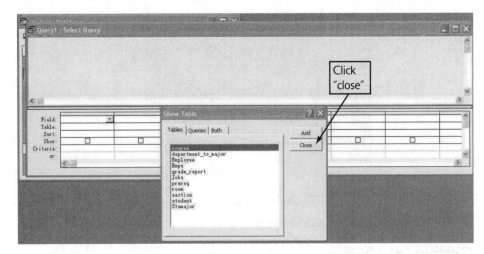

FIGURE 1.5 Closing the Show Table Dialog Box

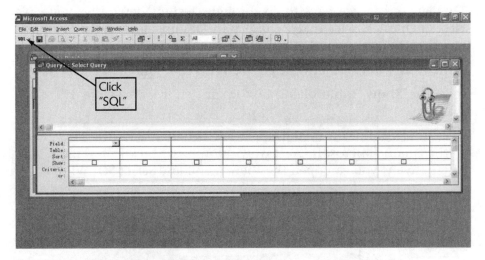

FIGURE 1.6 Getting into the SQL View Screen from Design View

Typing a Simple SQL Query

You are now in the Access screen called **SQL view** (Figure 1.7), into which you can type a SQL query.

Type the following SQL query on this screen (Figure 1.7):

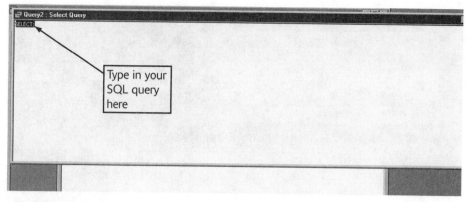

FIGURE 1.7 SQL View

```
SELECT  *
FROM    Student
WHERE   class = 4;
```

Running a SQL Query

To look at the output of the SQL query, you need to "run" the SQL query by clicking the red exclamation mark (!) button on the toolbar (see Figure 1.8).

Running the query shown in Figure 1.8 produces the output shown in Figure 1.9.

> You can also type the query in MS Word or Notepad, and copy and paste it into **SQL view**.

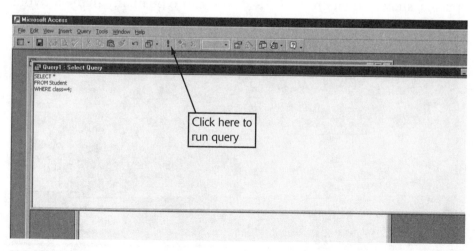

FIGURE 1.8 Running a SQL Query

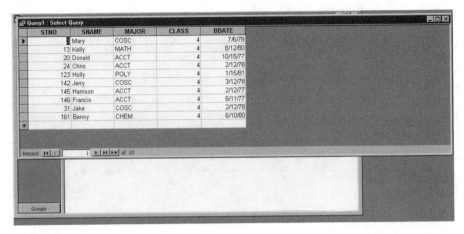

FIGURE 1.9 Output Screen

The number of rows (records) in the output is given at the bottom of this output screen. According to output screen in Figure 1.9, the query we ran (Figure 1.8), gave us 10 rows (records) of output.

Saving a SQL Query

You may save your query so that you can edit and re-run the query in the future. To save your query, first try to close the **Query1** window, which will prompt Access to ask you if you wish to save your query, as shown in Figure 1.10. You may now save your query by clicking **Yes**.

You now need to name the SQL query in the **Save As** dialog box that appears, shown in Figure 1.11. Here, you can type in any name for your

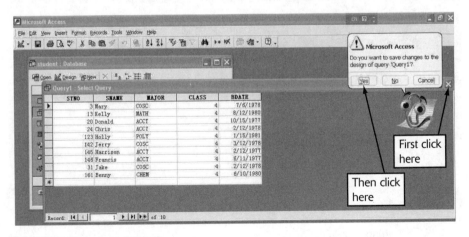

FIGURE 1.10 Saving a SQL Query

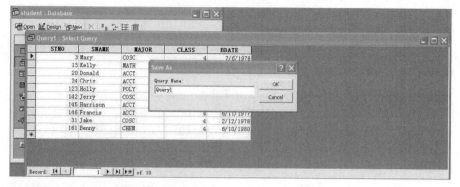

FIGURE 1.11 Naming the SQL Query

query, but we will assume for now that you will use the default name of "Query1." After you type in a name, click the **OK** button.

Access will now save your query as a SELECT query (note the icon for the SELECT query in Figure 1.12). There are many other types of queries in Access SQL, which we will look at in later chapters.

Editing a SQL Query

Once you have saved your query, you may want to retrieve your query and change it slightly.

First, make sure the **Queries** tab is selected in the **Objects** list. Then, click the query that you would like to edit, and then click the **Design** button located at the top of the screen (see Figure 1.12).

Your query now opens on your **SQL view** screen (as in Figure 1.7 or Figure 1.8), enabling you to edit your query and re-run it. For example, you might look at the students that are juniors (WHERE class = 3).

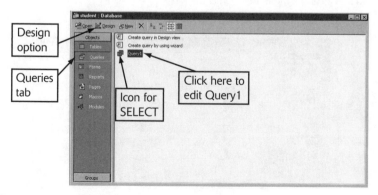

FIGURE 1.12 Selecting a SQL Query to Edit

When you are finished editing your SQL query, close the query and resave it if necessary.

Viewing Table Designs

Table designs provide information (like field names, field data types, field sizes, etc.) about the tables in the database. To view the design of a particular table in our database, click the **Tables** tab in the **Objects** list, click **Course** on the right (as shown in Figure 1.13), and then click the **Design** button.

You can now view the design of the Course table, as shown in Figure 1.14.

Close this view by closing this window, and you will now be on the screen shown in Figure 1.15.

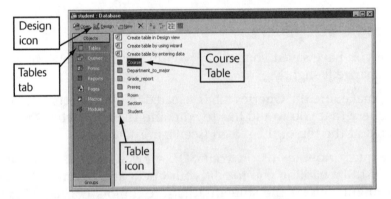

FIGURE 1.13 Selecting a Table to View Its Design

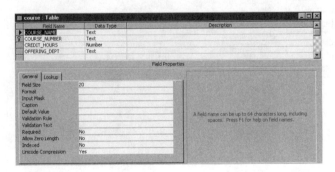

FIGURE 1.14 A Table Design View

Viewing Data in Tables

To view the data in a particular table, such as the Course table shown in Figure 1.15, you may either double-click the table that you would like to view, or highlight the table and click the **Open** button. Figure 1.16 shows data from the Course table.

Resizing Output Columns

You will notice that some of the columns in the output get cut off (as shown in Figure 1.15). To increase the column sizes (so that you can view the whole column), you need to adjust the column margins with your cursor. Place your cursor between the "COURSE_NAM" and "COURSE_NUM" columns (as shown by the arrow in Figure 1.15). Then, once you get a cross kind of cursor (instead of the arrow cursor), click and drag the column to the right, and make the column as long as you would like (as in the example shown in Figure 1.16).

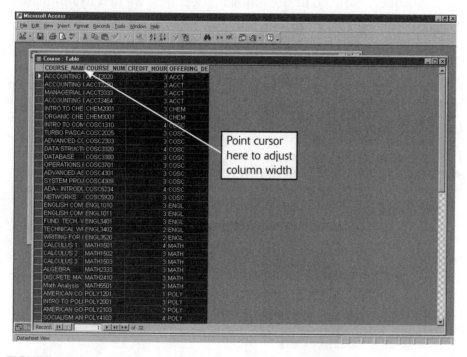

FIGURE 1.15 Data in a Table

COURSE_NAME	COURSE_NUMBER	CREDIT_HOURS	OFFERING_DEPT
ACCOUNTING I	ACCT2020	3	ACCT
ACCOUNTING II	ACCT2220	3	ACCT
MANAGERIAL FINANCE	ACCT3333	3	ACCT
ACCOUNTING INFO SYST	ACCT3464	3	ACCT
INTRO TO CHEMISTRY	CHEM2001	3	CHEM
ORGANIC CHEMISTRY	CHEM3001	3	CHEM
INTRO TO COMPUTER SC	COSC1310	4	COSC
TURBO PASCAL	COSC2025	3	COSC
ADVANCED COBOL	COSC2303	3	COSC
DATA STRUCTURES	COSC3320	4	COSC
DATABASE	COSC3380	3	COSC
OPERATIONS RESEARCH	COSC3701	3	COSC
ADVANCED ASSEMBLER	COSC4301	3	COSC
SYSTEM PROJECT	COSC4309	3	COSC
ADA - INTRODUCTION	COSC5234	4	COSC
NETWORKS	COSC5920	3	COSC
ENGLISH COMP I	ENGL1010	3	ENGL
ENGLISH COMP II	ENGL1011	3	ENGL
FUND. TECH. WRITING	ENGL3401	3	ENGL
TECHNICAL WRITING	ENGL3402	2	ENGL

Record: 1 of 32

FIGURE 1.16 Viewing Complete Data in a Table

Deleting Tables or Queries

> Be careful before you delete any tables. After you delete a table, you cannot run any queries that are dependent on it.

Since tables and queries are saved separately, you can delete a query without affecting the table in any way. But, if you delete a table first, you will not be able to run the queries that are dependent on it (even if you saved the query earlier). In the following sections, we first examine how to delete a query, and then how to delete tables.

Deleting a Query

To delete a query, first select the **Queries** tab in the **Objects** list and then click once on the query that you would like to delete, as shown in Figure 1.17. Once you have selected the query, to delete it, either right-click the query and select **Delete** from the shortcut menu (as shown in Figure 1.18), or click the "X" button on the top menu (beside the **New** button) as shown in Figure 1.17. Alternatively, once you have selected the query that you wish to delete, you can press the **Delete** key on your keyboard.

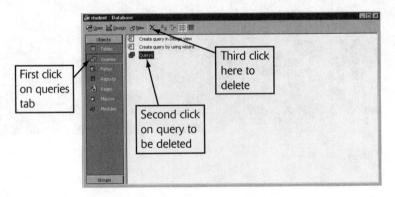

FIGURE 1.17 Selecting a Query to Delete

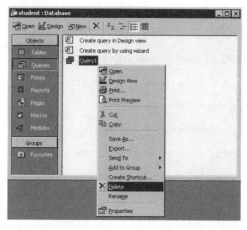

FIGURE 1.18 Deleting a Query Using the Right-click Shortcut Menu

Deleting a Table

Select the **Tables** tab (refer to Figure 1.13), and then click once on the table that you would like to delete. Once you have selected the table, to delete it, you may either right-click the table and select **Delete** from the shortcut menu, or click the "✗" button on the top menu (beside the **New** button).

> **Caution:** Do not actually perform these delete steps; otherwise you will have to reload the database. Just note this section for later reference when deleting tables in the future.

Printing SQL Code and Output from Access

In some versions of SQL running under a host system (for example, Oracle running under UNIX), one can "spool" output to a text file, which can then later be examined. Access does not have any way to create spool files. But, Access output can be directly printed from Access by selecting the **Print** key. SQL code, however, cannot be printed directly from Access. So, to print SQL code, you have to copy and paste the code into a word processing program, such as Notepad or Word, and then print it from the word processor.

To print the tables that the SQL code produces, click the **File** menu at the top of the word processor, and then choose **Print**.

CHAPTER 1 REVIEW QUESTIONS

1.   How do you type a SQL query in Access?

2.   How do you run a SQL query in Access?

3.   How do you save a SQL query in Access?

4. How do you edit a SQL query in Access?

5. How do you view table designs?

6. What information do table designs give us?

7. How do you view data in tables in Access?

8. How do you delete tables in Access?

9. How do you delete queries created in Access?

10. How do you print SQL code and output from Access?

11. Once you delete a query, does it affect a SQL table in any way?

12. Once you delete a table, can you run a query that was dependent on it (even if you had saved the query earlier)?

CHAPTER 1 EXERCISES

> Refer to Appendix 1 for a complete list of tables and fields in the student.mdb database.

1. The database provided with this book (student.mdb) has the following tables: Student, Grade_report, Section, Department_to_major, Course, Prereq, and Room, as well as two other tables that will be used later, Cap and Plants.

   a. View and print the design of each of these tables.

   b. View the data of each of these tables.

2. Write a SQL query to view all the columns and rows in the Room table. (Hint: To retrieve all columns, use SELECT * in your query; the * means "all columns." To see all rows, do not use a WHERE clause). To print the SQL code, copy and paste the results into a Notepad or Word file. Also, print the results. (Note: Just clicking the printer icon while your results are displayed on the screen will print just the output, not the SQL query.) Make sure you adjust the column sizes in your output so that you can read all of the data in the columns.

Beginning SQL Commands in Access

Topics covered in this chapter

SQL statements in Access must begin with one of the following commands: SELECT, INSERT, DELETE, UPDATE, or PROCE-DURE. SELECT is the most commonly used command in any version of SQL because SELECT signifies a query. In this chapter, we examine the SELECT command. The other commands will be covered in later chapters (but, we do not cover the PROCEDURE command in this book).

Chapter 1 explained how you get into SQL in Access, type in a query (SELECT), and execute it. In this chapter, we discuss how to write (build) simple SQL query statements in Access. We also examine how to retrieve data from a table by the use of SELECT statements, how to SELECT fields and rows from tables, how to use the ORDER BY and WHERE clauses, and how to use the AND, OR, and BETWEEN operators. The concept of COUNT and null values will also be introduced. Finally, to make writing queries simpler, we discuss how to use table and column aliases, table qualifiers, and a convention for writing SQL statements.

The SELECT Statement

SELECT is *usually* the first word in a SQL statement. The SELECT statement instructs the database engine to return information from the database as a set of records, or a **result set**. The SELECT statement displays the result on the computer screen, but does not save the results. The following is the simplest form of the SELECT syntax:

```
SELECT fields FROM Table;
```

This gives us a result set that is drawn from the list of fields (or columns or attributes) that are available in a table. In this syntax, "Table" is the name of the table from which the data will be taken, and "fields" shows only the selected fields from the table. Substituting an asterisk (*) in place of "fields" would list all the fields of the table. The keywords SELECT and FROM are *always* present in a SELECT statement.

As in most versions of SQL, SQL commands in Access have to be terminated by a semicolon. But, if you forget to add a semicolon to the end of a query, Access does not give an error message—Access automatically adds the semicolon to the end of a query. So, to stay with SQL convention, in this book we will place a semicolon at the end of every query.

> The "*" means "all fields" of the table, Student.

To display all the data from a table called Student from our database (student.mdb), you would enter the following in the SQL view screen (this screen is shown in Figure 1.7, in Chapter 1):

```
SELECT  *
FROM    Student;
```

Run or execute the preceding query by clicking the red exclamation mark (!) button on the toolbar (refer to "Running a SQL Query" in Chapter 1 for further help on running queries), and your output should include all fields (and all 48 rows) of the Student table.

Icon for a SELECT Query

As was illustrated in Chapter 1, a SELECT statement may be saved in Access SQL as a SELECT query. Figure 2.1 shows the icon for a SELECT query named **Query1**. Double-clicking on **Query1** will run the query.

If you click on **Query1** once, and then click the **Design** button, you will see the actual query statement that was typed in **Query1**, as shown in Figure 2.2.

SELECTing Fields

You do not have to show all the fields (a.k.a., attributes or columns) with a SELECT statement. You may select field names from a table, provided you know the names of the fields. In this section, we first show how to select one field, then how to select more than one field, and then how to select all fields.

SELECTing One Field

Before we can select fields from a particular table, we need to know what fields the table contains. Figure 2.3 shows the design of the Student table that we will be using.

> For instructions on how to view table designs, refer to Chapter 1.

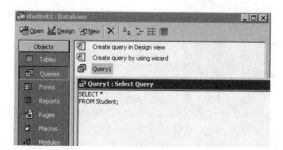

FIGURE 2.1 Icon for SELECT Query

FIGURE 2.2 Query Statement

> Refer to Appendix 1 for a complete list of tables and fields in the student.mdb database.

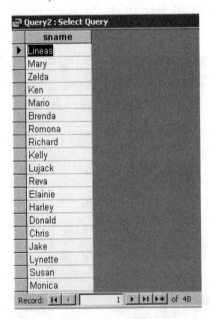

FIGURE 2.3 Design of Student Table

To SELECT or view one field or column, you would type the following in the SQL view screen :

```
SELECT field_name FROM table;
```

For example, to view a field called sname from our Student table, you type the following:

```
SELECT  sname
FROM    Student;
```

This produces 48 rows of output (of which the first 20 rows are shown below):

This window displaying the result set is resizable. You may move the cursor over the side or bottom of the output window and resize the window. We can see that we have 48 rows (records) in the output on the bottom of the output window.

SELECTing More Than One Field

To SELECT or view more than one field or column, the field names have to be separated by commas, as follows:

```
SELECT  sname, class
FROM    Student;
```

This query also produces 48 rows of output (of which we show the first 20 rows here):

sname	class
Lineas	1
Mary	4
Zelda	
Ken	
Mario	
Brenda	2
Romona	
Richard	1
Kelly	4
Lujack	1
Reva	2
Elainie	1
Harley	2
Donald	4
Chris	4
Jake	4
Lynette	1
Susan	3
Monica	3
Bill	

SELECTing All Fields

Sometimes, you will want to view all the fields in a table. To do so, you use a *. For example, the following produces an output of 48 rows and all the fields in the Student table:

```
SELECT   *
FROM     Student;
```

The * also comes in handy when you do not know the names of all the fields in a table, because the * lists all the fields anyway.

Using ORDER BY

A table maintains its data in order based on the primary key (if there is one). If there is no primary key, a table maintains the data in the order that the data was entered (in Access). If you wish to display the contents of a table in a more meaningful way in any other order, you may use the ORDER BY clause. For example, to order the Student table by the field class, you use the following:

> A primary key is used to uniquely identify a row in a table.

```
SELECT   sname, class
FROM     Student
ORDER    BY class;
```

This produces the following 48 rows of output, ordered by class:

sname	class
Lionel	
Bill	
Stephanie	
Thornton	
Genevieve	
Zelda	
Mario	
Romona	
Ken	
Smith	
Lineas	1
Lynette	1
George	1
Hillary	1
Fraiser	1
Steve	1
Elainie	1
Brad	1
Lujack	1

sname	class
Lindsay	1
Richard	1
Harley	2
Alan	2
Sadie	2
Jessica	2
Brenda	2
Reva	2
Jake	2
Cedric	2
Smithly	2
Sebastian	2
Gus	3
Phoebe	3
Cramer	3
Monica	3
Susan	3
Rachel	3
Losmith	3
Francis	4
Mary	4
Benny	4
Kelly	4
Jake	4
Chris	4
Harrison	4
Holly	4
Jerry	4
Donald	4

> In this output, since the output is ordered by class, the students that have no class assigned to them are at the top of the list.

Using ASC or DESC

To order output in ascending order, you may append the keyword, ASC, like this:

```
SELECT   sname, class
FROM     Student
ORDER    BY class ASC;
```

This will produce the same 48 rows of output as shown above since the default sorting sequence of the ORDER BY clause is ascending order.

To order output in descending order, you may append the keyword, DESC, like this:

```
SELECT   sname, class
FROM     Student
ORDER    BY class DESC;
```

This produces 48 rows of output in descending order of class (of which the first 22 rows are shown below):

sname	class
Mary	4
Jerry	4
Kelly	4
Harrison	4
Francis	4
Benny	4
Donald	4
Chris	4
Holly	4
Jake	4
Susan	3
Cramer	3
Losmith	3
Monica	3
Rachel	3
Gus	3
Phoebe	3
Alan	2
Sadie	2
Harley	2
Jessica	2
Reva	2

Ordering Within an Order

You may order within an order. For example, the following syntax orders the Student table principally by class in descending order, and then by sname within class:

```
SELECT   sname, class
FROM     Student
ORDER    BY class DESC, sname;
```

This produces the following 48 rows of output:

sname	class
Benny	4
Chris	4
Donald	4
Francis	4
Harrison	4
Holly	4
Jake	4
Jerry	4
Kelly	4
Mary	4
Cramer	3
Gus	3
Losmith	3
Monica	3
Phoebe	3
Rachel	3
Susan	3
Alan	2
Brenda	2
Cedric	2
Harley	2
Jake	2
Jessica	2
Reva	2
Sadie	2

sname	class
Sebastian	2
Smithly	2
Brad	1
Elainie	1
Fraiser	1
George	1
Hillary	1
Lindsay	1
Lineas	1
Lujack	1
Lynette	1
Richard	1
Steve	1
Bill	
Genevieve	
Ken	
Lionel	
Mario	
Romona	
Smith	
Stephanie	
Thornton	
Zelda	

SELECTing Rows (Tuples)

We will use the term "rows" to indicate a line of output. More theoretically oriented database literature uses the term "tuple" instead of row. Access often uses the word, record, to refer to a row of data. The word "row" is more common in relational database and hence we will refer to a line of output as "rows."

You do not have to show all rows with a SELECT statement. You can selectively choose rows that you wish to display. In this section, we will show you how to selectively choose rows using the WHERE clause. The WHERE clause may also use the logical operators AND and OR, and the BETWEEN operator.

The WHERE Clause

You may restrict the output of rows (tuples) in the result set by adding a WHERE clause. When the WHERE clause is used, the database engine selects the records (rows) from the table that meet the conditions listed in the WHERE clause. If no WHERE clause is used, the query returns all rows from the table. In other words, the WHERE clause acts as a *row filter*.

The following is a simple form of the WHERE clause:

```
SELECT fields or attributes or columns
FROM   Table
WHERE  criteria;
```

For example, consider the following query:

```
SELECT  *
FROM    Student
WHERE   class = 4;
```

This produces the following 10 rows of output:

STNO	SNAME	MAJOR	CLASS	BDATE
3	Mary	COSC	4	7/6/78
13	Kelly	MATH	4	8/12/80
20	Donald	ACCT	4	10/15/77
24	Chris	ACCT	4	2/12/78
123	Holly	POLY	4	1/15/81
142	Jerry	COSC	4	3/12/78
145	Harrison	ACCT	4	2/12/77
146	Francis	ACCT	4	6/11/77
31	Jake	COSC	4	2/12/78
161	Benny	CHEM	4	6/10/80

The result set in this query consists of all the fields in the table, Student, but only the rows WHERE the value of the class attribute is equal to 4 (seniors) are selected for the result set.

All of the comparison operators that can be used in a WHERE clause are listed here:

- > (greater than)
- <> not equal
- = equal
- >= greater than or equal to
- <= less than or equal to

To include multiple conditions in a WHERE clause, logical operators, AND and OR, and the BETWEEN operator may be used. The following sections discuss the use of the AND, OR, and BETWEEN operators in the WHERE clause.

Using AND

You may further restrict the output of rows (tuples) in the result set by using an AND clause, which in effect works like more than one WHERE clause. Using the AND clause is one way of combining conditions in a WHERE clause.

For example, consider the following query:

```
SELECT  *
FROM    Student
WHERE   class = 4
AND     major = 'ACCT';
```

This produces the following four rows of output:

STNO	SNAME	MAJOR	CLASS	BDATE
20	Donald	ACCT	4	10/15/77
24	Chris	ACCT	4	2/12/78
145	Harrison	ACCT	4	2/12/77
146	Francis	ACCT	4	6/11/77

> The reason 'ACCT' is in single quotes is that text or character data has to be included in quotes (there is an extensive discussion of data types in the next chapter). Numeric data (class = 4) should not be in quotes.

The result set in this query consists of all the fields in the table, Student, but only the rows WHERE the value of the class attribute is equal to 4 (seniors) *and* the major of the student is Accounting. The AND means that *both* the criteria, class = 4 and major = 'ACCT', have to be met for the row to be included in the result set.

Using OR

Another way to combine conditions in a WHERE clause is by using the OR operator. The OR operator can be used when either of the conditions can be met for a row to be included in the result set. For example, consider the following query:

```
SELECT  *
FROM    Student
WHERE   class = 4
OR      major = 'ACCT';
```

This produces the following 11 rows of output:

STNO	SNAME	MAJOR	CLASS	BDATE
3	Mary	COSC	4	7/6/78
13	Kelly	MATH	4	8/12/80
20	Donald	ACCT	4	10/15/77
24	Chris	ACCT	4	2/12/78
123	Holly	POLY	4	1/15/81
142	Jerry	COSC	4	3/12/78
145	Harrison	ACCT	4	2/12/77
146	Francis	ACCT	4	6/11/77
148	Sebastian	ACCT	2	10/14/76
31	Jake	COSC	4	2/12/78
161	Benny	CHEM	4	6/10/80

This result set is a list of all students who are accounting majors, as well those who are seniors (class = 4). The OR means that either of the criteria, class = 4 or major = 'ACCT', has to be met for the row to be included in the result set.

Using BETWEEN

An optional way to combine comparisons in a WHERE clause is by using the BETWEEN operator. BETWEEN allows you to determine whether a value occurs within a given range of values. The syntax of the BETWEEN operator can be written as follows:

```
SELECT. . .
FROM
WHERE
BETWEEN value1 AND value2;
```

If we want to find all the students between classes 1 and 3, we type the following:

```
SELECT   sname, class
FROM     Student
WHERE    class
BETWEEN  1 AND 3;
```

This produces 28 rows of output (of which the first 16 rows are shown):

sname	class
Lineas	1
Brenda	2
Richard	1
Lujack	1
Reva	2
Elainie	1
Harley	2
Lynette	1
Susan	3
Monica	3
Hillary	1
Phoebe	3
Sadie	2
Jessica	2
Steve	1
Brad	1

In Access SQL, **value1** in the BETWEEN clause does not have to be less than **value2**. In most other versions of SQL, **value1** has to be less than **value2**. Note that the end points of the comparison are included in the result set, so the BETWEEN that we illustrated may also be written as follows:

```
SELECT   sname, class
FROM     Student
WHERE    class >=1
AND      class <=3;
```

The COUNT Function

In this section we introduce the COUNT function and the concept of null values. It is often desirable to explore the *number* of rows that will be obtained in a result set without actually displaying all of the result set (output) itself. This is especially true for larger outputs. For larger tables, you may want to determine how many rows will be obtained in a result set, without actually displaying the result set itself. This can be done in SQL in Access with a "row-counter" function called COUNT.

For example, if you execute the following command:

```
SELECT   *
FROM     Student;
```

The output will include all the rows of the Student table plus all the values for all fields in those rows. If you want to know *only* the number of rows in the result set (rather than the actual rows themselves), you can use the following command:

```
SELECT   COUNT(*)
FROM     Student;
```

This produces the following output:

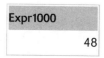

You can also count the occurrence of attributes. For example, if you type the following:

```
SELECT   COUNT(class)
FROM     Student;
```

It would give you:

COUNT(class) counts only the rows in which class is not null, meaning it counts only the rows that have a value. Therefore, the preceding output is 38 rows rather than 48 rows because the class field in the Student table includes 10 null values. If you want to use COUNT to count rows including null values, you must use COUNT(*). The next section discusses null values in more detail.

Null Values

Null values are used to designate missing data in tables. The IS NULL condition is the only condition that tests for nulls. Null values are ignored by all other conditions. Rows with null values cannot be retrieved by = NULL, since NULL signifies a missing value. Nulls are not considered like any other value in a table either, since nulls do not have data types. There is no distinction between nulls in numeric fields and nulls in text fields or date fields. The following query identifies student names and classes of students (from the Student table) that have null values for their class fields:

```
SELECT  sname, class
FROM    Student
WHERE   class IS NULL;
```

This produces the following 10 rows of output:

sname	class
Bill	
Genevieve	
Stephanie	
Thornton	
Lionel	
Zelda	
Mario	
Romona	
Ken	
Smith	

Using Aliases

We can enhance the output and readability of a query by using column and/or table aliases, both of which are discussed in this section.

Column Aliases

When writing a query, it is often useful to enhance its output and readability by using a **column alias**. A column alias is declared following the column designation in the result set part of a SELECT statement.

For purposes of comparison, the following is a query *without* a column alias:

```
SELECT  sname, major, class
FROM    Student
WHERE   class = 4;
```

This produces the following 10 rows of output:

sname	major	class
Mary	COSC	4
Kelly	MATH	4
Donald	ACCT	4
Chris	ACCT	4
Holly	POLY	4
Jerry	COSC	4
Harrison	ACCT	4
Francis	ACCT	4
Jake	COSC	4
Benny	CHEM	4

Note that the column headings for the result set are the field names from the Student table. To display more descriptive column headings, you can place column aliases just after the column name by using AS in the SELECT statement. The following is an example of a query *with* simple column aliases:

```
SELECT sname AS Student_name, major AS Student_major, class AS
Student_class
FROM    Student
WHERE   class = 4;
```

This produces the following 10 rows of output (note the change in column headings):

Student_name	Student_major	Student_class
Mary	COSC	4
Kelly	MATH	4
Donald	ACCT	4
Chris	ACCT	4
Holly	POLY	4
Jerry	COSC	4
Harrison	ACCT	4
Francis	ACCT	4
Jake	COSC	4
Benny	CHEM	4

You may also use more complex column aliases. For example, you can embed a blank in the column aliases by putting the column aliases in single or double quotes, as shown in the following example:

```
SELECT  sname AS "Student Name", major AS "Student Major",
class AS "Student Class"
FROM    Student
WHERE   class=4;
```

This produces the following 10 rows of output:

"Student Name"	"Student Major"	"Student Class"
Mary	COSC	4
Kelly	MATH	4
Donald	ACCT	4
Chris	ACCT	4
Holly	POLY	4
Jerry	COSC	4
Harrison	ACCT	4
Francis	ACCT	4
Jake	COSC	4
Benny	CHEM	4

Whereas some versions of SQL like Oracle will often wrap column headings, Access displays column headings on a single line, but note that these headings have quotes around them. To display the preceding column headings with no quotes around them, place them in brackets, [ ], as shown in the following query:

```
SELECT  sname AS [Student Name], major AS [Student Major],
class AS [Student Class]
FROM    Student
WHERE   class=4;
```

This produces the headings shown in the following output:

Student Name	Student Major	Student Class
Mary	COSC	4
Kelly	MATH	4
Donald	ACCT	4
Chris	ACCT	4
Holly	POLY	4
Jerry	COSC	4
Harrison	ACCT	4
Francis	ACCT	4
Jake	COSC	4
Benny	CHEM	4

Since this output looks a lot neater, from now on we will use brackets to enclose aliases.

Table Aliases

A *table alias* is a temporary name for a table that allows us to short-hand a table's name when we reference that table in a query. A table alias is usually used when the same table is used more than once in more complex queries. The following is an example of the previous query written with a one-letter table alias:

```
SELECT  s.sname
FROM    Student s
WHERE   s.class = 4;
```

This produces the following output (10 rows):

sname
Mary
Kelly
Donald
Chris
Holly
Jerry
Harrison
Francis
Jake
Benny

A table alias is defined by a letter *after* the table name (as shown in the previous query), so the table alias for Student is s. Thus, s could be used in place of Student if the table name needed to be used again in the query. Some people prefer a short, meaningful word or expression rather than a one-letter table alias, but the one-letter alias is very common among SQL users. We will use a lot of table aliases in future commands (Chapter 4 and onward), primarily in all multi-table queries.

Table Qualifiers

Table qualifiers are needed when more than one table is being used in a query, and the fields of different tables have the same name, such as FieldA. In such a case, without a table qualifier, Access will not know whether the query refers to FieldA of Table1 or FieldA of Table2. Therefore, we have to use a table qualifier in the form Table1.FieldA, where Table1 is the table qualifier (which is usually an alias).

Following is an example of an earlier query written with a table qualifier:

```
SELECT   *
FROM     Student
WHERE    student.class = 4;
```

In this query, student in the WHERE clause is the table qualifier.

A table qualifier may also be a table alias, as shown in the following query:

```
SELECT   *
FROM     Students
WHERE    s.class = 4;
```

Here, s (the table alias) is also the table qualifier.

The output of the preceding two queries will be the same as shown earlier (in the section, "The WHERE Clause"). As with table aliases, we will use a lot of table qualifiers in future commands (Chapter 4 and onward), primarily in all multi-table queries.

A Convention for Writing SQL Statements

Although no fixed rules exist for writing SQL commands which may contain multiple commands and lines, we suggest that you follow a few conventions that will help you as the commands you write become more involved:

• Use uppercase letters for the keywords, like SELECT, FROM, and WHERE. Use lowercase letters for the user-supplied words (since SQL in Access is not case sensitive for commands).

• Align the keywords SELECT, FROM, and WHERE on separate lines, like this:

```
SELECT   *
FROM     Student
WHERE    class = 4;
```

A Few Notes about SQL Syntax in Access

Below we provide some points that you need to know about SQL syntax in Access:

• Many versions of SQL allow the programmer to use "comments," non-executable words put in SQL statements to make the intent of a query clearer. Access does not allow comments in the SQL window.

• In Access SQL, single quotes and double quotes have the same meaning.

• Access allows blank lines in the SQL window, but does not allow any characters after the semicolon that marks the end of the SQL statement.

CHAPTER 2 REVIEW QUESTIONS

1. What is usually the first word in a SQL statement?

2. What is the ORDER BY used for?

3. What is the default order in an ORDER BY?

4. What kind of comparison operators can be used in a WHERE clause?

5. What are three major operators that can be used to combine conditions on a WHERE clause? Explain the operators with examples.

6. What are the two logical operators?

7. In a WHERE clause, do you need to enclose a text field in quotes? Do you need to enclose a numeric field in quotes?

8. Is a null value equal to anything? Can a space in a field be considered a null value? Why or why not?

9. Will COUNT(field) include fields with null values in its count?

10. What are column aliases? Why would you want to use column aliases? How can you embed blanks in column aliases?

11. What are table qualifiers? When should table qualifiers be used?

12. Are semicolons required at the end of Access SQL statements?

CHAPTER 2 EXERCISES

> Refer to Appendix 1 for a complete list of all tables (and their fields) available in the student.mdb database.

In writing out all the following queries, try to use the conventions for writing SQL statements. Also, for future reference, you may want to get into the practice of saving your queries by question number. For example, save the query you write for question 2a as **query2a**. Print the query and your results.

1. The student.mdb database used in this book has the following tables: Student, Course, Section, Prereq (for prerequisite), Grade_report, Department_to_major, and Room. Display the data from each of these tables by using the simple form of the SELECT * statement.

2. a. Display the student name and student number of all students who are juniors (Hint: class = 3).

   b. Display all the junior student names and numbers in descending order by name.

3. a. Display the course name and course number of all courses that are three credit hours.

   b. Display all the three-credit-hour course names and course numbers in ascending order by course name.

4. Display the building number, room number, and room capacity of all rooms in descending order by room capacity. Use appropriate column aliases to make your output more readable.

5. Display the course number, instructor, and building number of all courses that were offered in the Fall semester of 1998. Use appropriate column aliases to make your output more readable.

6. List the student number of all students who have grades of C or D.

7. List the student name of all students who have A grades but null values in their class field (of the `Student` table).

8. List the `offering_dept` of all courses that are more than three credit hours.

9. Display the student name of all students who have a major of "COSC."

10. Find the capacity of room 120 in Bldg 36.

11. Display a list of all student names ordered by major.

12. Display a list of all student names ordered by major, and by class within major. Use appropriate table and column aliases.

13. Count the number of departments in the `Department_to_major` table.

14. Count the number of buildings in the Room table.

15. What output will the following query produce?

```
SELECT COUNT(class)
FROM    Student
WHERE   class IS NULL;
```

Why do you get this output?

16. Use the BETWEEN operator to list all the sophomores, juniors, and seniors from the `Student` table.

Creating and Populating Tables

Topics covered in this chapter

In the Access database, data is stored in tables (also known as *relations* in relational database theory). Whereas Chapter 2 discussed how to write queries to retrieve data from *existing* tables by using the SELECT statement, in this chapter, we discuss how to open (create) a new database, create and populate *new* tables through SQL in Access by using the CREATE TABLE command, as well as how to alter and delete tables and their data by using SQL statements such as INSERT, UPDATE, and DELETE. Although Access's menu-oriented features are useful in creating and working with simple tables, if you wish to perform advanced operations while creating and populating tables, you need to have SQL knowledge. Therefore, we take a step-by-step approach to demonstrating how to create and manipulate table structures and populate and depopulate tables through SQL. Throughout the chapter, we also show the icons for the different types of SQL queries. In the final section of this chapter, we discuss the DATE data type and the formatting available for dates. (Chapter 5 covers calculations and manipulations with the DATE field.)

In a CREATE TABLE command, in addition to the field names, the data types and sizes of the fields have to be included, so before we get into the discussion of how to create or open a new database and then how to create and populate tables, we first discuss the data types available in Access SQL.

Data Types in Access

A field's **data type** determines what kind of information or values each field can contain and what operations can be performed on those values. Access supports 14 primary data types: TEXT, CHAR, INTEGER, REAL, FLOAT, DECIMAL, SMALLINT, TINYINT, MONEY, DATETIME, BINARY, BIT, IMAGE, and UNIQUEIDENTIFIER. These primary data types are the **internal names,** the names that are used when discussing the internals of the database engine.

Several of the primary data types also have valid synonyms that can be used instead of the regular data types. The synonyms are **external names** that are intended to make one SQL product compatible with another.

The more specific you are when selecting a data type for a field, the more accurate the information in your database will be. The following sections briefly describe each data type and its valid synonyms.

TEXT Type

The TEXT type should be used to enter

• text

• numbers that do not require any calculations, such as phone numbers or Zipcodes

• fields with a combination of text, numbers, and other symbols

A TEXT field can contain up to 2.14GB of information. Valid synonyms for the TEXT field are LONGTEXT, LONGCHAR, NOTE, NTEXT, and MEMO.

If the TEXT type is used without specifying the optional length, for example, TEXT, a LONGTEXT field is created. If the optional length is specified, for example, TEXT(20), the data type is equivalent to the CHAR data type.

> ANSI SQL does not support the TEXT type.

CHAR Type

The CHAR type should be used to enter

- text

- numbers that do not require any calculations, such as phone numbers or Zipcodes

- fields with a combination of text, numbers, and other symbols

A CHAR field can contain up to 255 characters per field. Valid synonyms for the CHAR field are TEXT(n), ALPHANUMERIC, CHARACTER, STRING, VARCHAR, CHARACTER VARYING, NCHAR, and NATIONAL CHARACTER.

Characters in fields defined as TEXT or CHAR are stored in Unicode representation format. Unicode requires 2 bytes to store each character.

NUMERIC Types

Access has several numeric data types: INTEGER, REAL, FLOAT, DECIMAL, SMALLINT, and TINYINT. A brief description of each of the numeric data types and their valid synonyms is provided next.

> ANSI SQL supports all the numeric types except TINYINT.

INTEGER Type

INTEGER is a long integer. It uses 4 bytes. The range of values is from −2,147,483,648 to 2,147,483,647.

Valid synonyms for INTEGER are LONG, INT, and INTEGER4.

REAL Type

REAL should be used for single-precision floating-point values. REALs use 4 bytes.

Valid synonyms for REAL are SINGLE, FLOAT4, and IEEESINGLE.

FLOAT Type

FLOAT should be used for double-precision floating-point values. FLOATs use 8 bytes.

Valid synonyms for FLOAT are DOUBLE, NUMBER, IEEEDOUBLE, and FLOAT8.

REAL and FLOAT data types are most often used in scientific calculations.

DECIMAL Type

DECIMAL is an exact numeric data type. With DOUBLE, you can define both precision (1–28) and scale (0–defined precision). The default precision and scale are 18 and 0, respectively. The DECIMAL type uses 17 bytes.

Valid synonyms for DECIMAL are NUMERIC and DEC.

SMALLINT Type

SMALLINT is an integer between –32,768 and 32,767. SMALLINT uses 2 bytes.

Valid synonyms for SMALLINT are SHORT and INTEGER2.

TINYINT Type

TINYINT is used to store integer values between 0 and 255. TINYINT uses 1 byte to store information.

Valid synonyms for TINYINT are INTEGER1 and BYTE.

MONEY Type

> ANSI SQL does not support the MONEY data type.

The MONEY type should be used when working with currency data. The MONEY type inserts the currency symbol and calculates numeric data with one to four decimal places. This data is accurate up to 15 digits on the left of the decimal point and up to 4 digits on the right of the decimal point. The MONEY type uses 8 bytes to store information.

A valid synonym for MONEY is CURRENCY.

DATETIME Type

The DATETIME type should be used to include data and time values between the years AD 100 and AD 9999. The DATETIME type is useful for calendar as well as clock data. It also allows you to calculate seconds, minutes, hours, days, months, and years. For example, a DATETIME field can be used to find the difference between two dates. The DATETIME type uses 8 bytes to store information.

Valid synonyms for the DATETIME type are DATE and TIME.

> ANSI SQL's equivalents to the DATETIME type are DATE, TIME, and TIMESTAMP.

BINARY Type

Any type of data may be stored in a field of this type, since the data in this field will be stored in binary form. No transformation of data is made in a field of this type. How the data has been input in a BINARY field dictates how it will appear in the output. BINARY types use 1 byte per character to store information. Access also has a LONGBINARY type (equivalent to Oracle's LOB data types), which can store up to 1.2GB of data.

BIT Type

This data type should be used for fields that store only one of two values, such as Yes/No, True/False, or On/Off. The BIT data type uses 1 byte to store information.

Valid synonyms for the BIT type are BOOLEAN, LOGICAL, and YESNO.

> ANSI SQL does not have an equivalent to Microsoft Jet SQL's BIT data type.

IMAGE Type

This is used for OLE objects (OLE stands for Object Linking and Embedding). An OLE object can contain an external object (Excel spreadsheet, Word document, or graphic image) that is linked or embedded into an Access table. A linked object is one where the source is not a part of the Access database. An embedded object is placed in the database as part of the data. An IMAGE type can hold up to 2.14GB of information.

Valid synonyms for IMAGE are LONGBINARY, GENERAL, and OLEOBJECT.

> ANSI SQL does not have an equivalent to Microsoft Jet SQL's IMAGE data type.

UNIQUEIDENTIFIER Type

A UNIQUEIDENTIFIER type is a unique identification number used with remote procedure calls. It uses 128 bits.

> ANSI SQL does not have an equivalent to Microsoft Jet SQL's UNIQUEIDENTIFIER data type.

Opening a Database

In Access, a table has to be created in a database. So, before we can create a table, we have to open a database. We have two options for opening a database—we could create a new database, or we could open an existing database. We will first show the steps for creating a new database to create a table, and then we will go over the steps for opening an existing database to create a new table.

Creating a New Database to Create a Table

To create a new table in a new, blank database, you have to first open a new, blank database following the steps below.

Once you start Access, click on **Blank Access database**, then click **OK** (as shown in Figure 3.1).

This will take you to the following screen (Figure 3.2). On this screen, first select the directory that you wish to work in, and then type in a name for your database. According to Figure 3.2, we are going to work in the Access directory, and the name of our new database will be work_database1.mdb. Once you have typed in a name for your database, click **Create**.

You will now be on a screen that you are familiar with (Figure 3.3). From this screen, select **Queries**, **Create query in Design View**, **New**, and then, in the **New Query** window that opens up, select **Design view** and then **OK** (as shown in Figure 1.4). Then **Close** the **Show Table** dialog box (as shown in Figure 1.5), and then click **SQL** (as shown in Figure 1.6).

FIGURE 3.1 Opening a New, Blank Database

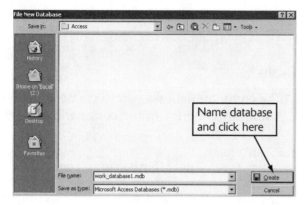

FIGURE 3.2 Naming a New, Blank Database

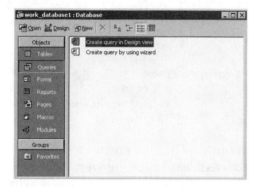

FIGURE 3.3 The work_database1.mdb Database

You are now ready to type in your query to create a new table in this new database. Next, follow the "Creating a Table" section.

Opening an Existing Database to Create a Table

A table can also be created in an existing database. In this section we will show you how to open an existing database to create a table.

For example, to create a new table in the existing student.mdb database, open student.mdb as shown in the "Opening the student.mdb Database" section of Chapter 1. Then, select **Queries**, **Create query in Design View**, **New**, and then, in the **New Query** window that opens up, select **Design view** and then **OK** (as shown in Figure 1.4). Then **Close** the **Show Table** dialog box (as shown in Figure 1.5), and then click **SQL** (as shown in Figure 1.6).

You are now ready to type in your query to create a new table in `student.mdb`.

Creating a Table

The CREATE TABLE command allows you to create a table in which you may store data. A simplified syntax of the command follows:

```
CREATE TABLE Tablename
  (attribute_name type,  attribute_name, type, .....);
```

To demonstrate how this command works, this section provides two examples.

For the first example, we will create a table called `Employee` that has four fields (attributes). First, type the following in a SQL view screen Figure 1.7:

```
CREATE TABLE  Employee (name             VARCHAR(20),
                        address          VARCHAR(20),
                        employee_number   NUMBER,
                        salary            CURRENCY);
```

Then, click the run button (**!**). This creates a table called `Employee` with four fields: `name`, `address`, `employee_number`, and `salary`. The data type of `name` is VARCHAR (varying character), with a maximum length of 20 characters (while CHAR in most versions of SQL means a fixed-length character string, CHAR and VARCHAR in Access are synonyms). The data type of `address` is CHAR, with a maximum length of 20 characters. The data type of `employee_number` is NUMBER, a synonym for FLOAT in Access. The data type of `salary` is CURRENCY, a synonym for the data type MONEY.

> Whereas most SQL implementations (other than Access) use CHAR for a fixed-length character field and VARCHAR for a variable-length character field, Access uses CHAR for a fixed-length field and *either* CHAR or VARCHAR for a variable-length field.

To look at the design of the table you just created, click the **Tables** tab in the **Objects** list, click the table Employee, and then click the **Design** button (as described in the "Viewing Table Designs" section of Chapter 1). This opens the screen shown in Figure 3.4.

For the second example, we will create a table called `Names`:

```
CREATE TABLE Names
   (name VARCHAR(20));
```

This table has only one field, `name`. Its data type is VARCHAR.

FIGURE 3.4 Design of Employee Table

Inserting Values into a Table

There are several ways to insert values into a table using SQL in Access. We will illustrate the two most commonly used ways: INSERT INTO .. VALUES and INSERT INTO .. SELECT.

Using INSERT INTO .. VALUES

One way to insert values into *one* row of a table is to use the INSERT INTO command with the VALUES option. As an example, using the Names table we created in the preceding section, you could type the following into a SQL view screen (Figure 1.7) and then run it:

```
INSERT INTO Names
VALUES ('Joe Smith');
```

where

- INSERT is the name of the command.

- INTO is a necessary keyword.

- Names is the name of an existing table.

- VALUES is another necessary keyword.

- "Joe Smith" is a string of letters corresponding to the data type (refer to the Names table example in the preceding section).

If you next type the following SQL query:

```
SELECT  *
FROM    Names;
```

You get the following result:

name
Joe Smith

The INSERT INTO .. VALUES command appends values to a table (that is, values are added to the end of the table). So, if you use INSERT INTO .. VALUES again as follows:

```
INSERT INTO Names
VALUES ('Sudip Kumar');
```

You get this result:

name
Joe Smith
Sudip Kumar

If you created a table with *n* attributes (columns), you usually would have *n* values in the INSERT INTO .. VALUES statement, in the order of the definition of the fields in the table. For example, to insert into the Employee table that you created earlier, the INSERT INTO .. VALUES statement to insert a row would have to match column for column and would look like this:

```
INSERT INTO Employee
VALUES ('Joe Smith', '123 4th St.', 101, 2500);
```

Note that CHAR data is entered with quotes around it. Numeric data does not use quotes (as shown by the 101 and 2500, both of which have been entered without quotes).

Now if you type:

```
SELECT  *
FROM    Employee;
```

You get the following:

name	address	employee_number	salary
Joe Smith	123 4th St.	101	$2,500.00

Notice that CHAR or TEXT data is left-justified by default, while numeric fields are right-justified, as shown by the fields employee_number and salary. Also, the salary field was automatically formatted with a "$" in the output since it was defined as a CURRENCY field. And, note that a comma automatically gets inserted into the CURRENCY field (`salary`), but not into the NUMERIC field (`employee_number`).

An INSERT statement in Access is stored as a SQL INSERT query. The icon for this query is shown in Figure 3.5.

An INSERT that looks like the following is incorrect because it does not include all four attributes of `Employee`:

```
INSERT INTO Employee
VALUES ('Joe Smith', '123 4th St.');
```

But you may write an INSERT like this to insert a row with less than all the attributes:

```
INSERT INTO Employee (name, address)
VALUES ('Joe Smith', '123 4th St.');
```

In this case, the row will contain nulls or default values for the values you left out, as shown here:

name	address	employee_number	salary
Joe Smith	123 4th St.		

An INSERT that looks like the following is incorrect because it does not have the values in the same order as the definition of the table:

```
INSERT INTO Employee
VALUES (2500, 'Joe Smith', 101, '123 4th St.');
```

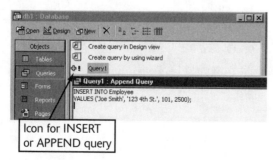

Icon for INSERT or APPEND query

FIGURE 3.5 Icon for INSERT or APPEND Query

If the data had to be specified in this order, the statement could be corrected by specifying the column names like this:

```
INSERT INTO Employee (salary, name, employee_number, address)
VALUES (2500, 'Joe Smith', 101, '123 4th St.');
```

The preceding query produces the following output:

name	address	employee_number	salary
Joe Smith	123 4th St.	101	$2,500.00

The following INSERT would also be legal if the address and the salary were unknown (null) when the row (tuple) was created, provided that the address and salary attributes allowed nulls:

```
INSERT INTO Employee
VALUES ('Joe Smith', null, 101, null);
```

The preceding query produces this output:

name	address	employee_number	salary
Joe Smith		101	

Now suppose we used the INSERT INTO .. VALUES command to insert valid data into the Employee table, so that the Employee table now looks as follows:

name	address	employee_number	salary
Joe Smith	123 4th St.	101	$2,500.00
Pradeep Saha	27 Shillingford	103	$3,300.00
Sumit Kumar	95 Oxford Rd	105	$1,200.00
Joya Das	23 Pesterfield Cr	114	$2,290.00
Terry Livingstone	465 Easter Ave	95	$3,309.00

Using INSERT INTO .. SELECT

With INSERT INTO .. VALUES, you insert only one row at a time into a table. With the INSERT INTO .. SELECT option, you may (and usually do) insert *many* rows into a table at one time.

To populate the Names table (which you created earlier) with the INSERT INTO .. SELECT, the general form of the command would be as follows:

```
INSERT INTO target_table(field)
  "SELECT    clause";
```

For example (if the Names table were empty), you could type the following:

```
INSERT INTO Names(name)
  SELECT  name
  FROM    Employee;
```

This would produce the following five rows of output:

name
Joe Smith
Pradeep Saha
Sumit Kumar
Joya Das
Terry Livingstone

The preceding query copies all the names from the Employee table to the Names table. We do not have to copy all the names from the Employee table. For example, if the Names table were empty, we could restrict the SELECT like this:

```
INSERT INTO Names(name)
  SELECT   name
  FROM     Employee
  WHERE    salary > 2600
```

This gives us only the following two rows in Names:

name
Pradeep Saha
Terry Livingstone

As with the INSERT INTO .. VALUES, if you create a table with *n* attributes, you usually would have *n* values in the INSERT INTO .. SELECT in the order of the table's definition.

For example, suppose we have a table named Emp1, created with three attributes:

```
Emp1 (addr, sal, empno),
```

The attributes stand for address, salary, and employee number, respectively.

Now suppose that we want to load an empty table called Emp1 from Employee with the appropriate attributes.

An INSERT INTO .. SELECT would look like this:

```
INSERT INTO Emp1(addr, sal, empno)
   SELECT   address, salary, employee_number
   FROM     Employee;
```

Emp1 would now have the following five rows:

addr	sal	empno
123 4th St	$2,500.00	101
27 Shillingford	$3,300.00	103
95 Oxford Rd	$1,200.00	105
23 Pesterfield Cr	$2,290.00	114
465 Easter Ave	$3,309.00	95

If we created a table, Emp2, with identical fields (or attributes) as Emp1, we could use the following INSERT to load the data from table Emp1 to Emp2:

```
INSERT INTO Emp2
   SELECT   *
   FROM     Emp1;
```

Emp2 would now have the following five rows:

> As with INSERT INTO .. VALUES, the INSERT INTO .. SELECT has to match column for column.

addr	sal	empno
123 4th St	$2,500.00	101
27 Shillingford	$3,300.00	103
95 Oxford Rd	$1,200.00	105
23 Pesterfield Cr	$2,290.00	114
465 Easter Ave	$3,309.00	95

Again, note that the Emp2 table has to exist before loading it with INSERT INTO .. SELECT.

Now Emp2 has the same data as Emp1.

An INSERT that looks as follows would fail, because Employee has four attributes and Emp1 has only three:

```
INSERT INTO Emp1
    SELECT   *
    FROM     Employee;
```

One caution: INSERT INTO .. SELECT could succeed if the types of the SELECT match the types of the attributes in the table to which we are inserting. For example, in the following statement, both sal and empno are numeric types:

```
INSERT INTO Emp1 (addr, sal, empno)
    SELECT   address, employee_number, salary
    FROM     Employee;
```

If you execute the preceding INSERT, the following output results:

addr	sal	empno
123 4th St	$101.00	2500
27 Shillingford	$103.00	3300
95 Oxford Rd	$105.00	1200
23 Pesterfield Cr	$114.00	2290
465 Easter Ave	$95.00	3309

The wrong information has been inserted in the Emp1 fields. The employee_number from Employee has been inserted into the sal field in Emp1, and the salary of Employee has been inserted into the empno field of Emp1.

Again, as you might guess from the last INSERT INTO .. VALUES example, you may load fewer attributes than the whole row of Emp1, with a statement like this:

```
INSERT INTO Emp1 (addr, sal)
   SELECT   address, salary
   FROM     Employee;
```

But, this would leave the other attribute, empno, with a value of null or with a default value, as shown here:

```
SELECT   *
FROM     Emp1;
```

This produces the following output:

addr	sal	empno
123 4th St	$2,500.00	
27 Shillingford	$3,300.00	
95 Oxford Rd	$1,200.00	
23 Pesterfield Cr	$2,290.00	
465 Easter Ave	$3,309.00	

Therefore, although you may load less than a "full row," you must be aware of the possibility of the resulting nulls.

In conclusion, be careful with this INSERT INTO .. SELECT command, because, unlike INSERT INTO .. VALUES (which inserts one row), you almost always insert multiple rows, and if types match, the insert will take place whether it makes sense or not.

The UPDATE Command

Another common command used for setting/changing data values in a table is the UPDATE command. As with INSERT INTO .. SELECT, you often UPDATE more than one row. To examine how the UPDATE command works, we will use the tables we created in the previous section. For example, if you want to set *all* salaries in the table Emp2 to zero, you may do so with one UPDATE command:

```
UPDATE Emp2
SET sal = 0;
```

This produces the following output:

addr	sal	empno
123 4th St	$0.00	101
27 Shillingford	$0.00	103
95 Oxford Rd	$0.00	105
23 Pesterfield Cr	$0.00	114
465 Easter Ave	$0.00	95

This commands sets all salaries in all rows of the Emp2 table to zero, regardless of previous values. This may be viewed as a dangerous command, because all rows are affected. Access will warn you when you are about to perform an UPDATE on a table, and you must accept the consequences if you really want to update all rows. Unlike some versions of SQL, there is no ROLLBACK command (that is, you cannot undo an UPDATE). Also, if you want to experiment with this command (or similar "dangerous" commands), you should first create a copy of the original table.

> There is no ROLL-BACK command in Access SQL.

It is often useful to include a WHERE clause in the UPDATE command so that you set values selectively. For example, you may UPDATE a particular employee from the Employee table with the following statement:

```
UPDATE   Employee
SET      salary = 0
WHERE    employee_number=101;
```

This produces the following output:

name	address	employee_number	salary
Joe Smith	123 4th St	101	$0.00
Pradeep Saha	27 Shillingford	103	$3,300.00
Sumit Kumar	95 Oxford Rd	105	$1,200.00
Joya Das	23 Pesterfield Cr	114	$2,290.00
Terry Livingstone	465 Easter Ave	95	$3,309.00

This updates only employee number 101's row. Once again, note that we do not need to use quotes around 101, since employee_number is defined as a NUMBER field. Quotes would have to be used around any CHAR field.

The icon for an UPDATE query is shown in Figure 3.6.

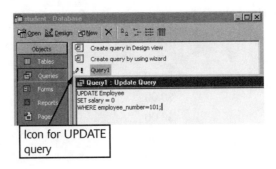

FIGURE 3.6 Icon for UPDATE Query

The ALTER TABLE Command

In addition to adding, changing, and updating rows in a table with INSERT and UPDATE, you also can add, change (modify), and delete *columns* in a table by using the ALTER TABLE command, as described in the following sections.

Adding a Column to a Table

The syntax for adding a column to a table is as follows:

```
ALTER TABLE Tablename
ADD column-name type;
```

For example, to add a column called `balance` (a NUMBER field) to the table `Employee`, you use the following:

```
ALTER TABLE Employee
ADD balance CURRENCY;
```

This command produces the table design for the `Employee` table shown in Figure 3.7.

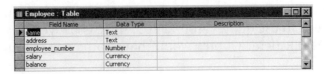

FIGURE 3.7 Field Added to Employee Table

Changing a Column's Type in a Table

The syntax for changing a column's type in a table is as follows:

```
ALTER TABLE Tablename
ALTER COLUMN column-name new_type;
```

> In other versions of SQL, such as SQL in Oracle, you cannot change the type if values exist that violate the data type.

For example, to change the data type of the `balance` field from CURRENCY to NUMBER, you would type the following:

```
ALTER TABLE EMPLOYEE
ALTER COLUMN balance NUMBER;
```

This produces the design for the `Employee` table shown in Figure 3.8.

Deleting a Column in a Table

The following is the syntax for deleting a column from a table:

```
ALTER TABLE Tablename
DROP column-name;
```

For example, to delete the column called `balance` from the table `Employee`, type the following:

```
ALTER TABLE Employee
DROP balance;
```

This produces the design for the `Employee` table shown in Figure 3.9, which is the original design for the table shown in Figure 3.4.

Field Name	Data Type	Description
name	Text	
address	Text	
employee_number	Number	
salary	Currency	
balance	Number	

FIGURE 3.8 Altered Column Type for balance in Employee Table

Field Name	Data Type	Description
name	Text	
address	Text	
employee_number	Number	
salary	Currency	

FIGURE 3.9 Design of Employee Table after Dropping Column

We will discuss several other uses of the ALTER TABLE command in subsequent chapters. For example, you can use it to define or change a default column value, enable or disable an integrity constraint, manage internal space, etc. You may add columns with little difficulty. If you modify a column, you may only make it bigger, not smaller; all the data in the database must conform to your modified type.

If you add a column, it will contain null values until you put data into it with an UPDATE command to change the values in the new column.

ALTER TABLE commands are known as *data definition queries* since they change the design of a table. The icon for a data definition query is shown in Figure 3.10.

This is the same icon that is used for the SELECT query with the CREATE TABLE command, since the CREATE TABLE command is also a data definition query.

The DELETE Command

In addition to inserting and updating rows in a table, it is also common to delete rows from a table. The following is the syntax of the DELETE command:

```
DELETE FROM Table
WHERE (condition);
```

The (condition) determines which rows of the table will be deleted.

> Again, because multiple rows can be affected by this command, it can be a dangerous command. Be careful when using it.

The following is an example of using the DELETE command on our original Employee table:

```
DELETE   *
FROM     Employee
WHERE    salary < 100;
```

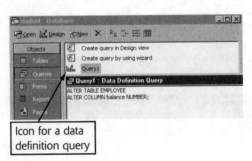

FIGURE 3.10 Icon for Data Definition Query

This produces the following four rows of output:

name	address	employee_number	salary
Pradeep Saha	27 Shillingford	103	$3,300.00
Sumit Kumar	95 Oxford Rd	105	$1,200.00
Joya Das	23 Pesterfield Cr	114	$2,290.00
Terry Livingstone	465 Easter Ave	95	$3,309.00

Before actually executing the deletion, Access warns you that the deletion is final and asks you to confirm the action.

The icon for a DELETE query is shown in Figure 3.11.

Deleting a Table

The SQL syntax to delete a table is:

```
DROP TABLE Tablename;
```

For example, to delete the table called `Names` from your database, you would use the following:

```
DROP TABLE Names;
```

The DATE Data Type and DATE Formatting

The DATE data type allows you not only to store dates but also to manipulate them (add dates, take differences between dates, format dates, and so on) by using a date function such as FORMAT.

> You can also delete a table as shown in the "Deleting Tables or Queries" section of Chapter 1, but here we show you the SQL syntax. It may also be a good idea to use the DROP TABLE command instead of DELETE to avoid accidental deletion of tables.

> The default date format in Access is mm/dd/yy.

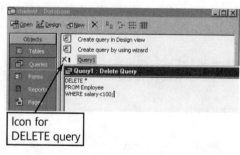

FIGURE 3.11 Icon for DELETE Query

Inserting Dates

> k5date is a field
that stands for
the date the child
first attended
kindergarten.

Suppose you define DATE types in a table like this:

```
CREATE TABLE DateTable    (birthdate    DATE,
                           k5date       DATE,
                           name         VARCHAR(20));
```

Data can now be entered into the birthday and k5date fields, which are both DATE fields, and into the name field. Access can accept dates in many formats.

Assuming that your CREATE TABLE is the same as the preceding example, then the following would be an example of an INSERT:

```
INSERT INTO DateTable
VALUES ('10-oct-01', '12/01/2006', 'Mala Sinha');
```

Note that quotes are required around date values.

Now, if you type the following

```
SELECT   *
FROM     DateTable;
```

> To get 12/01/06
instead of 12/1/06,
you need to use the
FORMAT com-
mand (discussed
later in this chapter).

the following appears in the DateTable table:

birthdate	k5date	name
10/10/01	12/1/06	Mala Sinha

Notice that DATE fields, like numeric fields, are, by default, aligned to the right.

Next we will insert dates using # instead of single quotes. The following INSERT statement

> If a date is entered
in a text string,
Access requires the
date to be enclosed
by the # sign;
Access then auto-
matically converts
the text string to a
date format.

```
INSERT INTO DateTable
VALUES ('10-oct-01', #12/01/2006#, 'Mala Sinha');
```

produces the same output:

birthdate	k5date	name
10/10/01	12/1/06	Mala Sinha

Invalid Dates

This section discusses what occurs when you enter an invalid value for a month or day. We first treat the situation in which an invalid value is entered for a month.

Suppose you type the following query, which has an invalid month, rwe, in the birthdate field:

```
INSERT INTO DateTable
VALUES ('10-rwe-01', '12/01/06', 'Mala Sinha');
```

You first get the message shown in Figure 3.12.

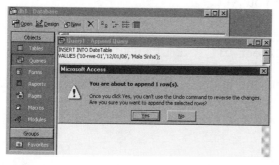

FIGURE 3.12 Appending a Row

If you click **OK**, you then get the "Type conversion failure" message shown in Figure 3.13.

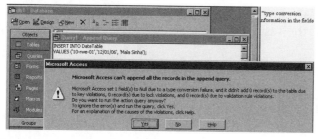

FIGURE 3.13 "Type conversion failure" Message

If you run the query anyway by clicking **Yes**, Access stores the record with the correct information in the k5date and name fields, but leaves the birthdate field null. So, if you now view the table by typing the following

```
SELECT  *
FROM    DateTable;
```

You get the following output:

birthdate	k5date	name
	12/1/06	Mala Sinha

Next, we look at how Access treats invalid days. If you use the following format (the birthdate field has '32-oct-01'), Access will reformat your date. Access thinks that you mean 10/1/32, and adds the field as such. In other words, you will not get a warning message that this may be an invalid date.

For example, if you type:

```
INSERT INTO DateTable
VALUES ('32-oct-01', '12/01/2006', 'Mala Sinha');
```

When you view the table, DateTable, the incorrect birthdate 10/1/32 appears:

birthdate	k5date	name
10/1/32	12/1/06	Mala Sinha

If you change the birthdate field to '32-oct-99' (as shown below), Access recognizes the incorrect day value and gives you the "type conversion failure" message previously shown in Figure 3.13. If you choose to run the query anyway by clicking **Yes**, Access again records the correct information in the rest of the fields but leaves the birthdate (incorrect date) field null.

So, if you type the following query

```
INSERT INTO DateTable
VALUES ('32-oct-99', '12/01/2006', 'Mala Sinha');
```

When you view the table, DateTable, the birthdate field now is null:

birthdate	k5date	name
	12/1/06	Mala Sinha

You get the same results if you change the `birthdate` to '32-oct-2001':

```
INSERT INTO DateTable
VALUES ('32-oct-2001', '12/01/2006', 'Mala Sinha');
```

When you view the table, `DateTable`, the `birthdate` field still is null:

birthdate	k5date	name
	12/1/06	Mala Sinha

Access is programmed to know how many days each month should have, so the following entry for the `birthdate` field (there is no September 31) would produce a "type conversion error," with similar consequences as above:

```
INSERT INTO DateTable
VALUES ('31-sep-01', '12/01/06', Mala Sinha);
```

When you view the table, `DateTable`, the `birthdate` field is null:

birthdate	k5date	name
	12/1/06	Mala Sinha

Using FORMAT

In Access, FORMAT is used to control the format in which a date will be displayed. All dates that are inserted in Access follow the same format (which is 2/1/01, with the year in a two-digit format), even if the dates were in a different format while being inserted (as can be seen in the various INSERT examples shown in the preceding section).

Suppose we populate the `DateTable` table with the following data:

birthdate	k5date	name
1/1/01	12/1/06	Mala Sinha
2/2/02	3/2/06	Mary Spencer
10/2/02	2/4/05	Bill Cox
12/29/98	5/5/04	Jamie Runner
6/16/99	3/3/03	Seema Kapoor

If we type the following query

```
SELECT  FORMAT (birthdate, 'mm-dd-yyyy') AS [DATE], name
FROM    DateTable;
```

we get the following output:

DATE	name
01-01-2001	Mala Sinha
02-02-2002	Mary Spencer
10-02-2002	Bill Cox
12-29-1998	Jamie Runner
06-16-1999	Seema Kapoor

Note the four-digit year format, resulting from the use of yyyy in the query.

The following are the date formats that are available in Access:

Format	Output
yyyy	2002 (four-digit year)
yy	02 (two-digit year)
mmmm	January (full name of month)
mmm	Jan (abbreviated name of month)
mm	01 (number of month)
dd	18 (day of month, 1 to 31)
dddd	Monday (day spelled out fully)
ddd	Mon (abbreviated name of day)
w	2 (number of the day of the week)
ww	34 (week of the year, from 1 to 54)

If we wish to format the birthdate field a little more—for example, in the following example we spell out the day of the week, include a two-digit date, spell out the month, and then include the four-digit year (and use a column alias for birthdate):

```
SELECT  FORMAT (Birthdate, 'dddd, dd mmmm, yyyy') AS [DATE],
name
FROM    DateTable;
```

This produces the following output:

DATE	name
Monday, 01 January, 2001	Mala Sinha
Saturday, 02 February, 2002	Mary Spencer
Wednesday, 02 October, 2002	Bill Cox
Tuesday, 29 December, 1998	Jamie Runner
Wednesday, 16 June, 1999	Seema Kapoor

Calculations can also be done with date fields. We will cover calculations on DATE fields in Chapter 5.

The FORMAT command does not work during inserts. For example, if you type the following INSERT:

```
INSERT INTO DateTable (Birthdate)
VALUES (FORMAT('2/1/2002', 'mm/dd/yyyy'));
```

The following would be stored in the table, DateTable:

birthdate	k5date	name
2/1/02		

CHAPTER 3 REVIEW QUESTIONS

1. The INSERT INTO .. VALUES command will insert values into the _____ of a table.

2. While you are inserting values into a table with the INSERT INTO .. VALUES command, does the order of the values in the INSERT statement have to be the same as the order of the values in the table?

3. While you are inserting values into a table with the INSERT INTO .. SELECT command, does the order of the values in the INSERT statement have to be the same as the order of the values in the table?

4. When would you use an INSERT INTO .. SELECT command versus an INSERT INTO .. VALUES command? Give an example of each.

5. What does the UPDATE command do?

6. Can you change the data type of a field in a table after the table has been created? If so, which command would you use?

7. How many primary data types does Access support?

8. Is there an ANSI equivalent of the TEXT data type?

9. Which numeric data type is not supported by ANSI SQL?

10. What is the default date format?

11. How do dates have to be entered in text strings in Access SQL?

12. What does the FORMAT command do?

13. Does Access SQL treat CHAR as a variable-length or fixed-length field? Do other SQL implementations treat it in the same way?

14. When columns are added to existing tables, what do they initially contain?

15. If you update a table in Access SQL, can you undo it?

16. What symbol does Access SQL require to enter dates in text strings?

CHAPTER 3 EXERCISES

1. a. Create a table called `Cust` with a customer number as a fixed-length character string of 3, an address with a variable-length character string of up to 20, and a numeric balance of five digits.

   b. Put values in the table with INSERT INTO .. VALUES. Use the form of INSERT INTO .. VALUES that requires you to have a value for each attribute; therefore, if you have a customer number, address, and balance, you must insert three values with INSERT INTO .. VALUES.

   c. Create at least five tuples (rows in the table) with customer numbers 101 to 105 and balances of 200 to 2000.

   d. Display the table with a simple SELECT.

   e. In the display of your `Cust` table, does your `balance` field show up with a $ symbol? If not, alter your table design so that a $ symbol is added to each of the balances.

   f. Show the balances for customers with customer numbers 103 and 104.

   g. Add a customer number 90 to your `Cust` table. Is it lined up with the rest of the customer numbers? Why or why not? If not, line it up with the rest of the customer numbers.

   h. Show a list of the customers in balance order (high to low), using ORDER BY in your SELECT. (Result: Five tuples or however many you created.)

2. From the Student table, display the student names, classes, and majors for freshmen or sophomores (class <= 2) in descending order.

3. From your Cust table, show a list of only the customer balances in ascending order where balance > 400. (You can choose some other constant or relation if you want, such as balance <= 600.) The results will depend on your data.

4. a. Create another two tables with the same data types as Cust but without the customer addresses. Call one table Cust1 and the other Cust2. Use attribute names cnum for customer number and bal for balance. Load the table with the data you have in the Cust table with one less tuple. Use an INSERT INTO .. SELECT with appropriate attributes and an appropriate WHERE clause.

    b. Display the resulting tables.

    c. Delete about half of your tuples from the Cust2 table ("DELETE FROM Cust2 WHERE bal < some value" [or bal > some value, etc.]).

    d. Show the Cust2 table after you have deleted the tuples.

5. a. Alter the Cust1 table by adding a date_opened column of type DATE. View the design of Cust1.

    b. Add some more data to the Cust1 table by using INSERT INTO .. VALUES.

    After each of the following, display the table.

    c. Set the date_opened value in all rows to "01-JAN-91".

    d. Set all balances to zero.

    e. Set the date_opened value of one of your rows to "21-OCT-60".

    f. Display the dates in the following format: four-digit year first, then the month (completely spelled out), then the date, and then the day of the week (completely spelled out).

    g. Change the type of the balance field in the Cust1 table to FLOAT (8,2). Display the table. Set the balance for one row to 888.88 and display the table again.

    h. Try changing the type of balance to INTEGER. What happens? Why?

    i. Delete the date_opened field of the Cust1 table.

    j. When you are finished with the exercise (but be sure you are finished), delete the tables Cust, Cust1, and Cust2.

Joins

Topics covered in this chapter

This chapter discusses joins. In Access, the "regular" join operations are called INNER JOINs, so we discuss and give examples of INNER JOINs first. Then, we show how the same join could also be achieved with a WHERE clause. The concepts of the Cartesian product, theta joins, equi-joins, self joins, and natural joins are also introduced. We also show how multiple table joins can be performed with nested INNER JOINs and with a WHERE clause. Finally, the concept of OUTER JOINs, with specific illustrations of the LEFT and RIGHT JOINs, is discussed.

The Join

Chapter 2 exposed you to some beginning SQL commands and demonstrated how to write simple query statements in SQL in Access. However, all the examples in Chapter 2 illustrated the use of just *one* table. In "real" databases, data is often spread over many tables. Thus, this chapter shows you how to join tables in a database so that you can easily retrieve data from more than one table. The join operation is used to combine related rows from two tables (relations) into a result set. The joining of more than one table (called a *join* function in relational databases) is fundamental to understanding relational databases, which are made up of relations (tables).

INNER JOINs

In Access SQL, the "regular" join operation is performed with the use of the INNER JOIN command. The INNER JOIN is the most common form of join used in Access. The INNER JOIN command is used in any FROM clause to combine records from two tables whenever there are matching values in a common field. The fields of the two tables being joined by the INNER JOIN are then matched using an ON clause.

The following is the simplest form of the INNER JOIN:

```
SELECT fields
FROM Table1 INNER JOIN Table2
ON Table1.field1=Table2.field1;
```

For example, from our database (`student.mdb`), if we want to find all the prerequisites of all the courses that have prerequisites, we have to join the `Prereq` table with the `Course` table. Before we can perform the join, we have to know which fields from the `Prereq` table and `Course` table can be joined. To make this determination, we first need to look at the descriptions of the `Prereq` and `Course` tables, shown in Figures 4.1 and 4.2, respectively.

Prereq : Table

Field Name	Data Type	Description
COURSE_Number	Text	
PREREQ	Text	

FIGURE 4.1 Description of Prereq Table

Field Name	Data Type	Description
COURSE_NAME	Text	
COURSE_NUMBER	Text	
CREDIT_HOURS	Number	
OFFERING_DEPT	Text	

FIGURE 4.2 Description of Course Table

From the descriptions, we can see that the Prereq table (which has attributes course_number and prereq) can be joined with the Course table (which has attributes course_name, course_number, credit_hours, and offering_dept) by the common field in both tables, course_number, as follows:

```
SELECT *
FROM Course c INNER JOIN Prereq p
ON c.course_number=p.course_number;
```

In the construction Course c, Course refers to the table, and c is the table alias. Typically, SQL programmers use single-letter table aliases. The table alias simplifies writing expressions. Note that this query could be written without the table alias as follows:

```
SELECT *
FROM Course INNER JOIN Prereq
ON Course.course_number=Prereq.course_number;
```

This query (with or without the alias) will display those rows (12 rows) that have course_number in the Course table equal to course_number in the Prereq table, as follows:

COURSE_NAME	c.Course_NUMBER	CREDIT_HOURS	OFFERING_DEPT	p.COURSE_NUMBER	PREREQ
MANAGERIAL FINANCE	ACCT3333	3	ACCT	ACCT3333	ACCT2220
DATA STRUCTURES	COSC3320	4	COSC	COSC3320	COSC1310
DATABASE	COSC3380	3	COSC	COSC3380	COSC3320
DATABASE	COSC3380	3	COSC	COSC3380	MATH2410
ADA - INTRODUCTION	COSC5234	4	COSC	COSC5234	COSC3320
ENGLISH COMP II	ENGL1011	3	ENGL	ENGL1011	ENGL1010

COURSE_NAME	c.Course_NUMBER	CREDIT_HOURS	OFFERING_DEPT	p.COURSE_NUMBER	PREREQ
FUND. TECH. WRITING	ENGL3401	3	ENGL	ENGL3401	ENGL1011
WRITING FOR NON MAJO	ENGL3520	2	ENGL	ENGL3520	ENGL1011
MATH ANALYSIS	MATH5501	3	MATH	MATH5501	MATH2333
AMERICAN GOVERNMENT	POLY2103	2	POLY	POLY2103	POLY1201
POLITICS OF CUBA	POLY5501	4	POLY	POLY5501	POLY4103
ORGANIC CHEMISTRY	CHEM3001	3	CHEM	CHEM3001	CHEM2001

Rows from the Course table without a matching row in the Prereq table are eliminated from the INNER JOIN result. This means that courses that do not have prerequisites are eliminated from the above join results. If there were nulls in the join attributes (in this case, course_number), the null rows would also be eliminated from the result of an INNER JOIN (since course_number in both tables is involved with the primary key, course_number could not be null).

Using a WHERE Clause Instead of an INNER JOIN

A second way of joining tables in Access is to use a WHERE clause (instead of using the INNER JOIN command). To perform a join with a WHERE clause, we list the tables to be joined in a FROM clause of a SELECT statement, and the "join condition" between the tables to be joined is specified in a WHERE clause.

The INNER JOIN from the preceding section instead could be written with a WHERE clause as follows:

```
SELECT   *
FROM     Course c, Prereq p
WHERE    c.course_number= p.course_number;
```

This will display the same 12 rows as shown above for the INNER JOIN.

Again, note the use of the table aliases in the query: c is used as a table alias for Course, and p is used as a table alias for Prereq. The table aliases are necessary because course_number is found in both tables. Without the table alias qualifier, the query will not work. As our queries get bigger and more complex, table aliases become even more useful. The explicit attribute qualifications (table aliases) will aid someone who may want to modify a query you wrote. We very strongly recommend using table aliases in all multi-table queries.

> In addition to using the WHERE clause to perform a JOIN, Access SQL also uses a newer clause introduced to perform joins, the INNER JOIN.

Field Types in Joins

Joins have to be performed on "like" fields (such as text to text, number to number, and so forth). Fields that are of Memo or OLE Object data types cannot be joined since these fields will generally not contain "like" fields.

The Cartesian Product

When joining tables by using a WHERE clause, you must be very careful not to get a Cartesian product of the two tables being joined. The Cartesian product is mathematically a binary operation in which two objects are combined in an "everything in combination with everything" fashion. The Cartesian product in SQL *per se* is usually not wanted-ed. If it is requested by accident, results are spurious.

Joining two tables together without using a WHERE clause and without using an INNER JOIN will produce a Cartesian product. An example of a Cartesian product would be:

```
SELECT   *
FROM     Course c, Prereq p;
```

The preceding command combines all the data in both tables and makes a new table. All rows in the Course table are combined with all rows in the Prereq table (a Cartesian product). The following shows only part of the result of this above Cartesian product:

COURSE_NAME	c.COURSE_NUMBER	CREDIT_HOURS	OFFERING_DEPT	p.COURSE_NUMBER	PREREQ
ACCOUNTING I	ACCT2020	3	ACCT	ACCT3333	ACCT2220
ACCOUNTING I	ACCT2020	3	ACCT	COSC3320	COSC1310
ACCOUNTING I	ACCT2020	3	ACCT	COSC3380	COSC3320
ACCOUNTING I	ACCT2020	3	ACCT	COSC3380	MATH2410
ACCOUNTING I	ACCT2020	3	ACCT	COSC5234	COSC3320
ACCOUNTING I	ACCT2020	3	ACCT	ENGL1011	ENGL1010
ACCOUNTING I	ACCT2020	3	ACCT	ENGL3401	ENGL1011
ACCOUNTING I	ACCT2020	3	ACCT	ENGL3520	ENGL1011
ACCOUNTING I	ACCT2020	3	ACCT	MATH5501	MATH2333
ACCOUNTING I	ACCT2020	3	ACCT	POLY2103	POLY1201
ACCOUNTING I	ACCT2020	3	ACCT	POLY5501	POLY4103
ACCOUNTING I	ACCT2020	3	ACCT	CHEM3001	CHEM2001
ACCOUNTING II	ACCT2220	3	ACCT	ACCT3333	ACCT2220
ACCOUNTING II	ACCT2220	3	ACCT	COSC3320	COSC1310
ACCOUNTING II	ACCT2220	3	ACCT	COSC3380	COSC3320
ACCOUNTING II	ACCT2220	3	ACCT	COSC3380	MATH2410
ACCOUNTING II	ACCT2220	3	ACCT	COSC5234	COSC3320
ACCOUNTING II	ACCT2220	3	ACCT	ENGL1011	ENGL1010
ACCOUNTING II	ACCT2220	3	ACCT	ENGL3401	ENGL1011
ACCOUNTING II	ACCT2220	3	ACCT	ENGL3520	ENGL1011
ACCOUNTING II	ACCT2220	3	ACCT	MATH5501	MATH2333
ACCOUNTING II	ACCT2220	3	ACCT	POLY2103	POLY1201
ACCOUNTING II	ACCT2220	3	ACCT	POLY5501	POLY4103
ACCOUNTING II	ACCT2220	3	ACCT	CHEM3001	CHEM2001
MANAGERIAL FINANCE	ACCT3333	3	ACCT	ACCT3333	ACCT2220
MANAGERIAL FINANCE	ACCT3333	3	ACCT	COSC3320	COSC1310
MANAGERIAL FINANCE	ACCT3333	3	ACCT	COSC3380	COSC3320
MANAGERIAL FINANCE	ACCT3333	3	ACCT	COSC3380	MATH2410
MANAGERIAL FINANCE	ACCT3333	3	ACCT	COSC5234	COSC3320
MANAGERIAL FINANCE	ACCT3333	3	ACCT	ENGL1011	ENGL1010

Before creating a Cartesian product, it is usually a good idea to get a count of the number of rows this Cartesian product will produce. This can be done by:

```
SELECT COUNT(*) AS [COUNT OF CARTESIAN]
FROM Course c, Prereq p;
```

This produces the following output:

COUNT OF CARTESIAN
384

From these results, we can see that the results of a Cartesian join will be a relation, say Q, which will have $n*m$ rows (where n is the number of rows from the first relation, and m is the number of rows from the second relation). In the preceding example, the result set has 384 rows (32 times 12), with all possible combinations of rows from the Course table and the Prereq table. If we compare these results with the results of the earlier query (with the WHERE clause), we can see that both the results have the same structure, but the earlier one has been row-filtered by the WHERE clause to include only those rows where there is equality between Course.course_number and Prereq.course_number. Put another way, the earlier results make more sense because they present only those rows that correspond to one another. The Cartesian product produces extra, meaningless rows. The Cartesian product can be called a join with no join (WHERE) condition. Oftentimes, the Cartesian product is the result of a user having forgotten to use an appropriate WHERE clause in the SELECT statement.

No Cartesian Product with an INNER JOIN Statement

Fortunately, Access does not allow you to produce a Cartesian product with the INNER JOIN statement, since the INNER JOIN requires an ON clause after the FROM clause. Therefore, the following query will produce a syntax error in Access:

```
SELECT *
FROM Course c INNER JOIN Prereq p;
```

Once again, the ON clause tells the INNER JOIN which field to join by, and this is missing in the above query, hence this query will not work.

Theta Joins and Equi-joins

Joins with comparison operators such as =, >, >=, <, <=, and <> on the WHERE or ON clauses are called theta joins. Joins with an = operator are called equi-joins, and joins with an operator other than an = sign are called nonequi-joins.

Equi-joins

The most common join involves join conditions with equality comparisons. Such a join, where the comparison operator is = in the WHERE or ON clause, is called an equi-join. That is, an equi-join is used whenever we want to join two tables were `field1` of the first table is equal to `field1` of the second table. In an equi-join, all join columns are included in the result set. The following is an example:

```
SELECT   *
FROM     Course c INNER JOIN Prereq p
ON       c.course_number=p.course_number;
```

The output for this query has been shown earlier in this chapter. As per the output, you will see that this query displays all rows that have `course_number` in the Course table equal to `course_number` in the Prereq table. And, all the join columns have been included in this result set. This means that `course_number` has been shown twice—once as per the Course table, and once as per the Prereq table—and this duplicate column is of course redundant.

Nonequi-joins

Theta joins that do not test for equality are called nonequi-joins. Nonequi-joins are rare. The following section provides an example of a theta join without an equality (=) operator (a nonequi-join).

Self Joins

On rare occasions, you will need to join a table with itself. Joining a table with itself is known as a self join.

The following is an example of a self join in which we are trying to find all the students who are more senior than other students (so we are joining the Student table with itself). First we open the Student table as **x**, and then we open another instance of the Student table as **y**. Then we join where x.class is greater than y.class (where y.class is 3, so this effectively gives us only the seniors). The use of the > sign is an example of a nonequi-join.

```
SELECT  x.sname + ' is more senior than ' + y.sname
FROM    Student AS x, Student AS y
WHERE   y.class = 3
AND     x.class > y.class;
```

This produces the 70 rows of output (of which we show the first 25 rows):

Expr1000
Mary is more senior than Susan
Mary is more senior than Monica
Mary is more senior than Phoebe
Mary is more senior than Rachel
Mary is more senior than Cramer
Mary is more senior than Losmith
Mary is more senior than Gus
Kelly is more senior than Susan
Kelly is more senior than Monica
Kelly is more senior than Phoebe
Kelly is more senior than Rachel
Kelly is more senior than Cramer
Kelly is more senior than Losmith
Kelly is more senior than Gus
Donald is more senior than Susan
Donald is more senior than Monica
Donald is more senior than Phoebe
Donald is more senior than Rachel
Donald is more senior than Cramer
Donald is more senior than Losmith
Donald is more senior than Gus
Chris is more senior than Susan
Chris is more senior than Monica
Chris is more senior than Phoebe
Chris is more senior than Rachel

In this join, all the rows where x.class is greater than y.class (which is 3) are joined to the rows that have y.class = 3. So, Mary, the first row that has x.class = 4, is joined to the first row greater than 3, which is Susan, and then is joined to the next row with y.class=3, which is Monica, and then Phoebe (whose y.class = 3), and so on. Then, the next row in the Student table with x.class = 4 is Kelly, so Kelly is joined to Susan (y.class = 3), and then to Monica (y.class = 3), and then to Phoebe (y.class = 3), and so on.

Natural Joins

The term "natural join" refers to an equi-join without the duplicate column and with the obvious join condition. The natural join on the Course and Prereq tables, would be as follows:

```
SELECT c.course_name, c.course_number, c.credit_hours,
c.offering_dept, p.prereq
FROM Course c INNER JOIN Prereq p
ON c.course_number=p.course_number;
```

This would produce the following 12 rows of output:

course_name	course_number	credit_hours	offering_dept	prereq
MANAGERIAL FINANCE	ACCT3333	3	ACCT	ACCT2220
DATA STRUCTURES	COSC3320	4	COSC	COSC1310
DATABASE	COSC3380	3	COSC	COSC3320
DATABASE	COSC3380	3	COSC	MATH2410
ADA – INTRODUCTION	COSC5234	4	COSC	COSC3320
ENGLISH COMP II	ENGL1011	3	ENGL	ENGL1010
FUND. TECH. WRITING	ENGL3401	3	ENGL	ENGL1011
WRITING FOR NON MAJO	ENGL3520	2	ENGL	ENGL1011

course_name	course_number	credit_hours	offering_dept	prereq
MATH ANALYSIS	MATH5501	3	MATH	MATH2333
AMERICAN GOVERNMENT	POLY2103	2	POLY	POLY1201
POLITICS OF CUBA	POLY5501	4	POLY	POLY4103
ORGANIC CHEMISTRY	CHEM3001	3	CHEM	CHEM2001

The implied join condition is the equality of `course_number` in the two tables, so it is displayed only once in the result set.

Using ORDER BY with a Join

The ORDER BY clause can be used in joins to order the output. For example, to order the output in the preceding section by `course_number`, we would type the following:

```
SELECT c.course_name, c.course_number, c.credit_hours,
c.offering_dept, p.prereq
FROM Course c INNER JOIN Prereq p
ON c.course_number=p.course_number
ORDER BY c.course_number;
```

Or this alternative:

```
SELECT c.course_name, c.course_number, c.credit_hours,
c.offering_dept, p.prereq
FROM Course c INNER JOIN Prereq p
ON c.course_number=p.course_number
ORDER BY 2;
```

This produces the same 12 rows as above, but ordered alphabetically in the order of `course_number`:

course_name	course_number	credit_hours	offering_dept	prereq
MANAGERIAL FINANCE	ACCT3333	3	ACCT	ACCT2220
ORGANIC CHEMISTRY	CHEM3001	3	CHEM	CHEM2001

course_name	course_number	credit_hours	offering_dept	prereq
DATA STRUCTURES	COSC3320	4	COSC	COSC1310
DATABASE	COSC3380	3	COSC	MATH2410
DATABASE	COSC3380	3	COSC	COSC3320
ADA - INTRODUCTION	COSC5234	4	COSC	COSC3320
ENGLISH COMP II	ENGL1011	3	ENGL	ENGL1010
FUND. TECH. WRITING	ENGL3401	3	ENGL	ENGL1011
WRITING FOR NON MAJO	ENGL3520	2	ENGL	ENGL1011
MATH ANALYSIS	MATH5501	3	MATH	MATH2333
AMERICAN GOVERNMENT	POLY2103	2	POLY	POLY1201
POLITICS OF CUBA	POLY5501	4	POLY	POLY4103

Joining More Than Two Tables

You will frequently need to perform a join in which you have to get data from more than two tables. A join is a pair-wise binary operation. In Access, you can join more than two tables in either of two ways: by using a nested INNER JOIN, or by using a WHERE clause.

Joining Multiple Tables Using a Nested INNER JOIN

The simplest form of the nested INNER JOIN is as follows:

```
SELECT fields
FROM table1 INNER JOIN
(table2 INNER JOIN table3
ON table3.field3=table2.field2)
ON table1.field1=table2.field2;
```

For example, if we want to see the courses that have prerequisites and the departments offering those courses, we have to first join the Course table with the Prereq table, and then join that result to the Department_to_major table. To determine which fields of the

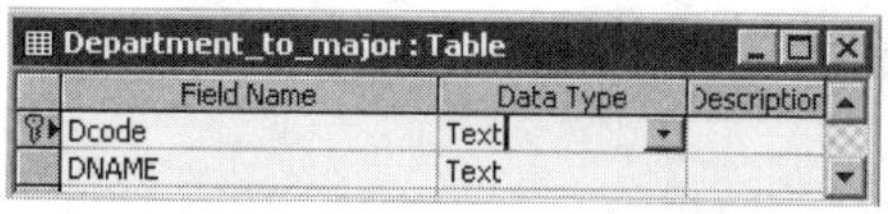

FIGURE 4.3 Description of `Department_to_major` Table

`Department_to_major` table can be used in the join, we have to also look at the description of the `Department_to_major` table, which is shown in Figure 4.3.

The following is the query to join the `Course` table to the `Prereq` table to the `Department_to_major` table:

```
SELECT c.course_name, c.course_number, d2m.dname
FROM Department_to_major d2m INNER JOIN
(course c INNER JOIN prereq  p
ON c.course_number=p.course_number)
ON c.offering_dept=d2m.dcode;
```

In the above nested INNER JOIN, the part within the parentheses, (course c INNER JOIN prereq p ON c.course_number=p.course_number), is done first, the result of which then is used to join to the third table, `Department_to_major`.

The result of the join is the following 12 rows:

course_name	course_number	dname
MANAGERIAL FINANCE	ACCT3333	Accounting
DATA STRUCTURES	COSC3320	Computer Science
DATABASE	COSC3380	Computer Science
DATABASE	COSC3380	Computer Science
ADA – INTRODUCTION	COSC5234	Computer Science
ENGLISH COMP II	ENGL1011	English
WRITING FOR NON MAJO	ENGL3520	English
AMERICAN GOVERNMENT	POLY2103	Political Science
POLITICS OF CUBA	POLY5501	Political Science
FUND. TECH. WRITING	ENGL3401	English
ORGANIC CHEMISTRY	CHEM3001	Chemistry
MATH ANALYSIS	MATH5501	Mathematics

Which join is performed first has performance implications. The same query can be written as follows:

```
SELECT c.course_name, c.course_number, d.dname
FROM (Course c INNER JOIN Department_to_major d
ON c.offering_dept = d.dcode)
INNER JOIN prereq p
ON p.course_number = c.course_number;
```

Joining Multiple Tables Using the WHERE Clause

Multiple tables can also be joined using a WHERE clause. For example, the nested INNER JOIN query in the preceding section could also be written as follows:

```
SELECT c.course_name, c.course_number, d.dname
FROM Course c, Prereq p, Department_to_major d
WHERE c.course_number=p.course_number
AND c.offering_dept = d.dcode;
```

Again, a join is a pair-wise operation. This "triple join" is actually either ((the Course table join the Prereq table) join the Department_to_major table) or (the Course table join (the Prereq table join the Department_to_major)), depending on the database engine. In this case, the result of this join would be exactly the same as shown in the preceding section using the nested INNER JOIN, but performance may be enhanced by tinkering with the order of joining. In Access, the order of joins is most easily controlled using the INNER JOIN syntax.

OUTER JOINs

In an equi-join, rows without matching tuple values are eliminated from the join result. For example, with the following join, we have lost the information on any course that does not have a prerequisite:

```
SELECT *
FROM Course c, Prereq p
WHERE c.course_number = p.course_number;
```

In some cases, it may be desirable to include rows from one table although it does not have matching rows in the other table. This is done by the use of OUTER JOINs. OUTER JOINs are used when we want to keep all the rows from the first relation, Course, or all the rows from the sec-

> Access SQL does not use the (+) to signify an OUTER JOIN (as is used in Oracle and other versions of SQL). Rather, Access SQL uses the terms LEFT JOIN and RIGHT JOIN.

ond relation, Prereq, regardless of whether or not they have matching rows in the other relation. In Access, an OUTER JOIN in which we want to keep all the rows from the first relation (or left relation) is called a LEFT JOIN, and an outer join in which we want to keep all the rows from the second relation (or right relation) is called a RIGHT JOIN.

The term FULL OUTER JOIN is used to designate the union of the LEFT and RIGHT OUTER JOINs. This means that the FULL OUTER JOIN includes the rows that are joined from both tables, the remaining rows from the first table, and the remaining rows from the second table.

> Access SQL does not explicitly support the FULL OUTER JOIN.

The LEFT JOIN

LEFT OUTER JOINs include all the records from the first (left) of the two tables, even if there are no matching values for the records in the second (right) table. LEFT OUTER JOINs are performed in Access using a LEFT JOIN statement.

> LEFT JOIN is the same as LEFT OUTER JOIN. The inclusion of the word OUTER is optional in Access SQL, so we will use LEFT JOIN instead of LEFT OUTER JOIN.

The following is the simplest form of a LEFT JOIN statement:

```
SELECT fields
FROM table1 LEFT JOIN table2
ON table1.field1=table2.field1;
```

For example, if we want to list all the rows in the Course table (the left, or first table), even if these courses do not have prerequisites, we type the following LEFT JOIN statement:

```
SELECT *
FROM Course c LEFT JOIN Prereq p
ON c.course_number = p.course_number;
```

The LEFT JOIN is processed by joining all the records from the Course table that have course_number equal to the course_number in the Prereq table. When a record (course_number) from Course (first table) has no match in Prereq (second table), the records from the Course table are added to the result set with a row of null values joined to the right side. This means that the courses that do not have prerequisites will get a set of null values for prerequisites. So, the output of a LEFT JOIN includes all rows from the left (first) table, which in this case is the Course table.

Therefore, the above query will produce the following 33 rows of output:

COURSE_NAME	c.COURSE_NUMBER	CREDIT_HOURS	OFFERING_DEPT	p.COURSE_NUMBER	PREREQ
ACCOUNTING I	ACCT2020	3	ACCT		
ACCOUNTING II	ACCT2220	3	ACCT		
MANAGERIAL FINANCE	ACCT3333	3	ACCT	ACCT3333	ACCT2220
ACCOUNTING INFO SYST	ACCT3464	3	ACCT		
INTRO TO COMPUTER SC	COSC1310	4	COSC		
TURBO PASCAL	COSC2025	3	COSC		
ADVANCED COBOL	COSC2303	3	COSC		
DATA STRUCTURES	COSC3320	4	COSC	COSC3320	COSC1310
DATABASE	COSC3380	3	COSC	COSC3380	COSC3320
DATABASE	COSC3380	3	COSC	COSC3380	MATH2410
OPERATIONS RESEARCH	COSC3701	3	COSC		
ADVANCED ASSEMBLER	COSC4301	3	COSC		
SYSTEM PROJECT	COSC4309	3	COSC		
ADA - INTRODUCTION	COSC5234	4	COSC	COSC5234	COSC3320
NETWORKS	COSC5920	3	COSC		
ENGLISH COMP I	ENGL1010	3	ENGL		
ENGLISH COMP II	ENGL1011	3	ENGL	ENGL1011	ENGL1010
WRITING FOR NON MAJO	ENGL3520	2	ENGL	ENGL3520	ENGL1011
ALGEBRA	MATH2333	3	MATH		
DISCRETE MATHEMATICS	MATH2410	3	MATH		
CALCULUS 1	MATH1501	4	MATHII		

COURSE_NAME	c.COURSE_NUMBER	CREDIT_HOURS	OFFERING_DEPT	p.COURSE_NUMBER	PREREQ
AMERICAN CONSTITUTIO	POLY1201	1	POLY		
INTRO TO POLITICAL S	POLY2001	3	POLY		
AMERICAN GOVERNMENT	POLY2103	2	POLY	POLY2103	POLY1201
SOCIALISM AND COMMUN	POLY4103	4	POLY		
POLITICS OF CUBA	POLY5501	4	POLY	POLY5501	POLY4103
TECHNICAL WRITING	ENGL3402	2	ENGL		
FUND. TECH. WRITING	ENGL3401	3	ENGL	ENGL3401	ENGL1011
INTRO TO CHEMISTRY	CHEM2001	3	CHEM		
ORGANIC CHEMISTRY	CHEM3001	3	CHEM	CHEM3001	CHEM2001
CALCULUS 2	MATH1502	3	MATH		
CALCULUS 3	MATH1503	3	MATH		
MATH ANAYSIS	MATH5501	3	MATH	MATH5501	MATH2333

Note the nulls added to the courses like ACCOUNTING I, ACCOUNTING II, ACCOUNTING INFO SYST, and so on, which are the courses (in the Course table) that do not have prerequisites.

The RIGHT JOIN

RIGHT OUTER JOINs include all the records from the second (right) of the two tables, even if there are no matching values for the records in the first (left) table. RIGHT OUTER JOINs are performed in Access using a RIGHT JOIN statement.

> RIGHT JOIN is the same as RIGHT OUTER JOIN. The inclusion of the word OUTER is optional in Access SQL, so we will use RIGHT JOIN instead of RIGHT OUTER JOIN.

The following is the simplest form of a RIGHT JOIN statement:

```
SELECT fields
FROM table1 RIGHT JOIN table2
ON table1.field1=table2.field1;
```

For example, if we want to list all the rows in the Course table (the right, or second table), even if these courses do not have prerequisites (similar to what we did in the preceding section with the LEFT JOIN statement), we type the following RIGHT JOIN statement:

```
SELECT *
FROM Prereq p RIGHT JOIN Course c
ON p.course_number = c.course_number;
```

The RIGHT JOIN is processed by joining all the records from the Prereq table that have course_number equal to the course_number in the Course table. When a record (course_number) from Course (second table) has no match in Prereq (first table), the records from the Course table are added to the result set with a row of null values joined to the left side. This means that the courses that do not have prerequisites will get a set of null values joined to the left side. So, the output of a RIGHT JOIN includes all rows from the right (second) table, which in this case is the Course table, producing output similar to that obtained in the previous section.

The output consists of 33 rows (of which the first 19 rows are shown):

Chapter Four

p.COURSE_NUMBER	PREREQ	COURSE_NAME	c.COURSE_NUMBER	CREDIT_HOURS	OFFERING_DEPT
		ACCOUNTING I	ACCT2020	3	ACCT
		ACCOUNTING II	ACCT2220	3	ACCT
ACCT3333	ACCT2220	MANAGERIAL FINANCE	ACCT3333	3	ACCT
		ACCOUNTING INFO SYST	ACCT3464	3	ACCT
		INTRO TO COMPUTER SC	COSC1310	4	COSC
		TURBO PASCAL	COSC2025	3	COSC
		ADVANCED COBOL	COSC2303	3	COSC
COSC3320	COSC1310	DATA STRUCTURES	COSC3320	4	COSC
COSC3380	COSC3320	DATABASE	COSC3380	3	COSC
COSC3380	MATH2410	DATABASE	COSC3380	3	COSC
		OPERATIONS RESEARCH	COSC3701	3	COSC
		ADVANCED ASSEMBLER	COSC4301	3	COSC

p.COURSE_NUMBER	PREREQ	COURSE_NAME	c.COURSE_NUMBER	CREDIT_HOURS	OFFERING_DEPT
		SYSTEM PROJECT	COSC4309	3	COSC
COSC5234	COSC3320	ADA - INTRODUCTION	COSC5234	4	COSC
		NETWORKS	COSC5920	3	COSC
		ENGLISH COMP I	ENGL1010	3	ENGL
ENGL1011	ENGL1010	ENGLISH COMP II	ENGL1011	3	ENGL
ENGL3520	ENGL1011	WRITING FOR NON MAJO	ENGL3520	2	ENGL
		ALGEBRA	MATH2333	3	MATH

Nested LEFT and RIGHT OUTER JOINs

In Access, a LEFT JOIN or a RIGHT JOIN can be nested inside an INNER JOIN, but an INNER JOIN cannot be nested inside a LEFT JOIN or a RIGHT JOIN.

CHAPTER 4 REVIEW QUESTIONS

1. What is a join? Why do you need a join?

2. What is an INNER JOIN?

3. Which clause can be used in place of the INNER JOIN in Access SQL?

4. What is the Cartesian product?

5. What would be the Cartesian product of a table with 15 rows and another table with 23 rows?

6. What is an equi-join?

7. What is a theta join? Give an example of a theta join.

8. What is a self join? Give an example of a self join.

9. What command is used to perform a LEFT OUTER JOIN in Access SQL?

10. What command is used to perform a RIGHT OUTER JOIN in Access SQL?

11. What is a LEFT OUTER JOIN?

12. What is a RIGHT OUTER JOIN?

13. What is a full outer join?

14. Can a full outer join be explicitly performed in Access SQL?

15. Does Access SQL allow the use of (+) to perform outer joins?

16. The fields that are being used in a join have to be _____.

17. What is the maximum number of rows that a self join can produce?

CHAPTER 4 EXERCISES

1. Create two tables, Stu(name, majorCode) and Major(majorCode, majorDesc), with the following data. Use CHAR(2) for codes and appropriate data types for the other fields.

Stu	
name	majorCode
Jones	CS
Smith	AC
Evans	MA
Adams	CS
Sumon	
Sudip	

Major	
majorCode	majorDesc
AC	Accounting
CS	Computer Science
MA	Math
HI	History

a. Display the Cartesian product (no WHERE clause) of the two tables. Use SELECT *.... How many rows did you get? How many rows will you always get when combining two tables with *n* and *m* rows in them (Cartesian product)?

b. Display an equi-join of the Stu and Major tables on majorCode. First do this using the INNER JOIN, and then display the results using the equi-join with an appropriate WHERE clause. Use appropriate table aliases. How many rows did you get?

c. Display whatever you get if you leave off the column qualifiers (the aliases) on the equi-join in step b. (Note: This will give an error because of ambiguous column names.)

d. Use the COUNT(*) function instead of SELECT * in the query. Use COUNT to show the number of rows in the result set of the equi-join.

e. Display the name, majorCode, and majorDesc of all students regardless of whether or not they have a declared major (even if the major field is null). (Hint: You need to use a LEFT JOIN here if Stu is the first table in your equi-join query.)

f. Display a list of majorDescs available (even if the majorDesc does not have students yet) and the students in each of the majors. (Hint: You need to use a RIGHT JOIN here.)

2. Create two tables, T1(name, jobno) and T2(jobno, jobdesc). Let jobno be data type NUMBER, and use appropriate data types for the other fields. Put three rows in T1 and two rows in T2. Give T1.jobno values 1, 2, 3 for the three rows: <..., 1>,<..., 2,>,<..., 3>, where ... represents any value you choose. Give T2.jobno the values 1, 2: <1,...>,<2,...>.

a. How many rows are in the equi-join (on jobno) of T1 and T2?

b. If the values of T2.jobno were <2,...>, <2,...> (with different jobdesc values), how many rows would you expect to get and why? Why would the rows have to have different descriptions?

c. If the values of T2.jobno were 4, 5 as in <4,...>,<5,...>, how many rows would you expect to get?

d. If the values of T1.jobno were <..., 1>,<..., 1>,<..., 1> (with different names) and the values of T2.jobno were <1,...>,<1...> with different descriptions, how many rows would you expect to get?

So, if you have two tables, what is the number of rows you may expect from an equi-join operation (and with what conditions)? A Cartesian product?

Edit the following statement into your homework with blanks filled in:

The answer to the equi-join question in this problem is as follows: The number of rows in an equi-join of two tables, whose sizes are m and n rows, is from ___ to ___ depending on these conditions: _____.

3. Use tables T1 and T2 from exercise 2. Create another table called T3(jobdesc, minpay). Let minpay be type NUMBER. Populate the table with at least one occurrence of each jobdesc from table T2 plus one more jobdesc that is not in T2. Write and display the result of a triple equi-join of T1, T2, and T3. Use an appropriate comment on each of the lines of the WHERE clause on which there are equi-join conditions. (Note: You will need two equi-join conditions.)

a. How many rows did you get in the equi-join?

b. Use the COUNT(*) function and display the number of rows in the equi-join.

c. How many rows would you get in this meaningless, triple Cartesian product (use COUNT(*))?

d. In an equi-join of *n* tables, you always have _____ equi-join conditions in the WHERE clause.

In the preceding three exercises, you created tables T1, T2, T3, Stu, and Major. These are temporary tables you used for testing. When you have completed the three exercises, delete these tables.

Answer questions 4 through 8 by using the student.mdb database.

4. Display a list of course names for all of the prerequisite courses.

5. Use an INNER JOIN to join the Section and Course tables.

    a. For each instructor, list the name of each course he or she teaches and the semester and year in which he or she taught that course.

    b. For each course, list the name of the instructor and the name of the department in which it is offered.

6. Use a LEFT JOIN to join the Section and Course tables.

    a. For each instructor, list the name of each course he or she teaches and the semester and year in which he or she taught that course. Order in descending order by instructors.

    b. For each course, list the name of the instructor and the name of the department in which it is offered.

7. Use a RIGHT JOIN to join the Section and Course tables.

    a. For each instructor, list the name of each course he or she teaches and the semester and year in which he or she taught that course.

    b. For each course, list the name of the instructor and the name of the department in which it is offered.

8. Are there any differences in the answers for questions 5, 6, and 7? Why? Explain.

9. Discuss the output that the following query would produce:

```
SELECT  *
FROM    Course AS c, Prereq AS p
WHERE   c.course_number<>p.course_number;
```

10. Find all the sophomores who are more senior than other students. (Hint: Use a self join.)

11. Find all the courses that have more credit_hours than other courses. (Hint: Use a self join.)

Functions

Topics covered in this chapter

Functions perform a predefined task. SQL in Access has several built-in functions, which can be divided into aggregate functions and row-level functions. In this chapter, we introduce some of these built-in functions.

Row-level functions operate on single rows at a time, whereas aggregate functions operate on multiple rows at once. There are two types of row-level functions. The first type of row-level functions are numeric row-level functions that are used in calculations on fields, for example, a ROUND function, which rounds numbers in a field. The second type of row-level functions are used for manipulations of rows, for example, string functions like MID, which are used to extract are number of characters from a string.

There are also two types of aggregate functions. The first type of aggregate function are numeric aggregate functions that are used in calculations on a group of numbers, for example, SUM or AVG, which stands for the sum or average of a group of numbers, respectively. The second type of aggregate functions can be used for other manipulations of multiple rows, for example, TOP or DISTINCT, in which we try to obtain a smaller set from multiple rows.

Calculations with dates are also fundamental to the operations of a database. So, although DATE functions can also be considered row-level functions, we cover DATE functions separately toward the end of the chapter. We look at some of the important built-in functions available for the manipulation and calculation of dates in SQL in Access.

Aggregate Functions

A function that returns a result based on multiple rows is called an *aggregate function* or a *group function*. We prefer the term "aggregate," because it avoids confusion. In Chapter 9, we will study the SELECT statement's GROUP BY option, which is designed to use aggregates, but aggregates can be used without using GROUP BY. An aggregate function combines or distills multiple rows into a smaller set. For example, aggregate functions can be used to calculate the number of rows, find the sum or average of all the entries in a given column, and find the largest or smallest of the entries in a given column. In SQL, these functions are called COUNT, SUM, AVG, MAX, and MIN, respectively. In this section we explore several of these more common aggregate functions used to manipulate a group (or rows) of numbers.

The COUNT Function

COUNT is a function that will generate a value of *how many* of something there are. COUNT, with an asterisk (*) as the argument, returns a count of the number of rows in the table(s) in the result of the query. For example, the following query returns a count of the number of tuples (all tuples or rows) in a table:

```
SELECT    COUNT(*)
FROM      table-name(s);
```

The following query counts the number of rows in the table Grade_report:

```
SELECT    COUNT(*) AS [Count]
FROM      Grade_report;
```

The following is its output:

COUNT(*) counts all rows, including rows that have some null values in some fields.

The design of the Grade_report table is shown in Figure 5.1.

Field Name	Data Type	Description
STUDENT_NUMBER	Number	
SECTION_ID	Number	
GRADE	Text	

FIGURE 5.1 Design of Grade_report Table

To count the number of grades in the Grade_report table, type the following:

```
SELECT    COUNT(grade) AS [Count of Grade]
FROM      Grade_report;
```

This produces the following output:

Count of Grade
114

Although the Grade_report table has 209 rows, you get a count of 114 grades rather than 209 grades because there are some null grades. COUNT(attribute) will not count the rows that have null values in the field (or attribute) being counted.

The COUNT feature can be quite useful because it can save you from unexpectedly long results. Also, you can use it to answer "how many" queries without looking at the rows directly. In Chapter 4, which showed how Cartesian products are generated, you learned that SQL does not prevent programmers from asking questions that have very long or even meaningless answers. Thus, when dealing with larger tables, it is good to first ask the question, "How many rows can I expect in my answer"? This question may be vital if a printout is involved. For example, consider the question, "How many rows are there in the Cartesian product of the Student, Section, and Grade_report tables in our database?" This can be answered by the following query:

```
SELECT   COUNT(*) AS Count
FROM     Student, Section, Grade_report;
```

The following output shows the count from this query, which should equal to the product of the table sizes of the three tables (the Cartesian product of the three tables). Obviously, in this example, it would be a good idea to first find out the number of rows in this result set before printing it.

Count
321024

Contrast the previous COUNTing query and its Cartesian product result to this query:

```
SELECT   COUNT(*) AS [Count]
FROM     Student, Grade_report, Section
WHERE    Student.stno = Grade_report.student_number
AND      Grade_report.section_id  = Section.section_id;
```

The following is the result of this query:

Count
209

What is requested here is a count of a three-way equi-join rather than a three-way Cartesian product, the result of which is something you probably would be much more willing to work with.

The syntax of SQL will *not* allow you to count two or more columns at the same time. The following query will not work:

```
SELECT  COUNT (grade, section_id)
FROM    Grade_report;
```

The SUM Function

The SUM function totals the values in a numeric field. For example, suppose you have a table called Employee that looks like this:

name	wage	hours
Sumon Bagui	10	40
Sudip Bagui	15	30
Priyashi Saha	18	
Ed Evans		10
Genny George	20	40

> The Employee table has not been created for you in the student.mdb database. You have to create it to run the following queries.

To find the sum of hours worked, use the SUM function as follows:

```
SELECT  SUM(Hours) AS [Total hours]
FROM    Employee;
```

This produces the following output:

Total hours
120

> AS [Total hours] is used in the query to give a title to the column.

Fields that contain null values are ignored by the SUM function (and *all* aggregate numeric functions except COUNT(*)).

The AVG Function

The AVG function calculates the arithmetic mean (the sum of non-null values divided by the number of non-null values) of a set of values contained in a numeric field (or attribute) in a query. For example, if you want to find the average hours worked from the Employee table, type:

```
SELECT   AVG(hours) AS [Average hours]
FROM     Employee;
```

This produces the following output:

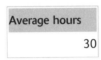

Average hours
30

Note that the null value is ignored (not used) in the calculation of the average, so the total hours (120) is divided by 4 rather than 5.

The MIN and MAX Functions

The MIN function finds the minimum from a numeric field, and the MAX function finds the maximum from a numeric field (once again, nulls are ignored). For example, to find the minimum wage and maximum wage from the Employee table, type the following:

```
SELECT  MIN(wage) AS [Minimum Wage], MAX(wage) AS [Maximum
Wage]
FROM Employee;
```

This produces the following output:

Minimum Wage	Maximum Wage
10	20

The FIRST and LAST Functions

The FIRST and LAST functions return a field value from the first or last row (tuple) in the result set returned by a query. For example, to obtain the name of the first employee from the Employee table, type:

```
SELECT  FIRST(name) AS [Employee Name]
FROM Employee;
```

This produces:

Employee Name
Sumon Bagui

Likewise, to obtain the last record or name from the Employee table, type:

```
SELECT  LAST(name) AS [Employee Name]
FROM    Employee;
```

This produces:

Employee Name
Genny George

There are several other aggregate functions available in SQL in Access, including STDEV to calculate the standard deviation and VAR to calculate the variance. These functions are less commonly used and thus won't be discussed.

Row-Level Functions

Whereas aggregate functions operate on multiple rows for a result, row-level functions operate on single rows at a time. In this section we look at row-level functions that are used in calculations; for example, row-level functions that are used to add a number to a field, the ROUND function, the NZ function, and other functions. We will discuss non-numeric row-level functions, like string functions, later in this chapter.

Adding a Number to a Field

A row-level function can be used to add a number to a field. For example, in the Employee table, if we wanted to increase each person's wage by 5, we would type the following:

```
SELECT  wage, (wage + 5) AS [wage + 5]
FROM    Employee;
```

In this query, from the Employee table, first the wage is displayed, then the wage is incremented by 5 with (wage + 5) and displayed.

This produces the following output:

wage	wage + 5
10	15
15	20
18	23
20	25

> Similarly, values can be subtracted (with the − operator), multiplied (with the * operator), and divided (with the / operator) to and from fields.

Once again note that the field with the null value in the wage is ignored in the calculations.

The ROUND Function

The ROUND function rounds numbers to a specified number of decimal places. For example, in the Employee table, if you wanted to divide each person's wage by 3 (a third of the wage), you would type (wage/3). Then, to round this, you would type ROUND(wage/3) and include the precision (number of decimal places) after the comma. In query form this would be:

```
SELECT   name, wage, ROUND((wage/3), 2) AS [wage/3]
FROM     Employee;
```

This produces the following output:

name	wage	wage/3
Sumon Bagui	10	3.33
Sudip Bagui	15	5
Priyashi Saha	18	6
Ed Evans		
Genny George	20	6.67

In this example, the value of (wage/3) is rounded up to two decimal places, because of the "2" after the comma after ROUND(wage/3).

The NZ Function

The result of the query in the preceding section shows not only that nulls are ignored, but that if a null is contained in a calculation on a row, the result is always null. To handle the null problem, Access provides a row-level function, NZ, which returns a value if a table value (or attribute) is null. The NZ function has the following form:

```
NZ(expression, ValueIfNull)
```

The NZ function basically says if the expression (or column value) *is not* null, return the value, but if the value *is* null, return ValueIfNull. For example, if you wanted to multiply wage by hours and avoid the null problem by making nulls act like zero, the correct statement would read:

```
SELECT  name, NZ(wage,0)*NZ(hours,0) AS [wage*hours]
FROM    Employee;
```

This would produce the following output:

name	wage*hours
Sumon Bagui	400
Sudip Bagui	450
Priyashi Saha	0
Ed Evans	0
Genny George	800

NZ does not have to have a ValueIfNull equal to zero. For example, if you want to assume that the number of hours is 100 if the value for hours is null, then you could use the following expression:

```
SELECT  name, hours, NZ(hours,100) AS [hours]
FROM    Employee;
```

This would produce the following output, in which 100 is substituted for null in the hours column for Priyashi Saha:

name	hours	hours
Sumon Bagui	40	40
Sudip Bagui	30	30
Priyashi Saha		100
Ed Evans	10	10
Genny George	40	40

Other row-level functions include ABS, which returns the absolute value of a numeric expression. For example, if we wanted to find the absolute value of –999.99, we would type the following:

```
SELECT ABS(-999.99) AS [Absolute Value];
```

This produces the following output:

Absolute Value
999.99

There are several other row-level functions available in Access SQL, including SIN, COS, TAN, LOG, and so forth. But, these functions are less commonly used and thus won't be discussed in this book.

Other Functions

This section discusses some other useful aggregate functions, such as TOP, TOP with PERCENT, DISTINCT, and DISTINCTROW. These functions help us in selecting rows from a larger set of rows.

The TOP Function

This function returns a certain number of records—records that fall at the top of a range specified by an ORDER BY clause. Suppose you want the names of the "top two" employees with the lowest wages from the Employee table ("top two" refers to the results in the first two rows). You would type:

```
SELECT   TOP 2 name, wage
FROM     Employee
ORDER    BY wage ASC;
```

This would produce the following output:

name	wage
Ed Evans	
Sumon Bagui	10

To get this output, first the wage field was ordered in ascending order, and then the top two names were selected from that ordered result set. The fields with the null wages are placed on top with the ascending (ASC) command.

With the TOP command, if you do not include the ORDER BY clause, the query will return rows based on the order in which they appear in the table, not in the order of the primary key (if there is a primary key) as you would naturally expect. For example, the following query does not include the ORDER BY clause:

```
SELECT  TOP 2 name, wage
FROM    Employee;
```

This returns the following output:

name	wage
Sumon Bagui	10
Sudip Bagui	15

Handling the "BOTTOM"

Since there is only a TOP command, and no similar "BOTTOM" command, if you want to get the "bottom" two employees (the values in the last two ordered rows) instead of the top two employees from the Employee table, the top two employees (the highest paid) would have to be selected from the table ordered in descending order, as follows:

```
SELECT  TOP 2 name, wage
FROM    Employee
ORDER   BY wage DESC;
```

This would produce the following output:

name	wage
Genny George	20
Priyashi Saha	18

Handling a Tie

This section answers an interesting question—what if there is a tie? For example, what if you are looking for the top two wages, and two employees have the same amount in the wage field? To demonstrate this example, make one change in the data in your Employee table, so that the value in the wage field of Sudip Bagui is 10 also:

name	wage	hours
Sumon Bagui	10	40
Sudip Bagui	10	30
Priyashi Saha	18	
Ed Evans		10
Genny George	20	40

Now type the following query (this is the first query used in the earlier section, "The TOP Function"):

```
SELECT  TOP 2 name, wage
FROM    Employee
ORDER   BY wage ASC;
```

Although you requested only the top two employees, this query produces three rows, because there was a tie in the field that you were looking for:

name	wage
Ed Evans	
Sudip Bagui	10
Sumon Bagui	10

Remember to change the data in your Employee table back to its original state if you are doing the exercises as you read the material.

The TOP Function with PERCENT

The PERCENT reserved word can be used to return a certain percentage of records that fall at the top of a range specified. For example, the following query selects the top 10 percent (by count) of the student names from the Student table based on the order of name:

```
SELECT  TOP 10 PERCENT sname
FROM    Student
ORDER   BY sname ASC;
```

This produces the following output:

sname
Alan
Benny
Bill
Brad
Brenda

Again, since there is no "BOTTOM PERCENT" function, to get the bottom 10 percent (by count), you would have to order the sname field in descending order as follows:

```
SELECT   TOP 10 PERCENT sname
FROM     Student
ORDER    BY sname DESC;
```

This would produce the following output:

sname
Zelda
Thornton
Susan
Steve
Stephanie

Now try the query without the use of ORDER BY:

```
SELECT   TOP 10 PERCENT sname
FROM     Student;
```

As output, this query returns the first 10 percent of the names based on the number of rows:

sname
Lineas
Mary
Brenda
Richard
Kelly

> Ties are handled here in the same way as discussed in the preceding section.

The DISTINCT Function

The DISTINCT function omits records that contain duplicate data in the selected fields. To be included in the result set of the query, the values for each field listed in the SELECT statement must be unique. To SELECT all grades from the `Grade_report` table, type:

```
SELECT   grade
FROM     Grade_report;
```

This results in 209 rows, all the grades in `Grade_report`.

To SELECT all *distinct* grades, type:

```
SELECT   DISTINCT grade
FROM     Grade_report;
```

This results in the following output:

grade
A
B
C
D
F

Observe that the syntax requires you to put the word DISTINCT first in the string of attributes because DISTINCT implies distinct rows in the result set. The preceding statement also produces a row for null grades (also regarded as a DISTINCT grade). Note also that the result set is sorted.

To COUNT the number of distinct grades, two steps are required. First, create a temporary table that has the distinct grades, as follows (temporary tables are covered in detail in Chapter 6):

```
SELECT   DISTINCT grade INTO Temp1
FROM     Grade_report;
```

This saves the result into a temporary table called `Temp1`, which gets created from the SELECT statement. It does not have to already exist.

Second, count the distinct grades from `Temp1` as follows:

```
SELECT   COUNT(grade) AS [Count of distinct grade]
FROM     Temp1;
```

This produces the count of distinct grades:

Count of distinct grade
5

Again, the preceding query does not count the null values.

> Access SQL does not allow the use of an expression like COUNT(DISTINCT column_name) or SUM(DISTINCT column_name).

The DISTINCTROW Function

The DISTINCTROW function omits rows based on entire duplicate records, not just duplicate fields. For example, if you type:

```
SELECT   DISTINCTROW prereq, course_number
FROM     Prereq;
```

You get the following 12 rows of output:

prereq	course_number
ACCT2220	ACCT3333
CHEM2001	CHEM3001
COSC1310	COSC3320
COSC3320	COSC3380
MATH2410	COSC3380
COSC3320	COSC5234
ENGL1010	ENGL1011
ENGL1011	ENGL3401
ENGL1011	ENGL3520
MATH2333	MATH5501
POLY1201	POLY2103
POLY4103	POLY5501

This output shows the whole Prereq table. Although it appears as if the DISTINCTROW command is being ignored, in fact there are no duplicate

```
```

rows in the table. So, it does not make sense to use DISTINCTROW when you are querying all attributes in only one table, since every table should have distinct rows.

Suppose that, in the result set, you wish to have all the output fields from multiple tables, as requested by this query:

```
SELECT DISTINCTROW
c.course_name,c.course_number,c.credit_hours,c.offering_dept,
p.prereq, p.course_number
FROM     Course AS c INNER JOIN Prereq AS p
ON       c.course_number=p.course_number;
```

This produces the following 12 rows of output:

course_name	c.course_number	credit_hours	offering_dept	prereq	p.course_number
MANAGERIAL FINANCE	ACCT3333	3	ACCT	ACCT2220	ACCT3333
DATA STRUCTURES	COSC3320	4	COSC	COSC1310	COSC3320
DATABASE	COSC3380	3	COSC	COSC3320	COSC3380
DATABASE	COSC3380	3	COSC	MATH2410	COSC3380
ADA – INTRODUCTION	COSC5234	4	COSC	COSC3320	COSC5234
ENGLISH COMP II	ENGL1011	3	ENGL	ENGL1010	ENGL1011
FUND. TECH. WRITING	ENGL3401	3	ENGL	ENGL1011	ENGL3401
WRITING FOR NON MAJO	ENGL3520	2	ENGL	ENGL1011	ENGL3520
MATH ANALYSIS	MATH5501	3	MATH	MATH2333	MATH5501
AMERICAN GOVERNMENT	POLY2103	2	POLY	POLY1201	POLY2103
POLITICS OF CUBA	POLY5501	4	POLY	POLY4103	POLY5501
ORGANIC CHEMISTRY	CHEM3001	3	CHEM	CHEM2001	CHEM3001

Again, if you select all rows from all tables for your result set (as in the preceding query), it will appear as if DISTINCTROW is not working. The preceding output is exactly the same as the output for the following query, which has no DISTINCTROW:

```
SELECT c.course_name,c.course_number,c.credit_hours,
c.offering_dept,p.prereq, p.course_number
FROM    Course AS c INNER JOIN Prereq AS p
ON      c.course_number=p.course_number;
```

Now, if you want only the DISTINCTROW offering_dept, type:

```
SELECT DISTINCTROW offering_dept
FROM    Course AS c INNER JOIN Prereq AS p
ON      c.course_number=p.course_number;
```

This produces these 11 rows:

offering_dept
ACCT
COSC
COSC
COSC
ENGL
ENGL
POLY
POLY
ENGL
CHEM
MATH

DISTINCTROW has an effect only when you select fields from some, but not all, of the tables used in the query.

To analyze the result of the preceding query, you could visualize that the database engine first created a table of c.course_number, p.course_number, and offering_dept, as follows:

```
SELECT  c.course_number, p.course_number, offering_dept
FROM    Course AS c INNER JOIN Prereq AS p
ON      c.course_number=p.course_number;
```

This would produce the following output:

c.course_number	p.course_number	offering_dept
ACCT3333	ACCT3333	ACCT
COSC3320	COSC3320	COSC
COSC3380	COSC3380	COSC
COSC3380	COSC3380	COSC
COSC5234	COSC5234	COSC
ENGL1011	ENGL1011	ENGL
ENGL3401	ENGL3401	ENGL
ENGL3520	ENGL3520	ENGL
MATH5501	MATH5501	MATH
POLY2103	POLY2103	POLY
POLY5501	POLY5501	POLY
CHEM3001	CHEM3001	CHEM

Then, the database engine selected all the DISTINCTROWs from this table, and there are 11 (row 3 and row 4 are duplicates).

Using similar reasoning, if you type the following query:

```
SELECT   DISTINCTROW prereq
FROM     Course AS c INNER JOIN Prereq AS p
ON       c.course_number=p.course_number;
```

This produces the following 12 rows of output:

prereq
ACCT2220
COSC1310
COSC3320
MATH2410
COSC3320
ENGL1010
ENGL1011
ENGL1011
MATH2333
POLY1201
POLY4103
CHEM2001

Again, to analyze the result of the preceding query, you could visualize that the database engine first created a table of c.course_number, p.course_number, and prereq, as follows:

```
SELECT  c.course_number, p.course_number, prereq
FROM    Course AS c INNER JOIN Prereq AS p
ON      c.course_number=p.course_number;
```

This produces the following 12 rows of output, which has all distinct rows:

c.course_number	p.course_number	prereq
ACCT3333	ACCT3333	ACCT2220
COSC3320	COSC3320	COSC1310
COSC3380	COSC3380	COSC3320
COSC3380	COSC3380	MATH2410
COSC5234	COSC5234	COSC3320
ENGL1011	ENGL1011	ENGL1010
ENGL3401	ENGL3401	ENGL1011
ENGL3520	ENGL3520	ENGL1011
MATH5501	MATH5501	MATH2333
POLY2103	POLY2103	POLY1201
POLY5501	POLY5501	POLY4103
CHEM3001	CHEM3001	CHEM2001

Then, the database engine selected all the DISTINCTROWs from this table, and there are 12 distinct rows of prereqs.

String Functions

SQL in Access has several string functions available for string concatenation and extraction, to find the length of a string, and to find and match characters in strings. In this section, we explore some of these useful string functions. String functions are not aggregates—they are all row-level functions, since they operate on one row at a time. String functions operate on one value in a row.

String Concatenation

String manipulations often require *concatenation,* which means to connect things together. In this section, we look at the string concatenation operators that are available in Access SQL, & and +.

To see an example of concatenation using the Employee table, first list the names of the employees through the following statement:

```
SELECT   name
FROM     Employee;
```

This produces the following output:

name
Sumon Bagui
Sudip Bagui
Priyashi Saha
Ed Evans
Genny George

Now, suppose you would like to concatenate each of the names with "Esq." Type the following:

```
SELECT   name&', Esq.' AS [Employee Names]
FROM     Employee;
```

This produces:

Employee Names
Sumon Bagui, Esq.
Sudip Bagui, Esq.
Priyashi Saha, Esq.
Ed Evans, Esq.
Genny George, Esq.

As another example, suppose you want to add ..... to the left side of the name field. Type:

```
SELECT   ('.....'+ name) AS [Employee Names]
FROM     Employee;
```

This produces the following output:

Employee Names
.....Sumon Bagui
.....Sudip Bagui
.....Priyashi Saha
.....Ed Evans
.....Genny George

Similarly, to add ..... to the right side of name field, type:

```
SELECT  (name & '.....') AS [Employee Names]
FROM    Employee;
```

This produces:

Employee Names
Sumon Bagui.....
Sudip Bagui.....
Priyashi Saha.....
Ed Evans.....
Genny George.....

String Extractors

SQL also has several string extractor functions. This section briefly describes some of the more useful string extractor functions, like MID, INSTR, LEFT/RIGHT, LTRIM/RTRIM, UCASE/LCASE, and LEN.

Before you start working with string extractors, you need to know a few things about how Access treats and presents data:

• Columns containing text data are left-justified, and columns containing numbers are right-justified.

• Access data is handled as if it were all uppercase, although it is displayed in mixed case (uppercase is used only for the first letter). This certainly makes it look nicer, but sometimes this can be misleading.

Now suppose the Employee table has the following data:

name	wage	hours
Sumon Bagui	10	40
Sudip Bagui	10	30
Priyashi Saha	18	
Ed Evans		10
Genny George	20	40

And, suppose you want to rearrange the names so that the last name is first, followed by the first letter of the first name (as shown below):

Employee Names
Bagui, S.
Bagui, S.
Saha, P.
Evans, E.
George, G.

To do this, you need string functions to break down the name into parts and then reassemble (concatenate) those parts. You can achieve this output by using a combination of the string functions MID, INSTR, and LEFT, as discussed next.

The MID Function

MID returns part of a string. The following is the format for the MID function:

```
MID(stringexpression, start, length)
```

Here, stringexpression is the field that we will be using, start tells Access where in the stringexpression to start retrieving from, and length tells Access how many characters to extract. If the length is absent, then the function returns the rest of the string from wherever you "started." For example, type the following:

```
SELECT  name, MID(name,2,4) AS [mid of name], MID(name,6) AS
[rest of name]
FROM    Employee;
```

This produces the following output:

name	mid of name	rest of name
Sumon Bagui	umon	Bagui
Sudip Bagui	udip	Bagui
Priyashi Saha	riya	shi Saha
Ed Evans	d Ev	ans
Genny George	enny	George

MID(name,2,4) started from the second position in the field, name, and extracted four characters starting from position 2.

MID(name,6) started from position 6 in name, and returned the rest of the name.

Strings in Access are indexed from 1 and not from 0. If you start at position 0, you will get an error. For example, the following query will produce an error:

```
SELECT  MID(name,0,2)
FROM    Employee;
```

The INSTR Function

INSTR (pronounced "in-string") finds the occurrence of some search-string pattern (third argument) in the string listed in the second argument. The following is the format for the INSTR function:

```
INSTR(start, source_string, search_string)
```

Here, start allows you to specify the position from which you would like to start reading source_string, which is the field you would like to search, and search_string is the field or value that you are looking for. For example, in the following query, we start at position 1 of the name field, and then look for the position of the space in the field. If there is no space in any particular name field, zero will be returned.

```
SELECT  name, INSTR(1,name, ' ') AS [position of blank in
name]
FROM    Employee;
```

This produces the following output:

name	position of blank in name
Sumon Bagui	6
Sudip Bagui	6
Priyashi Saha	9
Ed Evans	3
Genny George	6

Note in the preceding query that in INSTR(1,name, ' '), there is a space between the ' ' to denote a blank space.

Therefore, in the first name field, a space is found in the sixth position; in the second name field, a space is also found in the sixth position, and so on.

The LEFT/RIGHT Function

This function returns a portion of a string, starting from either the left or right side of a source_string. The following is the format for the LEFT/RIGHT function (where n is the number of characters that will be returned from the stringexpression or field):

```
LEFT(stringexpression, n)
```

Or

```
RIGHT(stringexpression, n)
```

The LEFT function starts from the LEFT of the stringexpression or field, and the RIGHT function starts from the right of the stringexpression or field.

For example, to get the first three characters from the name field, type:

```
SELECT  name, LEFT(name,3) AS [left]
FROM    Employee;
```

This produces:

name	left
Sumon Bagui	Sum
Sudip Bagui	Sud
Priyashi Saha	Pri
Ed Evans	Ed
Genny George	Gen

To get the last three characters from the name field (here the count will start from the right of the field, name), type:

```
SELECT  name, RIGHT(name,3) AS [right]
FROM    Employee;
```

This produces the last three characters of the name field:

name	right
Sumon Bagui	gui
Sudip Bagui	gui
Priyashi Saha	aha
Ed Evans	ans
Genny George	rge

Now that you know how to use the MID, INSTR, and LEFT string functions, you can combine them to produce the following output:

Employee Names
Bagui, S.
Bagui, S.
Saha, P.
Evans, E.
George, G.

The following is the query to achieve the preceding output:

```
SELECT MID([name],(INSTR(1,name,' ')+1),INSTR(1,name,' ')) &
',' & ' ' & LEFT(name,1) & '.' AS [Employee Names]
FROM Employee;
```

In this query, we get the last name with the MID([name], (INSTR(1,name,' ')+1),INSTR(1,name,' ')) portion, which says: from the name field, start at position (INSTR(1,name,' ')+1), and go to position INSTR(1,name,' '). We then concatenate this portion with the comma and a space, and then extract the first character of the first name with LEFT(name,1), and concatenate this with a period.

The LTRIM/RTRIM Function

LTRIM removes blanks from the beginning (left) of a string. For example, if three blank spaces appear to the left of Ranu in the name field, you can remove them with the following query:

```
SELECT LTRIM('   Ranu') AS name;
```

This produces:

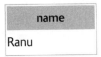

name
Ranu

Similarly, RTRIM removes blanks from the end (right) of a string. For example, if blank spaces appear to the right of Ranu in the name field, you could remove them using the RTRIM, and then concatenate "Saha" with the + sign, as shown below:

```
SELECT RTRIM('Ranu    ') + ' Saha' AS name;
```

This produces:

name
Ranu Saha

The UCASE/LCASE Function

To produce all the output in uppercase or all the output in lowercase, you can use the UCASE or LCASE functions, respectively. For example, to produce all the names in the Employee table in uppercase, type:

```
SELECT   UCASE(name) AS [NAMES IN CAPS]
FROM     Employee;
```

This produces the following output:

NAMES IN CAPS
SUMON BAGUI
SUDIP BAGUI
PRIYASHI SAHA
ED EVANS
GENNY GEORGE

To produce all the names in lowercase, type:

```
SELECT   LCASE(name) AS [NAMES IN SMALL]
FROM     Employee;
```

This produces:

NAMES IN SMALL
sumon bagui
sudip bagui
priyashi saha
ed evans
genny george

To produce, in all uppercase, the last name followed by the first letter of the first name, type:

```
SELECT UCASE(MID([name],(INSTR(1,name,' ')+1),INSTR(1,name,' '))
& ',' & ' ' & LEFT(name,1) & '.') AS [EMPLOYEE NAMES]
FROM Employee;
```

This produces the following output:

EMPLOYEE NAMES
BAGUI, S.
BAGUI, S.
SAHA, P.
EVANS, E.
GEORGE, G.

The LEN Function

The LEN function returns the length of a desired string. For example, to list the lengths of the full names (including the space) in the Employee table, type:

```
SELECT   name, LEN(name) AS [Length of Name]
FROM     Employee;
```

This produces the following output:

name	Length of Name
Sumon Bagui	11
Sudip Bagui	11
Priyashi Saha	13
Ed Evans	8
Genny George	12

In the Employee table, name was defined as VARCHAR(20) (a varying character field of size 20). If name were defined as a CHAR field or TEXT field of fixed length, then the preceding query would produce the following output:

Length of Name
20
20
20
20
20

Notice the fixed size of the name field (since name was defined as a CHAR(20)).

Matching Substrings Using LIKE

Often, we want to use part of a character attribute as a condition in a query. For example, consider the Section table, which has the following structure:

section_id	course_num	semyr	inst
85	MATH2410	FALL86	KING
86	MATH5501	FALL86	EMERSON

We might want to know something about math courses—courses with the prefix MATH; in this situation, we need an operator that can determine whether a substring exists in an attribute. A common way to handle this type of query is by using the LIKE function (we could combine MID and INSTR to get this result, but using LIKE is a little shorter).

Using LIKE as an "existence" match entails finding whether a character string exists in an attribute—if the string exists, the row is SELECTed for inclusion in the result set. Of course, we could use INSTR for this, but LIKE is a powerful and flexible alternative. This existence-type of the LIKE query is useful when the position of the character string sought may be in various places in the substring. Access uses the wildcard * at the beginning or end of a string, when looking for the existence of substrings. For example, suppose we want to find all names that have "Smith" in our Student table. Type the following:

```
SELECT  *
FROM    Student
WHERE   sname = 'Smith';
```

This produces the following output:

STNO	SNAME	MAJOR	CLASS	BDATE
88	Smith			10/15/79

Note that the case (upper or lower) in the statement WHERE sname = 'Smith' does not matter because Access data is handled as if it were all uppercase, although it is displayed in mixed case (and even if it had been entered in mixed case). In other words, we can say that Access data is *not* case sensitive.

To count how many people have a name of "Smith":

```
SELECT   COUNT(*) AS Count
FROM     Student
WHERE    sname = 'Smith';
```

This produces:

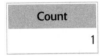

Count
1

Using * on both ends, you will find "Smith" and people who have names with "Smith" in it, like Losmith, Smithfield, Smithson, and so forth. So, if you type the following query:

```
SELECT   *
FROM     Student
WHERE    sname LIKE '*Smith*';
```

This produces the following output, showing any "Smith" pattern in sname:

STNO	SNAME	MAJOR	CLASS	BDATE
147	Smithly	ENGL	2	5/13/80
151	Losmith	CHEM	3	1/15/81
88	Smith			10/15/79

To find any pattern starting with "Smith", you would type:

```
SELECT   *
FROM     Student
WHERE    sname LIKE 'Smith*';
```

This produces:

STNO	SNAME	MAJOR	CLASS	BDATE
147	Smithly	ENGL	2	5/13/80
88	Smith			10/15/79

To find the math courses (any course_num starting with MATH), you could pose a wildcard match with a LIKE as follows:

```
SELECT   *
FROM     Section
WHERE    course_num LIKE 'MATH*';
```

This produces the following output:

SECTION_ID	COURSE_NUM	SEMESTER	YEAR	INSTRUCTOR	BLDG	ROOM
107	MATH2333	SPRING	00	CHANG	36	123
85	MATH2410	FALL	98	KING	36	123
112	MATH2410	FALL	99	CHANG	36	123
158	MATH2410	SPRING	98		36	123
86	MATH5501	FALL	98	EMERSON	36	123
109	MATH5501	FALL	99	CHANG	36	123

Finding a Range of Characters

The keyword LIKE can be used to find a range of characters. For example, to find all grades between C and F in the Grade_report table, type:

```
SELECT   DISTINCT student_number, grade
FROM     Grade_report
WHERE    grade LIKE "[c-f]"
AND      student_number > 100;
```

This produces:

> Square brackets, [ ],
are used to enclose
the range of values.

Student_number	grade
125	C
126	C
127	C
128	F
130	C
131	C
145	F
147	C
148	C
151	C
153	C
158	C
160	C
161	C
163	C

To find all grades that are *not* between C and F, we use a ! before the range we do not want to find:

```
SELECT   DISTINCT student_number, grade
FROM     Grade_report
WHERE    grade LIKE "[!c-f]"
AND      student_number > 100;
```

This produces the following:

Student_number	grade
121	B
122	B
123	A
123	B
125	A
125	B
126	A
126	B
127	A
127	B
129	A
129	B
132	B
142	A
143	B
144	B
146	B
147	B
148	B
155	B
157	B

To find a character that is not a digit, the following syntax may be used:

```
LIKE '[!0-9]'
```

> The ! as used here signifies a "NOT."

Finding a Single Character or Single Digit

To find a single character, a question mark, ?, is used as a wildcard. For example, the following will return x2x or xBx:

```
LIKE 'x?x'
```

A single digit can be found by using a pound sign, #. For example, to find all students with student_numbers in the 130s range from the Student table, type:

```
SELECT   DISTINCT student_number, grade
FROM     Grade_report
WHERE    student_number LIKE '13#';
```

This produces the following:

student_number	grade
130	C
131	C
132	B

Finaly we give an example that can be used to find a combination of characters and digits with LIKE. LIKE 'x[!c-m]#' will return anything that starts with "x" in a field, that has something other than c-m in the second character position, and that has a number at the end; for example, xb9 or x55.

DATE Functions

This section looks at some of the important functions available for the manipulation and calculation of dates. We will reuse the date table, DateTable, that we created and used in Chapter 3, with the following data:

> The DateTable table has not been created for you. You need to create it to run the queries that follow.

birthdate	k5date	name
1/1/01	12/1/06	Mala Sinha
2/2/02	3/2/06	Mary Spencer
10/2/02	2/4/05	Bill Cox
12/29/98	5/5/04	Jamie Runner
6/16/99	3/3/03	Seema Kapoor

In this table, birthdate and k5date were defined as DATE fields, and name was defined as a CHAR field.

The YEAR Function

The YEAR(number) function will extract the year from a date. For example, to extract the year from the field k5date, type:

```
SELECT   YEAR(k5date) AS [Kindergarten Year], name
FROM     Datetable;
```

This produces the following output:

Kindergarten Year	name
2006	Mala Sinha
2006	Mary Spencer
2005	Bill Cox
2004	Jamie Runner
2003	Seema Kapoor

We can also use the YEAR function in date calculations. For example, if you want to find out the number of years between when a person was born (birthdate) and when the person went to kindergarten (the K5date field) from the table DateTable, type the following query:

```
SELECT   YEAR(k5date)-YEAR(birthdate) AS [Age in K5], name
FROM     DateTable;
```

This produces the following output:

Age in K5	name
5	Mala Sinha
4	Mary Spencer
3	Bill Cox
6	Jamie Runner
4	Seema Kapoor

This is an example of subtracting one date from another. Here, the YEAR(birthdate) was subtracted from YEAR(k5date).

The MONTH Function

The MONTH function will extract the month from a date. Then, to add six months to the month, we first extract the month by MONTH(birthdate), and then add 6 to it, as shown below:

```
SELECT birthdate, MONTH(birthdate) AS [Birth Month],
((MONTH(birthdate)) + 6 ) AS [Sixth month], name
FROM DateTable;
```

This produces the following output:

birthdate	Birth Month	Sixth month	name
1/1/01	1	7	Mala Sinha
2/2/02	2	8	Mary Spencer
10/2/02	10	16	Bill Cox
12/29/98	12	18	Jamie Runner
6/16/99	6	12	Seema Kapoor

The DAY Function

The DAY function extracts the day of the month from a date. Again, to find the day of the birthdate, type the following query:

```
SELECT  birthdate, DAY([birthdate]) AS [Date], name
FROM    DateTable;
```

This produces the following output:

birthdate	Date	Name
1/1/01	1	Mala Sinha
2/2/02	2	Mary Spencer
10/2/02	2	Bill Cox
12/29/98	29	Jamie Runner
6/16/99	16	Seema Kapoor

The WEEKDAY Function

The WEEKDAY function extracts the day of the week from a date. Sunday is regarded as day 1. So, the following query extracts the day of the week:

```
SELECT  WEEKDAY(birthdate) AS [Day of week], birthdate, name
FROM    DateTable;
```

This produces the following output:

Day of week	birthdate	Name
2	1/1/01	Mala Sinha
7	2/2/02	Mary Spencer
4	10/2/02	Bill Cox
3	12/29/98	Jamie Runner
4	6/16/99	Seema Kapoor

Inserting the Current Date or Time

The function DATE() gives the current date. In the following query, we are inserting the current date for the birthdate, and we are adding five years to the current date for the K5date field:

```
INSERT INTO DateTable
VALUES (DATE(), DATE()+YEAR(5), 'Arpan Bagui');
```

This produces the following output (note the insertion of a sixth row):

birthdate	k5date	name
1/1/01	12/1/06	Mala Sinha
2/2/02	3/2/06	Mary Spencer
10/2/02	2/4/05	Bill Cox
12/29/98	5/5/04	Jamie Runner
6/16/99	3/3/03	Seema Kapoor
12/12/01	2/24/07	Arpan Bagui

The function NOW() gives the present date and time. In the following query, we are inserting the current date and time for the birthdate (done on 12/12/01), and we are adding five days to the current date for the date in the K5date:

```
INSERT INTO DateTable
VALUES (NOW(), NOW()+DAY(5), 'Arpan Bagui');
```

This produces the following output (again, note the insertion of the last row):

birthdate	k5date	name
1/1/01	12/1/06	Mala Sinha
2/2/02	3/2/06	Mary Spencer
10/2/02	2/4/05	Bill Cox
12/29/98	5/5/04	Jamie Runner
6/16/99	3/3/03	Seema Kapoor
12/12/01 10:31:01 PM	12/16/01 10:31:01 PM	Arpan Bagui

Likewise, the function TIME() gives only the current time.

CHAPTER 5 REVIEW QUESTIONS

1. What are functions?

2. What are aggregate functions? Give examples of aggregate functions. What is another term for "aggregate function"?

3. What are row-level functions? Give examples of row-level functions.

4. Is COUNT an aggregate function or a row-level function? Explain why. Give at least one example of when the COUNT function may come in handy. Does the COUNT function take nulls into account?

5. Is AVG an aggregate function or a row-level function?

6. What is the NZ function? Explain.

7. How does the TOP function handle ties?

8. How does the DISTINCTROW function work?

9. Are string functions aggregate functions or row-level functions?

10. Give examples of some characters that are used in matching substrings.

11. What is the INSTR function used for?

12. What function would you use to find the leftmost characters in a string?

13. What are the LTRIM/RTRIM functions used for?

14. What function would produce output in all lowercase?

15. What function would you use to find the length of a string?

16. What characters or symbols are most commonly used as wildcard characters?

17. What are the concatenation operators in Access SQL?

18. What does the YEAR function do?

19. What does the MONTH function do?

20. Correct the following query:

```
SELECT ('.....'+ name) AS [name]
FROM Employee;
```

21. Does Access SQL allow an expression like COUNT(DISTINCT column_name)?

CHAPTER 5 EXERCISES

Use appropriate column headings when displaying your output.

1. Display the COUNT of tuples (rows) in each of the tables Grade_report, Student, and Section. How many rows would you expect in the Cartesian product of all three tables? Display the COUNT (*not* the resulting rows) of the Cartesian product of all three and verify your result (use SELECT COUNT(*) ...).

2. Display the COUNT of section-ids from the Section table. Display the COUNT of DISTINCT section-ids from the Grade_report table. What does this information tell you? (Hint: section_id is the primary key of the Section table.)

3. Write, execute, and print a query to list student names and grades (just two attributes) using the table alias feature. Restrict the list to students that have either A's or B's in courses with ACCT prefixes only.

   Here's how to complete this problem:

   a. Get the statement to work as a COUNT of a join of the three tables, Student, Grade_report, Section. Use table aliases in the join condition. Note that *a join of* n *tables requires (n–1) join conditions,* so here you have to have two join conditions: one to join the Student and Grade_report tables, and one to join the Grade_report and Section tables. Note the number of rows that you get (expect no more rows than is in the Grade_report table). Why do you get this result?

   b. Modify the query and include the Accounting condition in the WHERE clause. Note the number of rows in the result—it should be a good bit less than in step a.

   c. Again, modify the query and add the grade constraints. The number of rows should decrease again. Note that if you have WHERE x *and* y *or* z, parentheses are optional, but then the criteria will be interpreted according to precedence rules.

The reason that we want you to "start small" and add conditions is that it gives you a check on what you ought to get and it allows you to output less nonsense. Your minimal starting point should be a count of the join with appropriate join conditions.

4. Using the Student table, answer the following questions:

    a. How many students have names like Smith?

    b. How many have names that contain the letter sequence SMITH?

    c. How many students have names that end in LD?

    d. Would SELECT * FROM Student WHERE sname LIKE 'SMITH#' find someone whose name is:

       (i) LA SMITH

       (ii) SMITH-JONES

       (iii) SMITH JR.

       (iv) SMITH, JR

5. List the junior-level COSC courses (like COSC3xxx) and the name of the courses. Use the Course table.

6. Using the COUNT feature, determine whether or not there are duplicate names or student numbers in the Student table.

7. Assume that all math courses start with MATH. How many math courses are listed in the Section table? From the count of courses, does it appear that there any math courses in the Section table that are not in the Course table? Again, using COUNTs, are there any math courses in the Course table that are not in the Section table? Does it appear that there are any courses at all that are in the Grade_report, Section, or Course tables that are not in the others? (We will study how to ask these questions in SQL in a later chapter.) Note that a query like the following would not work:

```
SELECT  g.section_id
FROM    Grade_report g, Section t
WHERE   g.section_id <> t.section_id;
```

Explain why WHERE .. <> .. will not work to produce the desired output.

8. For every table in the student.mdb database, we would like to compile the following information: attributes, number of rows, number of distinct rows, and rows without nulls. Find this information using different queries and compile the information in a table as shown on the following page:

Table	Attribute	Rows	Distinct Rows	Rows Without Nulls
Student	stno		48	48
	sname		47	0
	major		8	3
	class		etc., etc.	
Section	section_id		etc.	

The other tables in the `student.mdb` database are `Grade_report`, `Section`, `Room`, `Course`, `Prereq`, and `Department_to_major`.

Hint: You can use the following query:

```
SELECT   COUNT(*)
FROM     Student
WHERE    sname IS NULL
```

9. **a.** Find the average, minimum, and maximum capacity of the rooms in the database.

   b. Where there is a null value for the capacity, assume the capacity to be 40, and find the average room size again.

10. **a.** Using the `Student` table, display the first 10 rows with an appended initial. For the appended initial, choose the halfway letter of the name, so that if a name is Evans, the initial is A (half of the length +1). If the name is Conway, the initial is W (again, (half of the length +1)). You do not need to round up or down, just use (LEN(Name)/2)+1 as the starting place. Use appropriate column aliases. Your result should look like this (actual names may vary depending on the current database):

PERSON#	NAMES
1	Lineas, E.
2	Mary, R.
3	Brenda, N.
4	Richard, H.
5	Kelly, L.
6	Lujack, A.
7	Reva, V.
8	Elainie, I.
9	Harley, L.
10	Donald, A.

    b. Display the preceding output in all capital letters.

11.   **a.** Find the names of the bottom 50 percent of the students, ordered by grade.

    b. Find the names of the top 25 percent of the seniors, ordered by grade.

12. Count the number of courses each instructor taught.

13. Count the number of classes each student is taking.

14. Display all the names that are fewer than five characters long from the `Student` table.

15. List all the students with student numbers in the 140s range.

16. Find all the students (the student names should be listed only once) who made A's and B's.

17. Would you call TOP an aggregate function? Why or why not?

18. Add a asterisk (*) to the names of all juniors and seniors who made at least one A. (This question will take a few steps, and you will have to approach this problem in a step-by-step manner.)

19. In Chapter 3, we created a table called `Employee`. Add a `birthdate` field and an `employment_date` field to the `Employee` table. Insert values into both the fields.

    a. Display the current ages of all the employees.

    b. Find the youngest employee.

    c. Find the oldest employee.

    d. Find the youngest employee at the time of employment.

    e. Find the oldest employee at the time of employment.

    f. Add five years to the current ages of all employees. Will any of the employees be over 65 in five years?

    g. List the birth months and the names of all employees.

Query Development and Derived Structures

Topics covered in this chapter

A problem in SQL, and in all programming for that matter, is the development of long queries or statements. One way to create long statements is to begin modestly and to incrementally build or develop the query of interest. This is the approach described in this chapter, which we will illustrate by developing a query or two. As you'll find out, the appropriate placement of parentheses within the query is often also required.

Another way to develop queries is to use derived structures—a pseudo-table, if you will. In Access SQL, derived structures include views (both real and inline views) and temporary tables, both of which enable us to easily manipulate partial displays of tables. The partial displays can then be connected to answer a complicated database query. This chapter discusses derived structures, focusing specifically on views and temporary tables, and how query development can be aided with the use of derived structures.

Query Development

Queries sometimes are developed after some initial experimentation, while other times they are the result of modifying previously stored queries. The best way to understand how the query building process works is to look at an example. Suppose we want to find the names of all students in the standard `student.mdb` database who major in computer science (COSC) and have earned a grade of B in some course. To do so, follow these steps:

1. Type the following query to find students who major in computer science:

```
SELECT   *
FROM     Student
WHERE    major = 'COSC';
```

This produces the following output:

ST NO	SNAME	MAJOR	CLASS	BDATE
3	Mary	COSC	4	7/6/78
8	Brenda	COSC	2	8/13/77
14	Lujack	COSC	1	2/12/77
17	Elainie	COSC	1	8/12/76
121	Hillary	COSC	1	7/16/77
128	Brad	COSC	1	9/10/77
130	Alan	COSC	2	7/16/77
142	Jerry	COSC	4	3/12/78
31	Jake	COSC	4	2/12/78
5	Zelda	COSC		2/12/78

2. To find those students in the preceding output who have earned a B in a course, we first need to add the `Grade_report` table, shown in Figure 6.1, with a join (to get the grades of those students who are computer science majors).

Grade_report : Table

Field Name	Data Type	Description
STUDENT_NUMBER	Number	
SECTION_ID	Number	
GRADE	Text	

FIGURE 6.1 Description of Grade_report Table

The join query now looks as follows (note the choice of fields in the SELECT statement, so that we can see the student names, majors, and their grades):

```
SELECT  stu.sname, stu.major, g.section_id, g.grade
FROM    Student stu, Grade_report g
WHERE   stu.major = 'COSC'
  AND   stu.stno = g.student_number;
```

This produces the following 48 rows of output:

sname	major	section_id	grade
Mary	COSC	85.00	A
Mary	COSC	87.00	B
Mary	COSC	90.00	B
Mary	COSC	91.00	B
Mary	COSC	92.00	B
Mary	COSC	96.00	B
Mary	COSC	101.00	
Mary	COSC	133.00	
Mary	COSC	134.00	
Mary	COSC	135.00	
Brenda	COSC	85.00	A
Brenda	COSC	92.00	A
Brenda	COSC	94.00	C
Brenda	COSC	95.00	B
Brenda	COSC	96.00	C
Brenda	COSC	102.00	B
Brenda	COSC	133.00	
Brenda	COSC	134.00	
Brenda	COSC	135.00	
Brenda	COSC	201.00	
Lujack	COSC	91.00	A
Lujack	COSC	102.00	B

sname	major	section_id	grade
Lujack	COSC	112.00	
Lujack	COSC	135.00	
Lujack	COSC	145.00	B
Lujack	COSC	158.00	B
Elainie	COSC	112.00	
Elainie	COSC	119.00	
Elainie	COSC	135.00	
Hillary	COSC	90.00	B
Hillary	COSC	94.00	B
Hillary	COSC	95.00	B
Brad	COSC	90.00	F
Brad	COSC	94.00	F
Brad	COSC	95.00	F
Alan	COSC	90.00	C
Alan	COSC	94.00	C
Alan	COSC	95.00	C
Jerry	COSC	88.00	
Jerry	COSC	89.00	A
Jerry	COSC	90.00	A
Jerry	COSC	100.00	
Jerry	COSC	107.00	
Jerry	COSC	202.00	
Jake	COSC	90.00	C
Zelda	COSC	90.00	C
Zelda	COSC	94.00	C
Zelda	COSC	95.00	B

3. To add the condition for B's, we need to add another AND clause in the WHERE condition, by adding a fifth line to the query:

```
SELECT  stu.sname, major, section_id, grade
FROM    Student stu, Grade_report g
WHERE   stu.major = 'COSC'
  AND   stu.stno = g.student_number
  AND   g.grade = 'B';
```

This produces the following 14 rows of output:

sname	major	section_id	grade
Mary	COSC	87.00	B
Mary	COSC	90.00	B
Mary	COSC	91.00	B
Mary	COSC	92.00	B
Mary	COSC	96.00	B
Brenda	COSC	95.00	B
Brenda	COSC	102.00	B
Lujack	COSC	102.00	B
Lujack	COSC	145.00	B
Lujack	COSC	158.00	B
Hillary	COSC	90.00	B
Hillary	COSC	94.00	B
Hillary	COSC	95.00	B
Zelda	COSC	95.00	B

4. To get only the student names from the preceding output, type the following:

```
SELECT  stu.sname
FROM    Student AS stu, Grade_report AS g
WHERE   stu.major = 'COSC'
  AND   stu.stno = g.student_number
  AND   g.grade = 'B';
```

This produces the following output, a list of all the students who are majoring in COSC and received a grade of B:

sname
Mary
Mary
Mary
Mary
Mary

sname
Brenda
Brenda
Lujack
Lujack
Lujack
Hillary
Hillary
Hillary
Zelda

The point of this process is that it allows us to test as we go, verify that the query works up to that point, and ensure that we have a reasonable result before we move on to the next enhancement.

A final presentation using DISTINCT (to find the distinct names) and ORDER BY (to order by names) could be added to the query if desired.

Parentheses in SQL Expressions

As queries get longer, they can become very ambiguous without the appropriate use of parentheses. In programming languages like C, you can write a statement like this:

```
x = y + z * w
```

What does this compute? The answer depends on precedence rules. Usually in programming languages (and in SQL), clauses in parentheses have the highest precedence. The authors of this book advocate *fully* parenthesized expressions for three reasons:

• It makes the expression easier to debug.

• It tells anyone else who looks at your expression that it is written as you intended, because you explicitly and unambiguously wrote the expression in a fully parenthesized way.

• There is no guarantee that another version of SQL will behave like the one you learned.

In SQL, the precedence problem occurs when AND and OR are used in the same query. For example, what does the following query request?

Does AND or OR have precedence or is the rule "left to right"? (The answer to this is left as an end-of-chapter exercise).

```
SELECT    *
FROM      Student
WHERE     class = 3 OR class = 4 AND stno < 100;
```

This produces the following output (12 rows):

ST NO	SNAME	MAJOR	CLASS	BDATE
3	Mary	COSC	4	7/6/78
13	Kelly	MATH	4	8/12/80
20	Donald	ACCT	4	10/15/77
24	Chris	ACCT	4	2/12/78
49	Susan	ENGL	3	3/11/80
62	Monica	MATH	3	10/14/80
122	Phoebe	ENGL	3	4/15/80
131	Rachel	ENGL	3	4/15/80
143	Cramer	ENGL	3	4/15/80
31	Jake	COSC	4	2/12/78
151	Losmith	CHEM	3	1/15/81
160	Gus	ART	3	10/15/78

The point is, you do not have to know the rule to write an unambiguous expression. If you use parentheses appropriately, you make the expression clear and unambiguous. Consider the following examples. If we type the following:

```
SELECT    *
FROM      Student
WHERE     class = 3 OR (class = 4 AND stno < 100);
```

The result is the following output (12 rows):

ST NO	SNAME	MAJOR	CLASS	BDATE
3	Mary	COSC	4	7/6/78
13	Kelly	MATH	4	8/12/80
20	Donald	ACCT	4	10/15/77
24	Chris	ACCT	4	2/12/78
49	Susan	ENGL	3	3/11/80
62	Monica	MATH	3	10/14/80
122	Phoebe	ENGL	3	4/15/80
131	Rachel	ENGL	3	4/15/80
143	Cramer	ENGL	3	4/15/80
31	Jake	COSC	4	2/12/78
151	Losmith	CHEM	3	1/15/81
160	Gus	ART	3	10/15/78

The preceding query has the parentheses around the AND clause, the result of which is that the AND is performed first. The following query has the parentheses around the OR clause, meaning the OR is performed first:

```
SELECT    *
FROM      Student
WHERE     (class = 3 OR class = 4) AND stno < 100;
```

This results in the following output (7 rows):

ST NO	SNAME	MAJOR	CLASS	BDATE
3	Mary	COSC	4	7/6/78
13	Kelly	MATH	4	8/12/80
20	Donald	ACCT	4	10/15/77
24	Chris	ACCT	4	2/12/78
49	Susan	ENGL	3	3/11/80
62	Monica	MATH	3	10/14/80
31	Jake	COSC	4	2/12/78

As the preceding two query statements demonstrate, appropriate placement of parentheses eliminates any ambiguity in queries that contain both OR and AND.

Derived Structures

Derived structures become very necessary as the queries we build get larger and we have to use a more step-by-step approach. Derived structures help us to build queries on top of other queries. In this section, we discuss two of the most commonly used derived structures—views and temporary tables.

> The way in which Access SQL handles derived structures is a little different from how standard SQL handles them.

Views

In SQL, a **view** (also called a *virtual table* or, in Access, a *saved query*) is a mechanism to procure a restricted subset of data that is accessible in ways akin to ordinary tables. We use the word "akin" because some operations on views (such as some updates and deletes) may be restricted where they otherwise would not be if performed on the underlying structure itself. A view serves several purposes: It is a convenient way to develop a query by isolating parts of it, and it is used to restrict a set of users from seeing part of the database in a multiuser system, which is a security feature. Another benefit of views is that they do not occupy much disk space, since they have no data of their own. When you use a view for queries, you use it just as you would use the underlying table(s). Therefore, views can also be used to create other views or queries.

> Views are typically a way of building queries on top of other queries.

Creating Views

In Access SQL, you cannot create a view as a SQL command. Instead, to create a view, you have to follow the steps outlined in the following example. This example creates a view called `namemaj`, which is a view of students' names and majors from the `Student` table:

1. Type the following command in a new query screen in the SQL view window.

```
SELECT   sname, major
FROM     Student;
```

2. In the main Access window, click the **File** menu and select **Save**, which will open the **Save As** dialog box, shown in Figure 6.2.

3. In the **Query Name** list box, type `namemaj`, and then click **OK**.

4. Close your SQL query screen.

Your view of the names and majors of students from the `Student` table is now ready to be used.

> Because of the way Access creates a view, Access uses the term "saved query" instead of "view." However, because views in ordinary SQL and saved queries in Access have the same effect, and because "view" is the commonly recognized term among SQL users, we will use the term "view."

159

Query Development and Derived Structures

FIGURE 6.2 Saving the View

Using Views

The new view can be used just like a table, in the FROM clause of any SELECT statement. Open a new query screen in SQL view (see Figure 6.3) and type the query shown in Figure 6.3.

FIGURE 6.3 Using the View

Click the red ! to run the query, which will output a list of names and majors (of which the first 19 rows of the 48 rows of output are shown below):

sname	major
Lineas	ENGL
Mary	COSC
Zelda	COSC
Ken	POLY
Mario	MATH
Brenda	COSC
Romona	ENGL
Richard	ENGL
Kelly	MATH
Lujack	COSC
Reva	MATH
Elainie	COSC

sname	major
Harley	POLY
Donald	ACCT
Chris	ACCT
Jake	COSC
Lynette	POLY
Susan	ENGL
Monica	MATH

Just like an ordinary table, a view can be filtered and used in a SELECT. For example, type the following query:

```
SELECT   n.major AS [Major], n.sname AS [Student Name]
FROM     namemaj AS n, Department_to_major AS d
WHERE    n.major = d.dcode
AND      d.dname LIKE 'COMP*';
```

This produces the following output:

Major	Student Name
COSC	Mary
COSC	Brenda
COSC	Lujack
COSC	Elainie
COSC	Hillary
COSC	Brad
COSC	Alan
COSC	Jerry
COSC	Jake
COSC	Zelda

ORDER BY in Views

If we want to order our output, we can add an ORDER BY to a view statement. For example, if we create a view called namemaj1, as follows:

```
SELECT   sname, major
FROM     Student
ORDER    BY sname;
```

And then type the following:

```
SELECT  sname, major
FROM    namemaj1
WHERE   major='COSC';
```

The output is ordered by name:

sname	major
Alan	COSC
Brad	COSC
Brenda	COSC
Elainie	COSC
Hillary	COSC
Jake	COSC
Jerry	COSC
Lujack	COSC
Mary	COSC
Zelda	COSC

The names are ordered because the view was ordered when it was created.

Column Aliases in Views

Column aliases can be used instead of column names in views. For example, type the following to create a view called namemaj2 with column aliases:

```
SELECT  sname AS [name], major AS [maj]
FROM    Student
WHERE   major = 'COSC';
```

Then type:

```
SELECT *
FROM    namemaj2;
```

This produces the following output, with the column aliases in the column headings:

name	maj
Mary	COSC
Brenda	COSC
Lujack	COSC
Elainie	COSC
Hillary	COSC
Brad	COSC
Alan	COSC
Jerry	COSC
Jake	COSC
Zelda	COSC

To use the column aliases in a query, the name of the view or table alias (in this case, a view alias) has to precede the column alias, as shown in this query:

```
SELECT  namemaj2.[name], namemaj2.[maj]
FROM    namemaj2
WHERE   namemaj2.[name] LIKE 'J*';
```

This query produces the following output:

name	maj
Jerry	COSC
Jake	COSC

The same query could also be written as follows, in which n is the table (view) alias:

```
SELECT  n.[name], n.[maj]
FROM    namemaj2 AS n
WHERE   n.[name] LIKE 'J*';
```

Data in Views

A view has no data of its own. Data is stored only in the table, not in the view. The view only stores the SELECT statement (rather than the actual data). Therefore, views depend on the underlying tables.

When data in the original table is changed, the view is automatically updated. Therefore, the view is always up-to-date. And, when data is changed through a view, the original (underlying) table is also automatically updated.

Changing Data in Views

To demonstrate how changing data through a view automatically updates the original table, begin with the following `Employee` table, which we created and used in Chapter 5:

name	wage	hours
Sumon Bagui	10	40
Sudip Bagui	15	30
Priyashi Saha	18	
Ed Evans		10
Genny George	20	40

1. Create a view called `Employee_view` from the `Employee` table, as follows:

```
SELECT  *
FROM    Employee;
```

2. To output the entire contents of the view, type the following query:

```
SELECT  *
FROM    Employee_view;
```

This produces the following output:

name	wage	hours
Sumon Bagui	10	40
Sudip Bagui	15	30
Priyashi Saha	18	
Ed Evans		10
Genny George	20	40

3. Viewing the data in a view is just like viewing the data in a table. So, following the "Viewing Table Designs" section of Chapter 1, to view the data of a particular view in your database, click the **Tables** tab from the **Objects** list, then double-click the view, `Employee_view`, and change some data; for example, change the third name in the preceding view from "Priyashi Saha" to "Mala Saha."

4. Close the screen. The data in the original `Employee` table automatically changes to match the change that you made in the view.

To test the results, type the following query:

```
SELECT   *
FROM     Employee;
```

This now produces the following output, with the third name changed in the `Employee` table:

name	wage	hours
Sumon Bagui	10	40
Sudip Bagui	15	30
Mala Saha	18	
Ed Evans		10
Genny George	20	40

If a record were added or deleted from the view, `Employee_view`, the same change would also appear in the original table.

Therefore, when adding, changing, or deleting data in views, you should always be very careful because you do not want to unintentionally change the original table. Remember that a view may sometimes only be a section of a table.

Changing Data in Tables

If data is changed in the original table, `Employee`, the same data in all the views related to that table also gets changed.

Temporary Tables

If you were going to use the view of names, student numbers, and department names of freshmen and sophomore computer science (COSC) majors often, and you did not need absolutely current information, you might want to create a ***temporary table*** rather than a view. A drawback of the temporary table is that if the underlying table data is changed, it is not changed in the temporary table, whereas in a view, since there is no extra table, whatever "happens" in the table "happens" in the view. On the plus side, a temporary table can be indexed, queries can change the ORDER BY (or not), and views of the temporary table can be made—sort of a hierarchy of views.

> Indexing is discussed in detail in Chapter 11.

As an example of how to create a temporary table in Access, type the following SELECT query:

```
SELECT   s.sname, s.stno, d.dname, s.class INTO Temp1
FROM     Student s, Department_to_major d
WHERE    s.major = d.dcode
AND      (s.class = 1 or s.class = 2)
AND      s.major = 'COSC';
```

Running this query creates the temporary table, Temp1, because of the statement fragment INTO Temp1. To view the temporary table, type the following:

```
SELECT   *
FROM     Temp1;
```

This produces the following output:

sname	stno	dname	class
Brenda	8	Computer Science	2
Lujack	14	Computer Science	1
Elainie	17	Computer Science	1
Hillary	121	Computer Science	1
Brad	128	Computer Science	1
Alan	130	Computer Science	2

Note the icon of the SELECT query that creates a temporary table, shown in Figure 6.4.

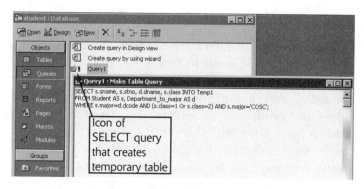

FIGURE 6.4 Icon of SELECT Query That Creates Temporary Table

To access the temporary tables directly, click the **Tables** tab, and then click the temporary table (for help on this, refer to "Viewing Table Designs" in Chapter 1). The icon for a temporary table is the same as the icon for a regular table.

Data in Temporary Tables

Unlike what happens when you change the data in a view, if you change data in a temporary table, it does not affect the original table. For exam-

sname	stno	dname	class
Brenda	8	Computer Science	2
Lujack	14	Computer Science	1
Elainie	17	Computer Science	1
Hillary	121	Computer Science	1
Brad	128	Computer Science	1
Alan	130	Computer Science	2
Brandon	330	Computer Science	2

ple, suppose we changed Temp1 so that we now have the following data (a row has been added at the end):

This does not change the original table, Student, but any queries using Temp1 now have the preceding seven rows.

Query Development with Derived Structures

In this section, we will discuss how derived structures such as views and temporary tables can be used in query development. To illustrate this process, we will list from our standard database, student.mdb, the name, student number, and department name of students who are freshmen or sophomores and computer science majors. In Step 1 we will develop a query, and in Step 2 we will show how to use this query with derived structures. In Step 2, Option 1 shows how the query can be turned into a view; Option 2 shows how an inline view can be used instead of a regular view; and Option 3 shows how to use a temporary table.

Step 1: Develop a Query Step by Step

1. The first step is to see which fields we need and in which tables these fields are found. We need student names (sname) and numbers (stno), which are found in the Student table. Department names (dname) are found in the Department_to_major table. To find the department names that correspond to the student majors, we have to join the Student and Department_to_major tables. To join these two tables, we have to join where major from the Student table joins with the dcode from the Department_to_major table as follows (since the statements eventually will be filtered by class, we will include class in the result set):

```
SELECT   s.sname, s.stno, d.dname, s.class
FROM     Student s, Department_to_major d
WHERE    s.major = d.dcode;
```

After we type the query and run it, we get the following output:

sname	stno	dname	class
Lineas	2	English	1
Mary	3	Computer Science	4
Brenda	8	Computer Science	2
Richard	10	English	1
Kelly	13	Mathematics	4
Lujack	14	Computer Science	1
Reva	15	Mathematics	2
Elainie	17	Computer Science	1
Harley	19	Political Science	2

sname	stno	dname	class
Donald	20	Accounting	4
Chris	24	Accounting	4
Lynette	34	Political Science	1
Susan	49	English	3
Monica	62	Mathematics	3
Bill	70	Political Science	
Hillary	121	Computer Science	1
Phoebe	122	English	3
Holly	123	Political Science	4
Sadie	125	Mathematics	2
Jessica	126	Political Science	2
Steve	127	English	1
Brad	128	Computer Science	1
Cedric	129	English	2
Alan	130	Computer Science	2
Rachel	131	English	3
George	132	Political Science	1
Jerry	142	Computer Science	4
Cramer	143	English	3
Fraiser	144	Political Science	1
Harrison	145	Accounting	4
Francis	146	Accounting	4
Smithly	147	English	2
Sebastian	148	Accounting	2
Jake	31	Computer Science	4
Losmith	151	Chemistry	3
Genevieve	153		
Lindsay	155		1
Stephanie	157	Mathematics	
Benny	161	Chemistry	4
Gus	160	Art	3
Zelda	5	Computer Science	
Mario	7	Mathematics	
Romona	9	English	
Ken	6	Political Science	
Jake	191	Mathematics	2

2. Close the output window and save the query as `stucosc`.

3. Select the **Queries** tab in the **Objects** list, as shown in Figure 6.5, click once on `stucosc`, and then click the **Design** button to open `stucosc` in SQL view, as shown in Figure 6.6.

4. To find all the freshmen and sophomores (classes 1 and 2) from the `Student` table, add `AND (s.class = 1 or s.class = 2)` to the end of `stucosc`, as shown in Figure 6.6.

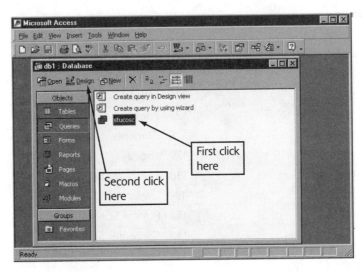

FIGURE 6.5 Accessing a View

FIGURE 6.6 SQL View of stucosc Screen

Running this query produces the following 21 rows of output:

sname	stno	dname	class
Lineas	2	English	1
Brenda	8	Computer Science	2
Richard	10	English	1
Lujack	14	Computer Science	1
Reva	15	Mathematics	2
Elainie	17	Computer Science	1

sname	stno	dname	class
Harley	19	Political Science	2
Lynette	34	Political Science	1
Hillary	121	Computer Science	1
Sadie	125	Mathematics	2
Jessica	126	Political Science	2
Steve	127	English	1
Brad	128	Computer Science	1
Cedric	129	English	2
Alan	130	Computer Science	2
George	132	Political Science	1
Fraiser	144	Political Science	1
Smithly	147	English	2
Sebastian	148	Accounting	2
Lindsay	155		1
Jake	191	Mathematics	2

5. Now that we have the department names of all the freshmen and sophomores, we need to find the computer science majors from this group, so we add AND s.major = 'COSC' to the query stucosc as follows:

```
SELECT   s.sname, s.stno, d.dname, s.class,
FROM     Student s, Department_to_major d
WHERE    s.major = d.dcode
AND      (s.class = 1 or s.class = 2)
AND      s.major = 'COSC';
```

This produces the following output, which finally gives us the student name, student number, and department name of students who are freshmen or sophomores and computer science majors:

sname	stno	dname	class
Brenda	8	Computer Science	2
Lujack	14	Computer Science	1
Elainie	17	Computer Science	1
Hillary	121	Computer Science	1
Brad	128	Computer Science	1
Alan	130	Computer Science	2

Step 2: Using a Derived Structure

This step shows how you can turn the `stucosc` query developed in Step 1 into a view, inline view, or temporary table. Each one of these derived structures will produce the same end results, so as you develop your own queries, you may use whichever derived structure you become most comfortable with. (Derived structures are also very useful when you wish to use functions within functions, an example of which is shown in the section "The COUNT Function" in Chapter 5.)

Option 1: Turning Your Query into a View

To create a view (called `vustu`) by editing `stucosc`, follow these steps:

1. Select the **Queries** tab and click once on `stucosc`.

2. Click the **Design** button to open `stucosc` in SQL view. (In case you are not in SQL view, click **View** on the main Access menu and select **SQL View**.)

3. When the following SQL code appears in SQL view, click the **File** menu and select **Save As**.

```
SELECT   s.sname, s.stno, d.dname, s.class
FROM     Student s, Department_to_major d
WHERE    s.major = d.dcode
AND      (s.class = 1 or s.class = 2)
AND      s.major = 'COSC';
```

4. Save the view as `vustu`.

You can now just SELECT from the view. For example, type the following query in a new SQL view screen:

```
SELECT   *
FROM     vustu
WHERE    sname LIKE 'BR*';
```

This produces the following output, which includes all the names in the view `vustu` that start with "Br":

sname	stno	dname	class
Brenda	8	Computer Science	2
Brad	128	Computer Science	1

Option 2: Using an Inline View

You can also put a query in the FROM clause of a SELECT statement and hence create what is called an *inline view.* An inline view exists only during the execution of a query. The main purpose of an inline view is to simplify the development of a query. In a typical development scenario, a person would probably devise the inline view, inner select, test it, examine the result, wrap it in parentheses, and continue with the development by using the inline view.

Let's look at an example of an inline view in our sample problem. In this example, we create the view inline—that is, we create the view on the fly, give it an alias, v, and use it just as we would use a stored table or view. To begin, open stucosc and edit it to read as follows:

```
SELECT  v.['name'], v.dname, v.class
FROM    [SELECT s.sname AS 'name', s.stno, d.dname, s.class
FROM    Student AS s, Department_to_major AS d
WHERE   s.major = d.dcode
  AND   (s.class = 1 or s.class = 2)
  AND   s.major = 'COSC']. AS v;
```

This produces the following output:

'name'	dname	class
Brenda	Computer Science	2
Lujack	Computer Science	1
Elainie	Computer Science	1
Hillary	Computer Science	1
Brad	Computer Science	1
Alan	Computer Science	2

Observe that a column alias is used for the student name ('name'), whereas the other columns in the inline view result set are not aliased. In the final result set of the outer query, the column names reference the names used or aliased in the inline view result set—v.['name'] corresponds to the alias of s.sname, 'name', and v.dname corresponds to d.dname.

It is better to use column aliases throughout in the inline view to avoid confusion. Thus, you should use something like the following:

```
SELECT v.['name'], v.['in_view_stno'], v.['in_view_dname'],
v.['in_view_class']
FROM [SELECT s.sname AS 'name', s.stno AS 'in_view_stno',
d.dname AS 'in_view_dname', s.class AS 'in_view_class'
FROM Student AS s, Department_to_major AS d
WHERE s.major = d.dcode
    AND (s.class = 1 or s.class = 2)
    AND s.major = 'COSC']. AS v;
```

This produces the following output:

'sname'	'in_view_stno'	'in_view_dname'	'in_view_class'
Brenda	8	Computer Science	2
Lujack	14	Computer Science	1
Elainie	17	Computer Science	1
Hillary	121	Computer Science	1
Brad	128	Computer Science	1
Alan	130	Computer Science	2

Option 3: Using a Temporary Table

To create a temporary table (called Temp2) using stucosc, follow these steps:

1. Select the **Queries** tab and click once on stucosc.

2. Click the **Design** button to open stucosc in SQL view. (In case you are not in SQL view, click **View** and select **SQL View**.)

3. Edit stucosc so that it reads as follows (note the addition of the clause INTO Temp2):

```
SELECT  s.sname, s.stno, d.dname, s.class INTO Temp2
FROM    Student s, Department_to_major d
WHERE   s.major = d.dcode
AND     (s.class = 1 or s.class = 2)
AND     s.major = 'COSC';
```

4. Run your query and save it. Once you run your query, you have created a temporary table called Temp2.

5. Open a new SQL query screen and type:

```
SELECT *
FROM Temp2;
```

You should get the following output, which should be exactly the same as you received in the other options:

sname	stno	dname	class
Brenda	8	Computer Science	2
Lujack	14	Computer Science	1
Elainie	17	Computer Science	1
Hillary	121	Computer Science	1
Brad	128	Computer Science	1
Alan	130	Computer Science	2

CHAPTER 6 REVIEW QUESTIONS

1. Which has precedence, an AND or an OR?

2. Why do we need derived structures?

3. List some advantages of using views.

4. List some advantages of using temporary tables.

5. Can temporary tables replace views in all cases?

6. Can views replace temporary tables in all cases?

7. If data is changed in a view, is it changed in the original table?

8. If data is changed in a temporary table, is it changed in the original table?

9. Why are inline views helpful?

CHAPTER 6 EXERCISES

1. Develop and execute a query to find the names of students who had HERMANO as an instructor and earned a grade of B or better in the class. Develop the query by first finding sections where HERMANO was the instructor. Save this query. Then, edit the query and modify it to join the Section table with the Grade_report table. Then, add the grade constraint.

2. Create from the Student table a duplicate table called Stutab that contains all rows from Student. Hint: Look at the design of the Student table to see the fields and their definitions. Create the

Stutab table with a CREATE TABLE command. Insert data into Stutab using the INSERT INTO.. SELECT.

a. List student names and majors from Stutab for students who are juniors or seniors only.

b. List student names and COSC majors from the Stutab table.

c. Create a view (call it vstu) that contains student names and majors, but only for COSC majors.

d. List the student names and majors from vstu in descending order by name.

e. Modify a row in your view of your table so that a student changes his or her major.

f. Re-execute the display of the view. Did modifying vstu also change the parent table, Stutab?

g. Try to modify the view again, but this time change the major to 'COMPSC'—an obviously invalid field in the Stutab table because the field was defined as four characters. Can you do it? What happens?

h. Create a temporary table (call it vstutemp) that contains student names and majors, but only for COSC majors.

i. List the student names and majors from vstutemp in ascending order by name.

j. Modify a row in vstutemp so that a student changes his or her major.

k. Re-execute the display of the temporary table. Did modifying your temporary table, vstutemp, also change the parent table, Stutab?

l. Try to modify the temporary table again, but this time change the major to 'COMPSC'—again, an obviously invalid field in Stutab because the field was defined as four characters. Can you do it? What happens?

m. Create an inline view (call it invstu) that contains student names and majors, but only for COSC majors.

3. Perform an experiment to determine the precedence in a query with three conditions linked by AND and OR. Does AND, OR, or left-to-right take precedence?

Run this query:

```
SELECT   *
FROM     Student
WHERE    stno < 100 AND major = 'COSC' OR major = 'ACCT';
```

Then run the following two queries and determine which one gives you the same output as the preceding nonparenthesized statement:

```
SELECT  *
FROM    Student
WHERE   (stno < 100 AND major = 'COSC') OR major = 'ACCT';
```

or:

```
SELECT  *
FROM    Student
WHERE   stno < 100 AND (major = 'COSC' OR major = 'ACCT');
```

What happens if you put the OR first instead of the AND and run the query without parentheses?

4. Develop a query to find the instructor name and course name for computer science courses (use the table). Order the table by instructor name.

   a. Convert your query into a view.

   b. Remove the ORDER BY clause and convert the query into an inline view with column aliases and test it.

   c. Put the ORDER BY clause outside of the inline view in the main query and run your query again.

Set Operations

Topics covered in this chapter

In Chapter 4, we looked at how data can be retrieved from multiple tables using joins. As we'll discuss in this chapter, data can also be retrieved from multiple tables by using set operations. We'll look at the set operations available in Access SQL. Because not all the SQL set operations are explicitly available in Access SQL, we'll also look at the IN and NOT..IN predicates, which are ways around the explicit set operations. In the final section, we'll look at the UNION operation in relation to the join operation, and how the UNION operation can be used to get the results of some joins.

Introducing Set Operations

A *set* is a collection of objects. In relational databases, a table (or relation) can be regarded as a set of rows, and a row can be regarded as a set of one or more columns. Elements in a set do not have to be ordered (in fact, in relational databases, rows are never considered ordered as stored). *Set operations* are used in SQL to retrieve data from multiple sets.

Three explicit set operations are used in SQL: UNION, INTERSECT, and MINUS (set difference). However, Access SQL only allows the explicit use of the UNION set operation. Since the other two set operations cannot be explicitly used in Access SQL, we will illustrate these two set operations by using the IN and NOT..IN predicates, which enable us to accomplish the same result as using INTERSECT and MINUS.

A *binary union* is a set operation on two sets, the result of which contains all the elements of both sets. Other set operations in SQL include a *binary intersection*, which generates values in common between two sets, and a *binary set difference*, which generates values in one set less those contained in another.

The format of a set statement is as follows:

```
set OPERATOR set
```

where OPERATOR is a UNION, INTERSECT, or MINUS, and where "set" is defined by a SELECT. In Access SQL, however, the OPERATOR can only be a UNION, since Access SQL does not explicitely support the INTERSECT or MINUS operations. The following is an example of a UNION:

```
SELECT *
FROM TableA
UNION
SELECT *
FROM TableB;
```

Set statements allow us to combine two distinct sets of data (two tables or two result sets) only if we ensure union compatibility.

Union Compatibility

Union compatibility, the commonly used SQL terminology for *set compatibility,* means that when we use set operations, both sets have to match in the number of items and have to have compatible data types. In other words, in order for a UNION to be successful, the data types of the two result sets being unioned must be compatible. The data types do not necessarily have to be exactly the same, meaning they may differ in length and type, but they have to be "compatible."

So, what does "compatible" mean? For union compatibility, the three basic data types are numbers, text, and dates. All numeric fields are compatible with one another, all text fields are compatible with one another, and all dates are compatible with one another. For numbers, SQL will convert integers, floating-point numbers, and decimals into a numeric data type, to make them compatible with one another. So, any numeric field (integers) can be unioned with any other numeric field (decimals). Likewise, fixed-length text and variable-length text will be converted to a text type and take on the largest size of the text fields being unioned. Similarly, date and time columns will be combined to a date data type.

> For union compatibility, the three basic data types are numbers, text, and dates.

Union compatibility can happen in several ways:

• by unioning two tables that have identical attributes (which implies the same domains, too)

• by taking two subsets from a table and combining them

• by using two views from two tables with the attributes chosen so that they are compatible

The UNION Set Operation

In Access SQL, a binary union is performed with the UNION set operation. A UNION takes output from two queries and returns all rows from both results sets (removing the duplicates). In this section, we show how a UNION works. Using the Student table from previous chapters, suppose we want to find the names of all students who are computer science (COSC) majors along with all students who are MATH majors. To do so, we write the following query:

```
SELECT sname
FROM Student
WHERE major = 'COSC'
   UNION
SELECT sname
FROM Student
WHERE major = 'MATH';
```

> The two sets being unioned have to have the same number of fields too.

While executing the UNION, SQL executes the first query:

```
SELECT sname
FROM Student
WHERE major = 'COSC';
```

This produces the following 10 rows of output:

sname
Mary
Brenda
Lujack
Elainie
Hillary
Brad
Alan
Jerry
Jake
Zelda

Then SQL executes the second query:

```
SELECT sname
FROM Student
WHERE major = 'MATH';
```

This produces the following 7 rows of output:

sname
Kelly
Reva
Monica
Sadie
Stephanie
Mario
Jake

> The maximum number of rows possible when a UNION is used is the sum of the two result sets (or tables).

SQL then combines the two sets of results (the UNION operation), which includes throwing out any duplicates (an extra Jake) and ordering the output alphabetically, the product of which is the following 16 rows of output:

sname
Alan
Brad
Brenda
Elainie
Hillary
Jake
Jerry
Kelly
Lujack
Mario
Mary
Monica
Reva
Sadie
Stephanie
Zelda

Note that when you save a UNION query, it has a different icon from other queries, as shown in Figure 7.1.

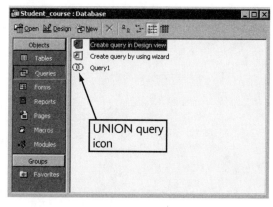

FIGURE 7.1 Icon for a UNION Query

The UNION ALL Set Operation

UNION ALL works exactly like UNION but does not expunge duplicates nor sort the results. Although this makes UNION ALL more efficient in execution, occasionally you may need to keep duplicates (just to keep all occurrences or records), in which case you can use UNION ALL.

The following is the same query previously shown for UNION, but using UNION ALL instead of UNION:

```
SELECT sname
FROM Student
WHERE major = 'COSC'
   UNION ALL
SELECT sname
FROM Student
WHERE major = 'MATH';
```

This results in 17 unsorted rows, including one duplicate, Jake (whereas using UNION produced 16 sorted rows with no duplicates):

sname
Mary
Brenda
Lujack
Elainie
Hillary
Brad
Alan
Jerry
Jake
Zelda
Kelly
Reva
Monica
Sadie
Stephanie
Mario
Jake

Performing UNIONs and UNION ALLs with an Unequal Number of Fields

All queries in a UNION or UNION ALL operation must request the same number of fields. If we want to union two sets that do not have the same number of fields, we can use NULL values in some of the field places as place holders. For example, from our student.mdb database, if we want to union the Course table and the Prereq table with all the fields, under normal circumstances, this would not be possible since the Course table has four fields and the Prereq table has only two fields. So, to perform a UNION ALL operation, we must place NULL values in the fields that will be empty, as follows:

```
SELECT c.*, NULL
FROM Course c
WHERE c.credit_hours = 4
UNION ALL
SELECT NULL, p.course_number, NULL, NULL, p.prereq
FROM Prereq p;
```

> In some versions of SQL, these results could also be achieved with a UNION JOIN operation, but Access SQL does not support the use of the UNION JOIN.

This produces the following output:

COURSE_NAME	COURSE_NUMBER	CREDIT_HOURS	OFFERING_DEPT	Expr1001
INTRO TO COMPUTER SC	COSC1310	4	COSC	
DATA STRUCTURES	COSC3320	4	COSC	
ADA - INTRODUCTION	COSC5234	4	COSC	
CALCULUS 1	MATH1501	4	MATH	
SOCIALISM AND COMMUN	POLY4103	4	POLY	
POLITICS OF CUBA	POLY5501	4	POLY	
	ACCT3333			ACCT2220
	COSC3320			COSC1310
	COSC3380			COSC3320
	COSC3380			MATH2410
	COSC5234			COSC3320

COURSE_NAME	COURSE_NUMBER	CREDIT_HOURS	OFFERING_DEPT	Expr1001
	ENGL1011			ENGL1010
	ENGL3401			ENGL1011
	ENGL3520			ENGL1011
	MATH5501			MATH2333
	POLY2103			POLY1201
	POLY5501			POLY4103
	CHEM3001			CHEM2001

The IN and NOT..IN Predicates

Although Access (and many other implementations of SQL) does not have MINUS (difference) or INTERSECT operators per se, it does have an IN predicate and a corresponding NOT..IN predicate that enable us to create intersections and differences. We will begin by looking at these predicates from a set point of view. In other words, if we find the objects from set A that are also in set B (or vice versa), we have found the intersection of sets A and B. If we find the objects from set A that are not in set B, we have found the difference of sets A and B.

Using IN

The following is a simple example of an IN predicate with constants in a SELECT statement:

```
SELECT   sname, class
FROM     Student
WHERE    class IN (3,4);
```

In this example, IN (3,4) is called a *subquery-set,* where (3,4) is the set in which we are testing membership. This query says: "Find all student names from the Student table where the class is in the set (3,4)." It produces the following 17 rows of output:

sname	class
Mary	4
Kelly	4
Donald	4
Chris	4
Susan	3
Monica	3
Phoebe	3
Holly	4
Rachel	3
Jerry	4
Cramer	3
Harrison	4
Francis	4
Jake	4
Losmith	3
Benny	4
Gus	3

The preceding query produces the same output as the following query:

```
SELECT  sname, class
FROM    Student
WHERE   class = 3 OR class = 4;
```

In other words, the IN (3,4) means belonging to either set (3) or set (4), as shown by the WHERE class = 3 OR class = 4.

Using IN as a Subquery

We can expand the IN predicate's subquery-set part to be an actual query. For example, consider the following query:

```
SELECT  Student.sname
FROM    Student
WHERE   Student.stno IN
   (SELECT  g.student_number
    FROM    Grade_report g
    WHERE   g.grade = 'A');
```

Note the following about this query:

- WHERE Student.stno references the name of the column (the attribute) in the Student table.

- g.student_number is the column name in the Grade_report table.

- stno in the Student table and student_number in the Grade_report table have the same domain.

Note also that you must have exact column headings (usually, qualified column names) and retrieve the information from the same domains (for purposes of union compatibility).

The preceding query produces the following 14 rows of output:

sname
Lineas
Mary
Brenda
Richard
Lujack
Donald
Lynette
Susan
Holly
Sadie
Jessica
Steve
Cedric
Jerry

You could view the preceding query as a result derived from the *intersection* of the sets A and B, where set A is the set of student numbers in the student set (the Student table) and set B is the set of student numbers in the grade set (the Grade_report table) that have A's.

To make this command behave like a set operator (for example, as if it were an INTERSECTION operator), you can add the qualifier DISTINCT to the result set as follows:

```
SELECT DISTINCT (Student.sname)
FROM Student
```

```
WHERE Student.stno IN
  (SELECT DISTINCT (g.student_number)
   FROM Grade_report g
   WHERE g.grade = 'A');
```

This produces the following 14 rows of output:

sname
Brenda
Cedric
Donald
Holly
Jerry
Jessica
Lineas
Lujack
Lynette
Mary
Richard
Sadie
Steve
Susan

Here, Access sorts the results for you and does not return duplicates. In this example the use of IN is preferable.

Using NOT..IN

If you use the NOT..IN predicate in your query, your query may perform poorly. The reason is that when NOT..IN is used, no indexing can be used, because the NOT..IN part of the query has to test the set with all values to find out what is *not* in the set. (For smaller tables, no difference in performance will likely be detected.) Nonetheless, we discuss how to use NOT..IN in this section so that you understand the logical negative of the IN predicate, which will help to complete your overall understanding of the SQL language. Instead of using NOT..IN, it is often preferable to use NOT EXISTS (discussed in a later chapter) or outer join techniques.

Sometimes the NOT..IN predicate may seem to more easily describe the desired outcome or may be used for a set difference. For a simple example, consider the following query:

> Indexing is discussed in detail in Chapter 11.

```
SELECT  sname, class
FROM    Student
WHERE   class IN (1,3,4);
```

This produces the following 28 rows of output:

sname	class
Lineas	1
Mary	4
Richard	1
Kelly	4
Lujack	1
Elainie	1
Donald	4
Chris	4
Lynette	1
Susan	3
Monica	3
Hillary	1
Phoebe	3
Holly	4
Steve	1
Brad	1
Rachel	3
George	1
Jerry	4
Cramer	3
Fraiser	1
Harrison	4
Francis	4
Jake	4
Losmith	3
Lindsay	1
Benny	4
Gus	3

Contrast the preceding query to the following query:

```
SELECT   sname, class
FROM     Student
WHERE    class NOT IN (2);
```

The output in this case is the same as the preceding output because the Student table only has classes 1, 2, 3, and 4. If counts (results) did not match, this would show that some value of class was not 1, 2, 3, or 4.

As another example, suppose you want the names of students who are not computer science (COSC) or math majors. The command would be the following:

```
SELECT   sname, major
FROM     Student
WHERE    major NOT IN ('COSC','MATH');
```

This produces the following output (28 rows):

sname	major
Lineas	ENGL
Richard	ENGL
Harley	POLY
Donald	ACCT
Chris	ACCT
Lynette	POLY
Susan	ENGL
Bill	POLY
Phoebe	ENGL
Holly	POLY
Jessica	POLY
Steve	ENGL
Cedric	ENGL
Rachel	ENGL
George	POLY
Cramer	ENGL
Fraiser	POLY
Harrison	ACCT

sname	major
Francis	ACCT
Smithly	ENGL
Sebastian	ACCT
Losmith	CHEM
Genevieve	UNKN
Lindsay	UNKN
Benny	CHEM
Gus	ART
Romona	ENGL
Ken	POLY

The above output gave all majors other than COSC and MATH. But, you must be very careful with the NOT..IN predicate because if nulls are present in the data, you get odd answers with NOT..IN.

As an example, consider the following table called Stumajor:

> The table, Stumajor, has not been created for you. You have to create it to run the queries that follow.

name	major
Mary	Biology
Sam	Chemistry
Alice	Art
Tom	

If you perform the following query

```
SELECT  *
FROM    Stumajor
WHERE   major IN ('Chemistry','Biology');
```

it produces the following output:

name	major
Mary	Biology
Sam	Chemistry

If you perform the following query:

```
SELECT   *
FROM     Stumajor
WHERE    major NOT IN ('Chemistry','Biology');
```

It produces the following output:

name	major
Alice	Art

The value, null, is not equal to anything. You might expect that NOT..IN would give you <Tom,null>, but it does not. Why? Because nulls in the selection field (here, major) are ignored with a NOT.. IN.

Using NOT..IN in a Subquery

A NOT..IN can also be used in a subquery. For example, assume that we have another table, called Instructor, as shown here:

iname	teaches
Richard	COSC
Subhash	MATH
Tapan	BIOCHEM

> The Instructor table has not been created for you. You have to create it to run the queries that follow.

Now, if we want to find all the departments that do not have instructors, we could type the following query:

```
SELECT   *
FROM     Department_to_major d
WHERE    d.dcode NOT IN
  (SELECT  dcode
   FROM     Department_to_major d, Instructor i
   WHERE    d.dcode=i.teaches);
```

This produces the following output (6 rows):

Set Operations

dcode	dname
ACCT	Accounting
ART	Art
ENGL	English
POLY	Political Science
UNKN	
CHEM	Chemistry

The Difference Operation

Because Access does not support the MINUS predicate, we will show the set difference operation using a NOT..IN. To illustrate the difference operation, suppose set A is the set of students in classes 2, 3, or 4 and set B is the set of students in class = 2. We could use the NOT..IN predicate to remove the students in set B from set A (a difference operation) by typing the following query:

```
SELECT  sname, class
FROM    Student
WHERE   class IN (2,3,4)
  AND NOT class IN (2);
```

This produces the following output (17 rows):

sname	class
Mary	4
Kelly	4
Donald	4
Chris	4
Susan	3
Monica	3
Phoebe	3
Holly	4
Rachel	3
Jerry	4
Cramer	3
Harrison	4
Francis	4
Jake	4
Losmith	3
Benny	4
Gus	3

To illustrate another difference operation, we will use views with the NOT..IN predicate to give the effect of a difference operation. Suppose you want to find names for those students who do not major in COSC or MATH, but delete from that set those students who have made an A in some course. First, we will create a view of the names of students who are not COSC or MATH majors using the following query:

```
SELECT   sname, major
FROM     Student
WHERE    major NOT IN ('COSC','MATH');
```

Save this query as **view1**.

This produces the same 28 rows of output as shown earlier in this chapter.

Then, to find the students who have made A's, we will use the following query:

```
SELECT   Student.sname, Student.major
FROM     Student
WHERE    Student.stno IN
```

```
(SELECT  g.student_number
 FROM    Grade_report g
 WHERE   g.grade = 'A');
```

Save this query as **view2**.

This produces the following output (14 rows):

sname	major
Lineas	ENGL
Mary	COSC
Brenda	COSC
Richard	ENGL
Lujack	COSC
Donald	ACCT
Lynette	POLY
Susan	ENGL
Holly	POLY
Sadie	MATH
Jessica	POLY
Steve	ENGL
Cedric	ENGL
Jerry	COSC

Now, to find the those students who are not majoring in COSC or MATH, and remove from that set those who made an A in some course, the difference operation could be approached as follows using views:

```
SELECT sname
FROM view1
WHERE sname NOT IN
   (SELECT sname
   FROM view2
   WHERE view1.sname=view2.sname);
```

This query has the same effect as **view1 – view2** (all students who are not majoring in COSC or MATH MINUS students who made an A in some course).

This produces the following output (19 rows):

sname
Harley
Chris
Bill
Phoebe
Rachel
George
Cramer
Fraiser
Harrison
Francis
Smithly
Sebastian
Losmith
Genevieve
Lindsay
Benny
Gus
Romona
Ken

The UNION and the Join

In this section, we first discuss some differences between the two operations, the UNION and the join. Although the UNION operation and the join operation are similar in that they both combine two tables or sets of data, the approaches used by the two operations are different. Then, we discuss how a UNION can be used to implement a full outer join.

Differences Between the UNION and the Join

We will first show the binary union. Relations or tables are *sets of rows*. We have two tables, TableA and TableB, as shown below:

TableA		
FieldA	**FieldB**	**FieldC**
X1	Y1	Z1
X2	Y2	Z2
X3	Y3	Z3

TableB		
FieldA	**FieldB**	**FieldC**
X4	Y4	Z4
X5	Y5	Z5
X6	Y6	Z6

Then, an SQL binary union can be shown as:

FieldA	**FieldB**	**FieldC**
X1	Y1	Z1
X2	Y2	Z2
X3	Y3	Z3
X4	Y4	Z4
X5	Y5	Z5
X6	Y6	Z6

Using a similar set of diagrams, the join operation could be shown as follows (joining `TableA` and `TableB` into `TableC`):

TableA		
FieldA	**FieldB**	**FieldC**
X1	Y1	Z1
X2	Y2	Z2
X3	Y3	Z3

TableB		
FieldA	FieldB	FieldC
X1	D1	E1
X2	D2	E2
X3	D3	E3

TableC					
FieldA	FieldB	FieldC	FieldA	FieldD	FieldE
X1	Y1	Z1	X1	D1	E1
X2	Y2	Z2	X2	D2	E2
X3	Y3	Z3	X3	D3	E3

The following are the major differences between UNIONs and joins:

• In a UNION, all the rows in the resulting tables (sets) being unioned have to be compatible; in a join, only the fields of the table being joined have to be compatible—the other fields may be different.

• In a UNION, no new columns can be added to the final result of the UNION; in a join, new columns can be added to the result of the join.

• In a UNION, the number of columns in the result set has to be the same as the number of columns in the sets being unioned; in a join, the number of columns in the result set may vary.

A UNION Used to Implement a Full Outer Join

A full outer join adds rows to the result set that would be dropped from both tables due to an inner join. Some SQL products directly support the full outer join, but Access does not directly support it. In Access, a UNION can be used to achieve a full outer join.

> In Access, if you want to use a full outer join, you have to construct it.

You can create a full outer join by writing a union of the left outer join and the right outer join as follows:

```
SELECT with right outer join
UNION
SELECT with left outer join
```

The order of the left outer join and the right outer join does not matter and can be reversed. To illustrate the workings of the full outer join, let us use the table called Instructor created earlier in the chapter:

iname	teaches
Richard	COSC
Subhash	MATH
Tapan	BIOCHEM

If we want to get a list of all instructors and the names of the departments for which they teach (which will be done by a regular equi-join); a list of the rest of the instructors, regardless of whether or not they belong to a department; and a list of the rest of the departments, regardless of whether or not they have instructors, we would write the following query to achieve the full outer join effect:

```
SELECT *
FROM Department_to_major AS d LEFT JOIN Instructor AS I
ON d.dcode=i.teaches
    UNION
SELECT *
FROM Department_to_major AS d RIGHT JOIN Instructor AS I
ON d.dcode=i.teaches;
```

This produces the following output (9 rows):

Dcode	dname	iname	teaches
		Tapan	BIOCHEM
ACCT	Accounting		
ART	Art		
CHEM	Chemistry		
COSC	Computer Science	Richard	COSC
ENGL	English		
MATH	Mathematics	Subhash	MATH
POLY	Political Science		
UNKN			

First, the LEFT JOIN was done, joining the Department_to_major table and the Instructor table (so all the rows of the Department_to_major table were added back to the result set after the join). Then, a RIGHT JOIN was done, again joining the Department_to_major table to the Instructor table (but this time all the rows of the Instructor table were added back to the result set after the join). Finally, a UNION of the two results sets was performed, creating the effect of a full outer join (where the rows from both the tables were added back after the join).

CHAPTER 7 REVIEW QUESTIONS

1. What are the major differences between the UNION operation and the join operation?

2. What is the major difference between the UNION and the UNION ALL?

3. What major set operators does Access SQL not have? How can these problems be resolved?

4. What does union compatibility mean?

5. What data types are union compatible?

6. What is the maximum number of rows that can result from a UNION?

7. What is the maximum number of rows that can result from a join?

8. How can a UNION be used to implement an outer join? Explain.

9. Does Access SQL support the INTERSECT or MINUS operations?

10. What is a full outer join? Does Access SQL directly support a full outer join?

11. Do you need the same number of fields to perform a union?

12. Do you need the same data types to perform a union?

13. Do you need the same number of fields to perform a join?

14. Does Access SQL support the UNION JOIN operation? From the example given in the chapter, what does the UNION JOIN appear to do?

CHAPTER 7 EXERCISES

1. In this exercise, you'll test the UNION statement. Having seen how the UNION statement works, demonstrate some permutations to see what will work "legally" and what won't. First, create two tables:

Table1	
A	**B**
x1	y1
r1	s1

Table2			
A	**B**	**C**	**D**
x2	y2	z2	w2
r2	s2	t2	u2

Let the type of A's and B's be CHAR(2). Let the type of C in `Table2` be VARCHAR(2) and D in `Table2` be VARCHAR(3).

Try the following statements and note the results:

```
SELECT * FROM Table1 UNION SELECT * FROM Table2;
SELECT * FROM Table1 UNION SELECT A,B FROM Table2;
SELECT * FROM Table1 UNION SELECT B,A FROM Table1;
SELECT * FROM Table1 UNION SELECT A,C FROM Table2;
SELECT * FROM Table1 UNION SELECT A,D FROM Table2;

CREATE VIEW viewx AS
SELECT A,B
FROM Table2;

SELECT *
FROM Table1
  UNION
SELECT *
FROM viewx;
```

Feel free to experiment with any other combinations that you deem appropriate or that you wonder about.

2. Create and print the result of a query that generates the names, class, and course numbers of students who have earned B's in computer science courses. Store this query as Q72. Then, revise Q72 to delete from the result set those students who are sophomores (class = 2). Use NOT..IN to SELECT those students who are sophomores.

3. Find the names, grades, and course numbers of students who have earned A's in computer science or math courses. Create a join of the `Section` and `Grade_report` tables (be careful to not create the Cartesian product), then UNION the set of "course numbers COSC* and A" with the set of "course number MATH* and A."

    Hint: Start with the query to get names, grades, and course numbers for COSC* and A, and then turn this into a view. Do the same for MATH* and A, and then execute the UNION statement as follows (using your view names):

```
SELECT *
FROM view1a
  UNION
SELECT *
FROM view1b;
```

4. Find the names and majors of students who have made a C in any course. Make the "who have made a C in any course" a subquery for which you use IN.

5. A less obvious example of a difference query is to find a difference that is not based on simple, easy-to-get sets. Suppose that set A is the set of students who have made A's and B's in computer science (COSC) courses. Suppose further that set B is the set of students who have taken math courses (regardless of what grade they earned).

   Then, set A minus set B would contain names of students who have made A's or B's in computer science courses, less those who have taken math courses. Similarly, set B minus set A would be the set of students who took math courses, less those who took COSC courses and made an A or a B in some COSC course.

   Build these queries into set difference queries as views based on student numbers and execute them, as follows:

   a. Write a query that gives the student number, name, course, and grade for each set. Save each query as Q75a and Q75b.

   b. Reconstruct each query into a view of just student numbers, verify that it works, and then create views to create set A and set B. Verify that you have the same number of tuples in set A as you have in Q75a, and the same number of tuples in set B as you have in Q75b.

   c. Display the student numbers of students in each set difference—show (set A minus set B) and (set B minus set A). Look at the original queries, Q75a and Q75b, to verify your result.

6. Create two tables, T1 and T2, that contain a `name` and a `salary`. In the first table, order the attributes as `name, salary`. In the second table, order the attributes as `salary, name`. Use the same types for each—VARCHAR(20) and NUMBER, for example. Populate the tables with two tuples each.

7. Can you UNION the two tables in the preceding question with the following query?

```
SELECT *
FROM T1
   UNION
SELECT *
FROM T2?
```

Why or why not? If not, can you force the union of the two tables? Illustrate how. Be sure to DROP the tables when you are finished.

8. Using the `Instructor` table you created in this chapter (as well as the tables supplied in the `student.mdb` database), find the following:

   a. All departments that have instructors. First do this using an IN predicate, and then using a regular join.

   b. Find all students who are also instructors.

   c. Find all instructors who are not students.

   d. Find all students who are not instructors.

   e. Find all students as well as instructors.

OPTIONAL EXERCISE

9. De Morgan's Theorem. Find the result set for all sections that are offered in building 13 and call this set A. Find the result set for all sections that are offered in building 36 and call this set B. Construct the SQL to find the following result sets:

   a. The result of set A OR set B (use WHERE building = 13 or building = 36).

   b. The result of the complement of (a): NOT(set A OR set B).

   c. The result of NOT(set A) AND NOT(set B).

   d. The count of all rows in the `Section` table.

   Is the count in d = a + b? Is the result of c the same as the result of b? Explain why or why not in each case (Hint: You may apply De Morgan's Theorem, which states that NOT(set A or set B) = NOT(set A) and NOT(set b).

Joins versus Subqueries

Topics covered in this chapter

The purpose of this chapter is to demonstrate the use of subqueries as alternatives to joins. There are two main issues to consider in choosing between subqueries and joins (and other techniques as well). First, you must consider how you get information, which often is subjective. By understanding the limitations of joins and subqueries (as well as sets and other techniques), you will broaden your choices regarding how to get information from the database. Second, you must also consider performance. You usually have choices of how to get information—joins, sets, subqueries, views, and so forth. On larger databases, you need to be flexible and consider other choices if a query performs poorly and is done often.

> Although set operations logically are also viable choices for retrieving data from multiple tables, set operations (Chapter 7) are less common and usually less efficient than joins and subqueries.

The IN Subquery

Suppose that a query requests a list of names of students (which are in the Student table in our student.mdb) who have made A's or B's in any course (grades are in the Grade_report table in our student.mdb). You can complete this query as either a subquery or a join. As a subquery, it will take the following form:

```
SELECT   Student.sname
FROM     Student
WHERE    "link to Grade_report"
   IN ("link to Student" - subquery involving Grade_report)
```

The link between the Student table and the Grade_report table is the student number. In the Student table, the appropriate field (attribute) is stno, and in the Grade_report table, it is student_number. In a link between tables with the IN subquery, the linking fields are all that can be mentioned in the WHERE..IN and in the result set of the subquery. Thus, the statement with a subquery is as follows:

```
SELECT   Student.sname, Student.stno
FROM     Student
WHERE    Student.stno
   IN (SELECT   gr.student_number
       FROM     Grade_report gr
       WHERE    gr.grade = 'B' OR  gr.grade = 'A')
ORDER BY Student.stno;
```

> The part of the query *before* the IN is often called the *outer query*. The part of the query *after* the IN is called the *inner query*.

This produces the following output (31 rows):

sname	stno
Lineas	2
Mary	3
Zelda	5
Ken	6
Mario	7
Brenda	8
Richard	10
Kelly	13
Lujack	14
Reva	15
Harley	19
Donald	20
Chris	24
Lynette	34
Susan	49
Hillary	121
Phoebe	122

sname	stno
Holly	123
Sadie	125
Jessica	126
Steve	127
Cedric	129
George	132
Jerry	142
Cramer	143
Fraiser	144
Francis	146
Smithly	147
Sebastian	148
Lindsay	155
Stephanie	157

The Subquery as a Join

An alternate way to perform the preceding query would be to form a joined relation, and not use a subquery, as follows:

```
SELECT   Student.sname
FROM     Student, Grade_report gr
WHERE    Student.stno = gr.student_number
AND      (gr.grade = 'B' OR gr.grade = 'A');
```

This produces 67 rows of output (of which we show the first 26 rows here):

sname
Lindsay
Phoebe
Lineas
Lineas
Lineas
Lineas
Mary
Mary

> Database systems such as Oracle parse queries and execute them according to plan, much like a programming language compiles source code and generates an object module for execution.

sname
Mary
Mary
Mary
Mary
Brenda
Brenda
Brenda
Richard
Kelly
Kelly
Lujack
Lujack
Lujack
Lujack
Reva
Reva
Reva
Harley

The question of which is more efficient, the join or the subquery, depends on which SQL you are using. If the join version is used, then any Student-Grade_report row (tuple) that has equal student numbers and a grade of A or B is SELECTed. Thus, you should expect many duplicate names in the output. To get the result without duplicates, add the qualifier DISTINCT to the join query, as follows:

```
SELECT   DISTINCT Student.sname
FROM     Student, Grade_report AS gr
WHERE    Student.stno = gr.student_number
AND      (gr.grade = 'B' OR gr.grade = 'A');
```

This produces the following output (31 rows):

sname
Brenda
Cedric
Chris
Cramer
Donald
Fraiser
Francis
George
Harley
Hillary
Holly
Jerry
Jessica
Kelly
Ken
Lindsay
Lineas
Lujack
Lynette
Mario
Mary
Phoebe
Reva
Richard
Sadie
Sebastian
Smithly
Stephanie
Steve
Susan
Zelda

> The use of DIS-
TINCT here is not
performance-
efficient, because of
internal sorting.

In the subquery version of the query, duplication of names does not occur in the output, because you are setting up a set (the subquery) from which you will choose names—a given name is either in the subquery set or it is not.

When the Join Cannot Be Turned into a Subquery

Our original query (the first query discussed in this chapter), requested the list of *names* of students who made A's or B's in any course. If this original query had asked for output from the Grade_report table, such as "list the names and grades of all students who have made A's or B's," the query would be asking for information from both the Student and Grade_report tables. In this case, you would join the two tables to get the information. Refer again to the original query example. It asks only for information from the Student table (student names). Although the query used the Grade_report table, nothing from the Grade_report table was in the outer result set. The following query asks for information from both the Student and Grade_report tables (a result set that lists both names and grades of all students who have made A's or B's in any course):

```
SELECT  DISTINCT Student.sname, gr.grade
FROM    Student, Grade_report gr
WHERE   Student.stno = gr.student_number
AND     (gr.grade = 'B' OR gr.grade = 'A');
```

This produces 41 rows of output (of which we show the first 25 rows here):

sname	grade
Brenda	A
Brenda	B
Cedric	A
Cedric	B
Chris	B
Cramer	B
Donald	A
Fraiser	B
Francis	B
George	B

sname	grade
Harley	B
Hillary	B
Holly	A
Holly	B
Jerry	A
Jessica	A
Jessica	B
Kelly	B
Ken	B
Lindsay	B
Lineas	A
Lineas	B
Lujack	A
Lujack	B
Lynette	A

As this example demonstrates, if information from a table is needed in a result set, then that table cannot be buried in a subquery—it must be in the outer query.

More Examples Involving Joins and IN

The purpose of this section is to demonstrate several queries that will and will not allow the use of the subquery. As we have discussed, some joins can be expressed as subqueries whereas others cannot. Further, all subqueries with the IN predicate can be re-formed as a join. How do you know whether you can use a subquery? It depends on the final, outer result set. Some examples will help clarify this point.

Example 1

In this example, we will find the names of all departments that offer a course with "INTRO" in the title. To formulate our query, we need to use the Course table (to find the course names) and the Department_to_major table (to find the names of the departments).

Begin by viewing the table designs.

> To view the design of a particular table in our database, click the **Tables** tab in the **Objects** list, select the table that you wish to view, and then click the **Design** button (as shown in the "Viewing Table Designs" section of Chapter 1).

The following is the design of the Course table:

The following is the design of the Department_to_major table:

We need in our query a department name (dname) from the Department_ to_major table. We also need course information from the Course table because our query depends on a course name; however, no course information appears in the result set. We did not ask for the names of the courses, just that they have INTRO in the title. The result set only asks for department names. We can find this result by using a subquery, with the Department_to_major table as the outer query, because all the information in the result set is contained in the outer query. The query would be as follows:

```
SELECT   d2m.dname
FROM     Department_to_major d2m
WHERE    d2m.dcode
  IN (SELECT   Course.offering_dept
      FROM     Course
      WHERE    Course.course_name LIKE '*INTRO*');
```

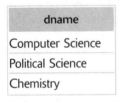

This produces the following output:

Example 2

In this example, we will list the student name, student major code, and section identifier of students who earned C's in courses taught by Professor Hermano (HERMANO).

First, we determine which tables are needed. We want to find the name, major code, and section identifier of students, so we need the Student, Grade_report, and Section tables. Again, it is usually a good idea to look at the table designs first.

The following is the design of the Student table:

The following is the design of the Grade_report table:

The following is the design of the Section table:

After we have determined which tables we want, we determine where the columns that are needed in the result set are located. We get the names and major codes from the Student table, and the section identifiers from the Grade_report table. So, the result set part of the query (the outer query) must contain the Student and Grade_report tables. The rest of the query can contain any other tables that we need to locate the columns. The resulting query may look like this:

```
SELECT   s.sname, s.major, g.section_id
FROM     Student s, Grade_report g
WHERE    g.student_number = s.stno
AND      g.grade = 'C'
AND      g.section_id IN
   (SELECT   t.section_id
    FROM     Section t
    WHERE    t.instructor LIKE 'HERMANO');
```

This produces the following output:

sname	major	section_id
Richard	ENGL	126

In this case, the query could also have been done as a three-table join, as follows:

```
SELECT  s.sname, s.major, t.section_id
FROM    Student s, Grade_report g, Section t
WHERE   s.stno = g.student_number
AND     g.section_id =t.section_id
AND     g.grade='C'
AND     t.instructor LIKE 'HERMANO';
```

Example 3

In this example, we will list the name and major code of students who earned C's in courses taught by Professor King (KING).

Again, we first want to determine which tables are needed. We want to collect student names and major codes, so we need to use the Student, Grade_report, and Section tables. (You can view the designs of these tables in the preceding exercise.) Then, we determine where the columns that are needed in the result set are located. In this example, they are all in the Student table.

Because the only table needed in the outer query is the Student table, we can structure the query in any of the following ways:

1. Student join Grade_report join Section [three-table join]

2. Student Sub (Grade_report join Section) [Student outer, join in subquery]

3. Student join Grade_report Sub (Section) [Similar to query 2 but with a different result set]

4. Student (Sub Grade_report (Sub Section)) [A three-level subquery]

Each of these queries could produce the same result with different efficiencies. We'll study them further in the exercises at the end of the chapter.

Using Subqueries with Operators

In this section, we will look at examples that demonstrate the use of subqueries with operators. These examples are based on the Room table, which has the following data:

BLDG	ROOM	CAPACITY	OHEAD
13	101	85	Y
36	120	25	N
36	121	25	N
36	122	25	N
36	123	35	N
58	110		Y
58	112	40	
58	114	60	
79	174	22	N
79	179	35	Y

In previous chapters, we have seen SELECTs with conditions like the following:

```
SELECT  *
FROM    Room
WHERE   capacity = 25;
```

In this example, 25 is a constant and = is an operator. The constant can be replaced by a subquery, and the operator can be any of the logical comparison operators (=, <>, <, >, <=, or >=). For example, we could devise a query to tell us which classrooms have a below-average capacity:

```
SELECT  *
FROM    Room
WHERE   capacity <
  (SELECT AVG(capacity)
   FROM   Room);
```

This produces the following output, showing six rooms with below-average capacity:

BLDG	ROOM	CAPACITY	OHEAD
36	123	35	N
79	179	35	Y
79	174	22	N
36	122	25	N
36	121	25	N
36	120	25	N

The only danger in using subqueries in this fashion is that *the subquery must return only one row*. If an aggregate function is applied to a table in the subquery in this fashion, you will always get only one row—even if there is a WHERE clause that excludes all rows, the subquery returns one row with a null value. For example, if we were to change the preceding query to the following

```
SELECT  *
FROM    Room
WHERE   capacity <
  (SELECT  AVG(capacity)
   FROM    Room
   WHERE   bldg = 99);
```

the query would run (no errors), but the result would be "no rows selected." If we were to change the query to the following

```
SELECT  *
FROM    Room
WHERE   bldg =
   (SELECT  bldg
    FROM    Room
    WHERE   capacity > 10);
```

> As with other queries that include derived results, the caveat to audit the result is always applicable.

we would get an error message from Access stating "At most one record can be returned by this subquery."

When operators are used, only single values are acceptable from the subquery. Again, to ensure that we get only one row in the subquery and hence a workable query, we can use an aggregate with no GROUP BY or HAVING (discussed in Chapter 9).

CHAPTER 8 REVIEW QUESTIONS

1. What is a subquery?

2. Which part of the query/subquery is considered the "inner query," and which part is considered the "outer query"?

3. Can a subquery be done as a join always? Why or why not?

4. Which predicate usually can be reformulated into a join?

5. When operators are used, are many values acceptable from a result of a subquery?

6. What can you do to ensure a working subquery?

CHAPTER 8 EXERCISES

Use the techniques from this chapter to construct and execute the following queries.

1. Find the student numbers of students who have earned A's or B's in courses taught in the fall semester. Do this in two ways: first using a subquery, and then using a join.

2. Find all students who took a course offered by the Accounting department. List the student name and student number, the course name, and the grade in that course. (Hint: Begin with Department_to_major and use an appropriate WHERE). Note that this cannot be done with a multilevel subquery. Why?

3. For all students who are sophomores (class = 2), find their name and the name of the department that includes their major.

4. Find the names of the departments that offer courses at the junior or senior levels (either one) but not at the freshman level. The course level is the first digit after the prefix; for example, AAAA3yyy is a junior course, and so on.

   Hint: Begin by creating the outer query—the names of departments that offer courses at the junior or senior levels. Save this query as q84. Then, construct the subquery—a list of departments that offer courses at the freshman level. Save the subquery as a view. Examine both lists of departments. When you have the outer query and the subquery results, recall the original query that you saved (q84) and add the subquery. Check your result with the department lists you just generated. Redo the last part of the experiment with your view. You should get the same result.

5. Find the names of courses that are prerequisites for other courses. List the course number and name, and the number and name of the prerequisite.

6. List the names of instructors who teach courses that have other than three-hour credits. Do the problem in two ways: once with IN and once with NOT..IN.

7. Create a table called `Secretary` with the attributes `dcode` (of type CHAR(4)) for department code and `name` (of type VARCHAR(20)) for the secretary name. Populate the table as follows:

Secretary	
dcode	name
ACCT	Beryl
COSC	Kaitlyn
ENGL	David
HIST	Christina
BENG	Fred
HINDI	Chloe

a. Create a query that lists the names of departments that have secretaries (use IN and the `Secretary` table in a subquery with the `Department_to_major` table in the outer query). Save this query as q87a.

b. Create a query that lists the names of departments that do not have secretaries (use NOT..IN). Save this query as q87b.

c. Add one more row to the `Secretary` table that contains <null,'Brenda'> (which you could do, for example, in a situation in which you have hired Brenda but have not yet assigned her to a department).

d. Recall q87a and rerun it. Recall q87b and rerun it.

   The behavior of NOT..IN when nulls exist may surprise you. If nulls may exist in the subquery, then NOT..IN either should not be used (Chapter 10 shows how to use another predicate, NOT EXISTS, which is a workaround to this problem) or should include AND whatever IS NOT NULL. If you use NOT..IN in a subquery, you must either ensure that nulls will not occur in the subquery or use some other predicate (such as NOT EXISTS). Perhaps the best advice is to avoid NOT..IN unless you cannot figure out another way to solve a problem.

e. To see a correct answer, add the phrase "WHERE dcode IS NOT NULL" to the subquery in the IN and NOT..IN cases and run them again.

Do *not* delete the `Secretary` table, because we will revisit this problem in Chapter 10.

8. Devise a list of course names that are offered in the fall semester in rooms where the capacity is equal to or above the average room size.

CHAPTER **9**

Aggregation and GROUP BY

Topics covered in this chapter

The SQL construction GROUP BY is a SELECT statement clause that is designed to be used in conjunction with aggregation (discussed in Chapter 5) to group data of similar types. An aggregate function is one that extracts information—such as a count of rows or an average, minimum, or maximum—by operating on multiple rows. We will first discuss using GROUP BY on one column and then on two columns. Then, we will look at how to use GROUP BY in conjunction with the ORDER BY, HAVING, and WHERE clauses. Finally, we will discuss aggregation with subqueries and the problems nulls present in aggregate functions and other queries.

The GROUP BY Clause

GROUP BY is used in conjunction with aggregate functions to group data of similar types. GROUP BY will return one row for each *value* of the column(s) that is grouped. You can use GROUP BY to group by one column or multiple columns.

As an example of how to GROUP BY one column, the following statement shows how you can use the aggregate COUNT to extract the number of class groups from the Student table:

```
SELECT    class, COUNT(*) AS [count]
FROM      Student
GROUP BY  class;
```

This produces the following output, which is grouped by one column, class:

class	count
	10
1	11
2	10
3	7
4	10

> You have to GROUP BY at least what you are aggregating.

This type of statement gives you a new way to retrieve and organize aggregate data. Other aggregate functions would have a similar syntax.

If a GROUP BY clause contains a two-column specification, the result is aggregated and grouped by two columns. For example, the following is the correct COUNT of class and major from the Student table:

```
SELECT    class, major, COUNT(*)  AS [count]
FROM      Student
GROUP BY  class, major;
```

This produces the following output (24 rows), which is grouped first by class and then by major:

jclass	major	count
		3
	COSC	1
	ENGL	1
	MATH	2
	POLY	2
	UNKN	1
1	COSC	4
1	ENGL	3
1	POLY	3
1	UNKN	1
2	ACCT	1
2	COSC	2
2	ENGL	2
2	MATH	3
2	POLY	2
3	ART	1
3	CHEM	1
3	ENGL	4
3	MATH	1
4	ACCT	4
4	CHEM	1
4	COSC	3
4	MATH	1
4	POLY	1

The sequence of the columns in a GROUP BY clause have no effect on the result of the counts. So, the following query will produce the same result as the previous one:

```
SELECT    class, major, COUNT(*)  AS [count]
FROM      Student
GROUP BY major, class;
```

However, a statement like the following will cause a syntax error (as shown in Figure 9.1) because it implies that you are to count both class and major, but GROUP BY class only:

```
SELECT    class, major, COUNT(*)
FROM      Student
GROUP BY  class;
```

To be syntactically and logically correct, you must have all the non-aggregate columns of the result set in the GROUP BY clause. In a similar vein, the following query would be improper because you must GROUP BY ohead to SUM capacities for each ohead value:

```
SELECT  ohead, SUM(capacity)
FROM    Room;
```

> ohead, an attribute in the Room table (in our Student.mdb), is short for rooms with overhead projectors.

This above query would also produce output similar to Figure 9.1.

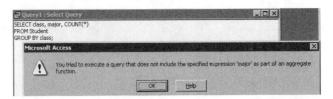

FIGURE 9.1 GROUP BY All Non-aggregate Columns

If you SELECT attributes *and* use an aggregate function, you must GROUP BY the non-aggregate attributes. The correct version of this statement is as follows:

```
SELECT    ohead, SUM(capacity) AS [sum]
FROM      Room
GROUP BY  ohead;
```

This produces the following output:

ohead	sum
	100
N	132
Y	120

This is the sum of room capacities for rooms that have no overhead projectors (N), rooms that do have overhead projectors (Y), and rooms in which the overhead projector capacity is unknown (null).

Observe that in the Room table, some rooms have null values for ohead, and the null rows are summed and grouped along with the non-null rows:

BLDG	ROOM	CAPACITY	OHEAD
13	101	85	Y
36	120	25	N
36	121	25	N
36	122	25	N
36	123	35	N
58	110		Y
58	112	40	
58	114	60	
79	174	22	N
79	179	35	Y

GROUP BY and ORDER BY

To enhance the display of a GROUP BY clause, you can combine it with an ORDER BY clause. Consider the following example:

```
SELECT    class, major, COUNT(*) AS [count]
FROM      Student
GROUP BY class, major;
```

This produces the following output (24 rows):

class	major	count
		3
	COSC	1
	ENGL	1
	MATH	2
	POLY	2
	UNKN	1
1	COSC	4
1	ENGL	3
1	POLY	3
1	UNKN	1
2	ACCT	1
2	COSC	2
2	ENGL	2
2	MATH	3
2	POLY	2
3	ART	1
3	CHEM	1
3	ENGL	4
3	MATH	1
4	ACCT	4
4	CHEM	1
4	COSC	3
4	MATH	1
4	POLY	1

The query orders the result set by class and then by major because of the internal sorting required to do the grouping. The result set can also be ordered by any other column from the result set using the ORDER BY. For example, the following example orders the output in descending order by COUNT(*):

```
SELECT  class, major, COUNT(*)  AS [count]
FROM    Student
GROUP BY class, major
ORDER BY COUNT(*) DESC;
```

This produces the following output (24 rows):

class	major	count
4	ACCT	4
1	COSC	4
3	ENGL	4
4	COSC	3
1	ENGL	3
1	POLY	3
		3
2	MATH	3
2	ENGL	2
	MATH	2
	POLY	2
2	COSC	2
2	POLY	2
4	POLY	1
1	UNKN	1
3	ART	1
3	CHEM	1
3	MATH	1
	UNKN	1
4	CHEM	1
4	MATH	1
	ENGL	1
	COSC	1
2	ACCT	1

GROUP BY and DISTINCT

When a SELECT clause includes all the columns specified in a GROUP BY clause, the use of the DISTINCT function is unnecessary, because the GROUP BY clause will group rows in such a way that the column(s) that are grouped will not have duplicate values.

The HAVING Clause

The GROUP BY and HAVING clauses are generally used together. The HAVING clause is used as a final filter (rather than as a conditional filter) on the output of a SELECT statement. In other words, the query has to be completed before the HAVING clause can be applied. For example, consider the following statement, which displays the count of students in various classes (classes of students = 1, 2, 3, 4, corresponding to freshman, sophomore, and so on):

```
SELECT    class, COUNT(*) AS [count]
FROM      Student
GROUP BY  class;
```

This produces the following output:

class	count
	10
1	11
2	10
3	7
4	10

If you are only interested in classes that have more than a certain number of students in them, you could use the following statement:

```
SELECT    class, COUNT(*) AS [count]
FROM      Student
GROUP BY class
HAVING COUNT(*) > 9;
```

This produces the following output:

class	count
	10
1	11
2	10
4	10

HAVING and WHERE

Whereas HAVING is a final filter in a SELECT statement, the WHERE clause, which excludes rows from a result set, is a conditional filter. Consider the following two queries:

```
SELECT   class, COUNT(*) AS [count]
FROM     Student
GROUP BY class
HAVING   class = 3;

SELECT   class, COUNT(*) AS [count]
FROM     Student
WHERE    class = 3
GROUP BY class;
```

Both queries produce the following output:

class	count
3	7

The first of these two queries is less efficient because the query engine has to complete the query before removing the WHERE class = 3 rows from the result. In the second version, the WHERE class = 3 rows are removed before grouping takes place. WHERE is not always a substitute for HAVING, but when it can be used instead of HAVING, it should be.

Consider the following query, its meaning, and the processing that is required to finalize the result set:

```
SELECT   class, major, COUNT(*) AS [count]
FROM     Student
WHERE    major = 'COSC'
GROUP BY class, major
HAVING COUNT(*) > 2;
```

This produces the following output:

class	major	count
1	COSC	4
4	COSC	3

In this example, all computer science (COSC) majors (per the WHERE clause) will be grouped and counted and then displayed only if COUNT(*) > 2. The query might erroneously be interpreted as "Group and count all COSC majors by class, but only if there are two in a class." This interpretation is wrong, because SQL applies the WHERE, then applies the GROUP BY, and, finally, filters with the HAVING criterion.

GROUP BY and HAVING: Functions of Functions

A "usual" GROUP BY has an aggregate and a column that are grouped like this:

```
SELECT    COUNT(stno) AS [count of student no], class
FROM      Student
GROUP BY class;
```

This produces a result set of counts by class:

count of student no	class
10	
11	1
10	2
7	3
10	4

While you must have class or some other attribute in the GROUP BY, you do not have to have the class in the result set. Consider the following query, which generates the same numeric information as the previous query but does not report the class in the result:

```
SELECT    COUNT(stno) AS [count of student no]
FROM      Student
GROUP BY class;
```

This produces the following output:

count of student no
10
11
10
7
10

This latter type query is useful when you want to determine aggregates of aggregates.

Suppose you want to find the **class** with the minimum number of students. You might try the following query:

```
SELECT MIN(COUNT(stno))
FROM Student
GROUP BY class;
```

However, this query will not work in SQL in Access (as shown in Figure 9.2).

FIGURE 9.2 Mismatch of Aggregation and Grouping

The MIN function is an aggregate function, and aggregate functions operate on tables that contain rows. In this case, the query is asking MIN to operate on a table of counted classes that have not yet been calculated. The point is that SQL in Access cannot handle this mismatch of aggregation and grouping.

To handle this mismatch of aggregation and grouping in Access SQL, you can use derived structures such as temporary tables, inline views, or even regular views (derived structures were covered in Chapter 6). Using either a temporary table or an inline view is the most logical way to solve this problem, so only these two choices are described.

> This mismatch of aggregation and grouping can be done in other SQL versions, such as SQL in Oracle.

Using a Temporary Table

The following steps describe how to use a temporary table to find the class with the minimum number of students:

1. Display the counts of classes, grouped by class:

```
SELECT     COUNT(stno) AS [count of students]
FROM       Student
GROUP BY   class;
```

This produces the following output:

count of students
10
11
10
7
10

2. To find the minimum number of students in a class, count the students (you could use stno for student number) grouped by class, and put this result in Temp1 (a temporary table), as follows:

```
SELECT (COUNT([stno])) AS [count] INTO Temp1
FROM Student
GROUP BY [class];
```

This produces the following output:

count
10
11
10
7
10

3. Find the minimum number of students in a class from the temporary table, Temp1, as follows:

```
SELECT  MIN(count)
FROM    Temp1;
```

This produces the following output:

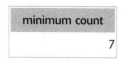

minimum count
7

4. Use this information in a subquery with a HAVING clause as follows:

```
SELECT COUNT(stno) AS [count of stno], class
FROM Student
GROUP BY class
HAVING COUNT(stno) =
(SELECT MIN(count) AS [Minimum count]
FROM Temp1);
```

This produces the desired output:

count of stno	class
7	3

Using an Inline View

As described in Chapter 6, you can put a query in the FROM clause of a SELECT statement to create an inline view. An inline view exists only during the execution of a query. The following steps describe how to use an inline view to find the class with the minimum number of students:

1. Count the stno in the FROM clause of the SELECT statement as follows:

```
SELECT MIN AS [min]
FROM (SELECT COUNT(stno) AS [c]
FROM Student
GROUP BY class);
```

This produces the following output:

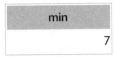

min
7

2. Save this query and then look at the **Design** view of this query. You will find that Access changes the query to the following:

```
SELECT MIN
FROM [SELECT COUNT(stno) AS [c]
FROM Student
GROUP BY class].AS [%$##@_Alias];
```

3. You can write the query in a subquery with a HAVING clause, as follows:

```
SELECT class, COUNT(*)
FROM Student
GROUP BY class
HAVING COUNT(*) =
(SELECT MIN
FROM (SELECT COUNT(stno) AS [c]
FROM Student
GROUP BY class));
```

This produces the desired output:

class	Expr1001
3	7

So, although SQL in Access cannot handle a mismatch of aggregation and HAVING, you can use your knowledge of temporary tables and inline views to work around the problem. Although this can also be done using regular views, it may not be the best option to select for this problem (once again, Chapter 6 covers the advantages and disadvantages of using each one of the derived structures).

Auditing in Subqueries

In this section, we consider the potential problem of using aggregation with subqueries. As with Cartesian products and joins, aggregation hides details and should always be audited. The two tables that follow will be used to illustrate this problem.

Table GG is similar to the `Grade_report` table and contains a student section identifier (`ssec`), grades (`gd`), and student names (`sname`):

> Tables GG and SS have not been created for you. You have to create them to run the queries that follow.

ssec	gd	sname
100	A	Brenda
110	B	Brenda
120	A	Brenda
200	A	Brenda
210	A	Brenda
220	B	Brenda
100	A	Richard
100	B	Doug
200	A	Richard
110	B	Morris

Table SS is similar to the `Section` table and contains a section identifier (`sec`) and an instructor name (`iname`):

sec	iname
100	Jones
110	Smith
120	Jones
200	Adams
210	Jones

Suppose you want to find out how many A's each instructor awarded. You might start with a join of the GG and SS tables. A normal equi-join would be as follows:

```
SELECT   *
FROM     GG, SS
WHERE    GG.ssec = SS.sec;
```

This produces the following output (9 rows):

ssec	gd	sname	sec	iname
100	B	Doug	100	Jones
100	A	Richard	100	Jones
100	A	Brenda	100	Jones
110	B	Morris	110	Smith
110	B	Brenda	110	Smith
120	A	Brenda	120	Jones
200	A	Richard	200	Adams
200	A	Brenda	200	Adams
210	A	Brenda	210	Jones

In addition, the following query tells you that there are six A's in the GG table:

```
SELECT   COUNT(*) AS [count of A's]
FROM     GG
WHERE    gd = 'A';
```

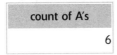

count of A's
6

Now, if you try this query

```
SELECT  SS.iname
FROM    SS, GG
WHERE   SS.sec = GG.ssec
  AND   GG.gd = 'A';
```

you get the following output:

iname
Jones
Jones
Adams
Jones
Jones
Adams

Now include a COUNT and GROUP BY as follows:

```
SELECT   SS.iname AS [iname], COUNT(*) AS [count]
FROM     SS, GG
WHERE    SS.sec = GG.ssec
  AND    GG.gd = 'A'
GROUP BY SS.iname;
```

This produces the following output:

iname	count
Adams	2
Jones	4

So far, so good. You may note that the final count/grouping has the same number of A's as the original tables—the sum of the counts equals 6. Now, if you had devised a count query with a sub-SELECT, you could get an answer that looks correct but in fact is not correct. For example, consider the following subquery version of the preceding join query:

```
SELECT   SS.iname AS [iname], COUNT(*) AS [count]
FROM     SS
WHERE    SS.sec IN
    (SELECT  GG.ssec
     FROM    GG
     WHERE   GG.gd = 'A')
GROUP BY SS.iname;
```

This produces the following output:

iname	count
Adams	1
Jones	3

The reason you get this output is that the second query is counting names of instructors and whether an A is present in the set of courses that this instructor teaches—not how many A's are in the set, just whether any exist. The join query gives you all the A's in the joined table and hence gives the correct answer to the question, "How many A's did each instructor award?" The sub-SELECTed query answers a different question: "In how many sections did the instructor award an A?"

The point in this example is that if you are SELECTing and COUNTing, *it is a very good idea to audit your results often*. If you want to count the number of A's by instructor, begin by first counting how many A's there are. Then, you can construct a query to join and count. You should be able to total and reconcile the number of A's to the number of A's by instructor.

Nulls Revisited

Nulls present a complication with regard to aggregate functions and other queries, because nulls are never equal, less than, greater than, or not equal to any value. Using aggregates by themselves on columns that contain nulls will ignore the null values. For example, suppose you have the following table called Sal:

> Table Sal has not been created for you. You have to create it to run the queries that follow.

name	salary
Joe	1000
Sam	2000
Bill	3000
Dave	

Consider the following query:

```
SELECT COUNT(*) AS [count], AVG(salary) AS [average],
SUM(salary) AS [sum], MAX(salary) AS [max], MIN(salary) AS
[min]
FROM Sal;
```

This produces the following output:

count	average	sum	max	min
4	2000	6000	3000	1000

COUNT(*) counts all rows, but the AVERAGE, SUM, and so forth ignore the nulled salary row in computing the aggregate. Counting columns indicates the presence of nulls. If you count by using the following query

```
SELECT   COUNT(name) AS [count of name]
FROM     Sal;
```

this produces:

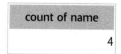

count of name
4

Or, if you use the "salary" column, you get:

```
SELECT   COUNT(salary) AS [count of salary]
FROM     Sal;
```

This produces:

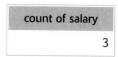

count of salary
3

This indicates that you have a null salary. If you want to include nulls in the aggregate, you can use the NZ function (discussed in Chapter 5). NZ returns a value if the value is null. NZ has the form NZ (column name, value if null), which is used in place of the column name. For example, if you type the following

```
SELECT   name, NZ(salary,0) AS [salary]
FROM     Sal;
```

this produces the following output:

name	salary
Joe	1000
Sam	2000
Bill	3000
Dave	0

If you type the following

```
SELECT  COUNT(NZ(salary,0)) AS [count of salary]
FROM    Sal;
```

this produces:

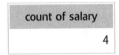

count of salary
4

If you type the following

```
SELECT  AVG(NZ(salary, 0)) AS [average of salary]
FROM    Sal;
```

this produces:

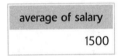

average of salary
1500

What seems almost contradictory to these examples is that when grouping is added to the query, nulls in the grouped column are included in the result set. So, if the Sal table had another column like this

name	salary	job
Joe	1000	Programmer
Sam	2000	
Bill	3000	Plumber
Dave		Programmer

and if you ran a query like this

```
SELECT   SUM(salary) AS [sum of salary], job
FROM     Sal
GROUP BY job;
```

you would get the following output

sum of salary	job
2000	
3000	Plumber
1000	Programmer

The aggregate will ignore values that are null, but grouping will compute a value for the nulled column value.

CHAPTER 9 REVIEW QUESTIONS

1. What do aggregate functions do?

2. How does the GROUP BY clause work?

3. What is the difference between a GROUP BY and ORDER BY?

4. What is the HAVING clause used for?

5. Can the WHERE clause always be considered a substitute for the HAVING clause? Why or why not?

6. How do functions of functions have to be handled in Access SQL? Why?

7. Will nulls in grouped columns be included in a result set?

8. How do aggregate functions treat nulls?

9. Does the sequence of the columns in a GROUP BY clause have an effect on the end result?

10. When would it not make sense to use the GROUP BY and DISTINCT functions together?

1. Display a list of courses (course names) that have prerequisites and the number of prerequisites for each course. Order the list by the number of prerequisites.

2. How many juniors (class = 3) are there in the Student table?

3. Group and count all MATH majors by class and display the count if there are two or more in a class. (Remember that class here refers to freshman, sophomore, and so on and is recorded as 1, 2, and so on.)

4. Print the counts of A's, B's, and so on from the Grade_report table.

   a. Using temporary tables, print the minimum counts of the grades (that is, if there were 20 A's, 25 B's, and 18 C's, you should print the minimum count of grades as C) from the Grade_report table.

   b. Using inline views, print the maximum counts of the grades (that is, if there were 20 A's, 25 B's, and 18 C's, you should print the maximum count of grades as B) from the Grade_report table.

   c. Why would you not want to use views for this problem?

5. Print the counts of course numbers offered in descending order by count. Use the Section table only.

6. Create a table with names and number-of-children (NOC). Populate the table with five or six rows. Use COUNT, SUM, AVG, MIN, and MAX on the NOC attribute in one query and check that the numbers you get are what you expect.

7. Create a table of names, salaries, and job locations. Populate the table with at least 10 rows and no fewer than three job locations. (There will be several employees at each location.) Find the average salary for each job location with one SELECT.

8. Print an ordered list of instructors and the number of A's they assigned to students. Order the output by number of A's (lowest to greatest). You can (and probably will) ignore instructors that assign no A's.

9. Create a table called Employees with a name, a salary, and job title. Include exactly six rows. Make the salary null in one row, the job title null in another, and both the salary and the job title/null in another. Use the following data:

Name	Salary	Title
Mary	1000	Programmer
Brenda	3000	
Stephanie		Artist
Alice		
Lindsay	2000	Artist
Christina	500	Programmer

   a. Display the table.

   b. Display count, sum, maximum, minimum, and average salary.

   c. Display count, sum, maximum, minimum, and average salary, counting salary as 0 if no salary is listed.

   d. Display the average salary grouped by job title on the table as is.

   e. Display the average salary grouped by job title when null salary is counted as 0.

   f. Display the average salary grouped by job title when salary is counted as 0 if it is null and include a value for "no job title."

10. Find the instructor and the course where the maximum number of A's were awarded.

11. Find the COUNT of the number of students by `class` who are taking classes offered by the computer science (COSC) department. Perform the query in two ways: once using a condition in the WHERE clause and once filtering with a HAVING clause. (Hint: These queries need a five-table join.)

Delete (DROP) all of your "scratch" tables (the ones you created just for this exercise: `Employees`, `NOC`, and any others you may have created).

Correlated Subqueries

Topics covered in this chapter

A *correlated subquery* is an inner subquery whose information is referenced by the main, outer query such that the inner query may be thought of as being executed repeatedly. In this chapter, we'll look at correlated subqueries in detail. We'll discuss existence queries and correlation as well as NOT EXISTS. We'll also take a look at SQL's universal and existential qualifiers. Before discussing correlated subqueries in detail, however, let's make sure that we understand what a non-correlated subquery is.

Non-Correlated Subqueries

A *non-correlated subquery* is a subquery that is independent of the outer query. In other words, the subquery could be executed on its own. The following is an example of a query that is not correlated:

```
SELECT   s.sname
FROM     Student s
WHERE    s.stno IN
            (SELECT   gr.student_number
             FROM     Grade_report gr
             WHERE    gr.grade = 'A');
```

The first part of the preceding query (the first three lines) is the main, outer query, and the second part (the part in parentheses) is the subquery (also referred to as an *inner, nested,* or *embedded query*). To demonstrate that this subquery is an independent entity, you could run it by itself:

```
SELECT    gr.student_number
FROM      Grade_report gr
WHERE     gr.grade = 'A';
```

This would produce the following output (17 rows):

student_number
2
3
8
8
10
14
20
129
142
129
34
49
123
125
126
127
142

The preceding subquery is thought of as being evaluated first, creating the set of student numbers who have A's. Then, the subquery's result set is used to determine which rows (tuples) in the main query will be SELECTed. So, the full query results in the following output (14 rows):

sname
Lineas
Mary
Brenda
Richard
Lujack
Donald
Lynette
Susan
Holly
Sadie
Jessica
Steve
Cedric
Jerry

Correlated Subqueries

As stated at the beginning of the chapter, a *correlated subquery* is an inner subquery whose information is referenced by the main, outer query such that the inner query may be thought of as being executed repeatedly.

Correlated queries present a different execution scenario to the database manipulation language (DML) than do ordinary, non-correlated subqueries. The correlated subquery cannot stand alone, as it depends on the outer query; therefore, completing the subquery prior to execution of the outer query is not an option. The efficiency of the correlated subquery varies; it may be worthwhile to test the efficiency of correlated queries versus joins or sets.

> One situation in which you cannot avoid correlation is the "for all" query, which is discussed later in this chapter.

To illustrate how a correlated subquery works, the following is an example of the non-correlated subquery from the previous section, revised as a correlated subquery:

```
SELECT   s.sname
FROM     Student s
WHERE    s.stno IN
  (SELECT  gr.student_number
   FROM    Grade_report gr
   WHERE   gr.student_number = s.stno
   AND     gr.grade = 'A');
```

This produces the following output (14 rows), which is the same as the output of the non-correlated subquery:

sname
Lineas
Mary
Brenda
Richard
Lujack
Donald
Lynette
Susan
Holly
Sadie
Jessica
Steve
Cedric
Jerry

In this example, the inner query (the part in parentheses) references the outer one—observe the use of s.stno in the WHERE clause of the inner query. Rather than thinking of this query as creating a set of student numbers that have A's, each row from the outer query can be considered to be SELECTed individually and tested against all rows of the inner query one at a time, until it is determined whether or not a given student number is in the inner set and whether or not that student earned an A.

This query was illustrated with and without correlation. You might think that a correlated subquery is less efficient than doing a simple subquery, because the simple subquery is done once, whereas the correlated subquery is done once for each outer row. However, the internal handling of how the query executes depends on the SQL and the optimizer for that database engine.

The correlated subquery acts like a nested DO loop in a programming language, where the first row from the Student table is SELECTed and tested against all the rows in the Grade_report table, and then the second Student row is SELECTed and tested against all rows in the Grade_report table. The following is the DO loop in pseudo-code:

```
LOOP1: For each row in Student  s  DO
            LOOP2: For each row in Grade_report  gr  DO
                        IF (gr.student_number = s.stno) THEN
                        IF (gr.grade = 'B') THEN TRUE
            END LOOP2;
        IF TRUE, THEN Student row is SELECTed
END LOOP1;
```

Existence Queries and Correlation

Correlated queries are often written so that the question in the inner query is one of existence. For example, suppose you want to find the names of students who have taken a computer science (COSC) class and have earned a grade of B in that course. This query can be written in several ways. For example, you can write it as a non-correlated subquery as follows:

```
SELECT   s.sname
FROM     Student s
WHERE    s.stno IN
  (SELECT   gr.student_number FROM Grade_report gr, Section
   WHERE    Section.section_id = gr.section_id
   AND      Section.course_num LIKE 'COSC*'
   AND      gr.grade = 'B');
```

This produces the following output (17 rows):

sname
Lineas
Mary
Brenda
Lujack
Reva
Harley
Chris
Lynette
Hillary

sname
Phoebe
Holly
George
Cramer
Fraiser
Francis
Lindsay
Stephanie

> This query could also be done by creating a double-nested subquery containing two INs, or it could be written using a three-table join.

You can think of this query as forming the set of student numbers of students who have made B's in COSC courses—the inner query result set. In the inner query, you must have both the Grade_report table (for the grades) and the Section table (for the course numbers). Once you form this set of student numbers (by completing the inner query), the outer query looks through the Student table and SELECTs only those students who are in the inner query set.

Had we chosen to write the query with an unnecessary correlation, it might look like this:

```
SELECT   s.sname
FROM     Student s
WHERE    s.stno IN
   (SELECT  gr.student_number
    FROM      Grade_report gr, Section
    WHERE     Section.section_id = gr.section_id
    AND       Section.course_num LIKE 'COSC*'
    AND       gr.student_number = s.stno
    AND       gr.grade = 'B');
```

The output of this query would be the same as the previous query. In this case, the use of the Student table in the subquery is unnecessary. Although correlation is unnecessary, this example is included to show the following:

• When correlation is necessary

• How to untangle unnecessarily correlated queries

• How you might migrate your thought process toward correlation, should it be necessary

First, let's look at situations in which the correlation of a subquery *is* necessary, and, in particular, introduce a new predicate: EXISTS.

Using EXISTS

In situations in which the correlation of a subquery *is* necessary, you can write the correlated subquery with the EXISTS predicate, which looks like this:

```
SELECT   s.sname
FROM     Student s
WHERE EXISTS
  (SELECT  1 FROM Grade_report gr, Section
   WHERE   Section.section_id = gr.section_id
   AND     Section.course_num LIKE 'COSC*'
   AND     gr.student_number  = s.stno
   AND     gr.grade = 'B');
```

The output of this query would be the same as the output (17 rows) of both of the previous queries.

Let's dissect this query. The EXISTS predicate says, "Choose the row from the Student table in the outer query if the subquery is true (that is, if a row in the subquery exists that satisfies the condition in the subquery WHERE clause)." Since no actual result set is formed, "SELECT 1" is used as a "dummy" result set to indicate that the subquery is true (1 is returned) or false (no rows are returned). In the non-correlated case, we tied the student number in the Student table to the inner query by the IN predicate as follows:

```
SELECT   s.stno
FROM     Student s
WHERE    s.stno IN
  (SELECT "student number ...)
```

When using the EXISTS predicate, we do not use any attribute of the Student table, but rather we are seeking only to find whether the subquery WHERE can be satisfied.

We have indicated that we are using EXISTS with (SELECT 1...). Using the EXISTS predicate, the subquery does not form a result set per se, but rather returns true or false. The use of SELECT * in the inner query is common among SQL programmers. However, from an "internal" standpoint, SELECT * causes the SQL engine to check the data dictionary unnecessarily. Since the actual result of the inner query is not important, it is strongly suggested that you use SELECT 'X' (or SELECT 1) ... instead of SELECT * ... so that a constant is SELECTed instead of some "sensible" entry. The SELECT 'X' ... or SELECT 1 ... is simply more efficient.

In the EXISTS case, we do not specify what attributes need to be SELECTed in the inner query's result set; rather, we use SELECT 1 to select something (a 1) if the subquery WHERE is satisfied (that is, true) and to select nothing (no rows would give false) if the condition in the subquery WHERE is not met. The EXISTS predicate forces us to correlate the query. To illustrate that correlation is usually necessary with EXISTS, consider the following query:

```
SELECT   s.sname
FROM     Student s
WHERE EXISTS
  (SELECT  'X' FROM Grade_report gr, Section t
   WHERE   t.section_id = gr.section_id
   AND     t.course_num like 'COSC*'
   AND     gr.grade = 'B');
```

This produces the following output (48 rows):

sname
Lineas
Mary
Brenda
Richard
Kelly
Lujack
Reva
Elainie
Harley
Donald
Chris
Lynette
Susan
Monica
Bill
Hillary
Phoebe
Holly

sname
Sadie
Jessica
Steve
Brad
Cedric
Alan
Rachel
George
Jerry
Cramer
Fraiser
Harrison
Francis
Smithly
Sebastian
Jake
Losmith
Genevieve
Lindsay
Stephanie
Thornton
Lionel
Benny
Gus
Zelda
Mario
Romona
Ken
Smith
Jake

This query uses EXISTS but has no correlation. This syntax infers that for each student row, we test the joined `Grade_report` and `Section` tables to see whether there is a course number like COSC and a grade of B (which, of course, there is). We unnecessarily ask the subquery question over and over again. The result from this latter, uncorrelated EXISTS query is the same as the following:

```
SELECT  s.sname
FROM    Student s;
```

The point is that the correlation is necessary when we use EXISTS.

Consider another example in which a correlation could be used. Suppose we want to find the names of all students who have three or more B's. A first pass at a query might be something like this:

```
SELECT  s.sname
FROM    Student s WHERE "something" IN
 (SELECT "something"
  FROM   Grade_report
  WHERE  "count of grade = 'B'" > 2);
```

This query can be done with a HAVING clause, as we saw previously, but we want to show how to do this in yet another way. Suppose we arrange the subquery to use the student number from the Student table as a filter and count in the subquery only when a row in the Grade_report table correlates to that student. The query (this time with an implied EXISTS) looks like this:

```
SELECT  s.sname
FROM    Student s
WHERE 2 < (SELECT COUNT(*)
           FROM    Grade_report gr
           WHERE   gr.student_number = s.stno
           AND     gr.grade = 'B');
```

This results in the following output (8 rows):

sname
Lineas
Mary
Lujack
Reva
Chris
Hillary
Phoebe
Holly

Although there is no EXISTS in this query, it is implied. The syntax of the query does not allow an EXISTS, but the sense of the query is "WHERE EXISTS a COUNT of 2 which is less than...". In this correlated subquery, we have to examine the Grade_report table for each member of the Student table to see whether or not the student has two B's. We test the entire Grade_report table for each student row in the outer query.

If it were possible, a subquery without the correlation would be more desirable. The overall query might be as follows:

```
SELECT    s.sname
FROM      Student s
WHERE     s.stno IN
  (subquery that defines a set of students who have made 3 B's)
```

Therefore, we might attempt to write the following query:

```
SELECT    s.sname
FROM      Student s
WHERE     s.stno IN
  (SELECT    gr.student_number
     FROM    Grade_report gr
    WHERE    gr.grade = 'B');
```

However, as the following output (27 rows) shows, this query would give us only students who earned at least one B:

sname
Lineas
Mary
Brenda
Kelly
Lujack
Reva
Harley
Chris
Lynette
Hillary
Phoebe
Holly
Sadie

sname
Jessica
Steve
Cedric
George
Cramer
Fraiser
Francis
Smithly
Sebastian
Lindsay
Stephanie
Zelda
Mario
Ken

To get a list of students who have earned three B's, we could try the following query:

```
SELECT   s.sname
FROM     Student s
WHERE    s.stno IN
  (SELECT   gr.student_number, COUNT(*)
   FROM     Grade_report gr
   WHERE    gr.grade = 'B'
   GROUP BY gr.student_number
   HAVING   COUNT(*) > 2);
```

However, this does not work, because the subquery cannot have two attributes in its result set unless the main query has two attributes in the WHERE .. IN, as shown in Figure 10.1.

Here, the subquery must have only gr.student_number to match s.stno. So, we might try to construct an inline view, as shown in the following query:

```
SELECT   s.sname
FROM     Student s
WHERE    s.stno IN
  (SELECT student_number
   FROM   (SELECT   student_number, COUNT(*)
```

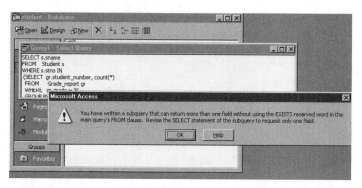

FIGURE 10.1 Error in Matching Attributes in Subquery

```
FROM      Grade_report gr
WHERE     gr.grade = 'B'
GROUP BY student_number
HAVING COUNT(*) > 2));
```

This query succeeds in Access, producing the following output (8 rows). Note that it is an example of the inline view, discussed in earlier chapters.

sname
Lineas
Mary
Lujack
Reva
Chris
Hillary
Phoebe
Holly

> This query also works in Oracle, but it may fail in some other SQL versions.

As you can see, several ways exist to query the database with SQL. In this case, the correlated subquery may be the easiest to see and perhaps the most efficient.

From IN to EXISTS

A simple example of converting from IN to EXISTS—uncorrelated to correlated (or vice versa)—would be to move the set test in the WHERE .. IN of the uncorrelated subquery to the WHERE of the EXISTS in the correlated query.

As an example, consider the following uncorrelated subquery:

```
SELECT  *
FROM    Student s
WHERE   s.stno  IN
   (SELECT  g.student_number
    FROM    Grade_report g
    WHERE   grade = 'B');
```

The following is the same query written as a correlated subquery:

```
SELECT  *
FROM    Student s
WHERE EXISTS
   (SELECT  g.student_number
    FROM    Grade_report g
    WHERE   grade = 'B'
    AND     s.stno = g.student_number);
```

This produces the following output (27 rows):

STNO	SNAME	MAJOR	CLASS	BDATE
2	Lineas	ENGL	1	4/15/80
3	Mary	COSC	4	7/6/78
8	Brenda	COSC	2	8/13/77
13	Kelly	MATH	4	8/12/80
14	Lujack	COSC	1	2/12/77
15	Reva	MATH	2	6/10/80
19	Harley	POLY	2	4/16/81
24	Chris	ACCT	4	2/12/78
34	Lynette	POLY	1	7/16/81
121	Hillary	COSC	1	7/16/77
122	Phoebe	ENGL	3	4/15/80
123	Holly	POLY	4	1/15/81
125	Sadie	MATH	2	8/12/80
126	Jessica	POLY	2	7/16/81
127	Steve	ENGL	1	3/11/80
129	Cedric	ENGL	2	4/15/80
132	George	POLY	1	4/16/81
143	Cramer	ENGL	3	4/15/80

STNO	SNAME	MAJOR	CLASS	BDATE
144	Fraiser	POLY	1	7/16/81
146	Francis	ACCT	4	6/11/77
147	Smithly	ENGL	2	5/13/80
148	Sebastian	ACCT	2	10/14/76
155	Lindsay	UNKN	1	10/15/79
157	Stephanie	MATH		4/16/81
5	Zelda	COSC		2/12/78
7	Mario	MATH		8/12/80
6	Ken	POLY		7/15/80

This example gives you a pattern to move from one kind of query to the other kind and to test the efficiency of both kinds of queries. Both of the preceding queries should produce the same output.

NOT EXISTS

As with the IN predicate, which has a NOT IN complement, EXISTS may also be used with NOT. In some situations, the predicates EXISTS and NOT EXISTS are vital. For example, if we ask a "for all" question, it must be answered by "existence" (actually, the lack thereof [that is, "not existence"]). In logic, the statement, "find x for all y" is logically equivalent to "do not find x where there does not exist a y." In SQL, there is no "for all" predicate. Instead, SQL uses the idea of "for all" logic with NOT EXISTS. (A word of caution, however: SQL is not simply a logic exercise, as we will see.) In this section we look at how EXISTS and NOT EXISTS work in SQL. In the following section, "SQL Universal and Existential Qualifiers," we will address the "for all" problem.

Consider the following query:

```
SELECT  s.sname
FROM    Student s
WHERE EXISTS
   (SELECT  'X'
    FROM    Grade_report gr
    WHERE   s.stno = gr.student_number
    AND     gr.grade = 'C');
```

This produces the following output (24 rows):

sname
Brenda
Richard
Reva
Donald
Susan
Monica
Bill
Sadie
Jessica
Steve
Alan
Rachel
Smithly
Sebastian
Jake
Losmith
Genevieve
Thornton
Lionel
Benny
Gus
Zelda
Mario
Ken

For this correlated subquery, "student names" are SELECTed when:

• The student is enrolled in a section (WHERE `s.stno = gr.student_number`).

• The same student has a grade of C (note the correlation in the WHERE clause in the inner query).

Both statements must be true for the student row to be SELECTed. Recall that we use SELECT 1 or SELECT X in our inner query because we want the subquery to return something if the subquery is true. Therefore, SELECT .. EXISTS "says" SELECT .. WHERE true. The inner query is true if any row is SELECTed in the inner query.

Now consider the preceding query with a NOT EXISTS in it instead of EXISTS:

```
SELECT   s.sname
FROM     Student s
WHERE NOT EXISTS
    (SELECT  'X'
     FROM    Grade_report gr
     WHERE   s.stno = gr.student_number
     AND     gr.grade = 'C');
```

This produces the following output (24 rows):

sname
Lineas
Mary
Kelly
Lujack
Elainie
Harley
Chris
Lynette
Hillary
Phoebe
Holly
Brad
Cedric
George
Jerry
Cramer
Fraiser
Harrison
Francis
Lindsay
Stephanie
Romona
Smith
Jake

In this query, we are still SELECTing with the pattern SELECT .. WHERE true because all SELECTs with EXISTS work that way. But, the twist is that the subquery has to be false to be SELECTed with NOT EXISTS. If the subquery is false, then NOT EXISTS is true and the outer row is SELECTed.

Now, logic implies that if either s.stno <> gr.student_number or gr.grade <> 'C', then the subquery "fails"—that is, it is false for that student row. Since the subquery is false, the NOT EXISTS would return a true for that row. Unfortunately, this logic is not quite what happens. Recall that we characterized the correlated subquery as follows:

```
LOOP1: For each row in Student  s  DO
        LOOP2: For each row in Grade_report DO
                    IF (gr.student_number = s.stno) THEN
                    IF (gr.grade = 'C') THEN TRUE
        END LOOP2;
      IF TRUE, THEN student row is SELECTed
END LOOP1;
```

Note that LOOP2 is completed before the next student is tested. In other words, just because a student number exists that is not equal, it will not cause the subquery to be false. Rather, the entire subquery table is parsed and the logic is more like this:

For the case .. WHERE EXISTS s.stno = gr.student_number ..., is there a gr.grade = 'C'? If, when the student numbers are equal, no C can be found, then the subquery *fails*—it is false for that student row. So, with NOT EXISTS, we will SELECT students who have student numbers equal in the Grade_report and Student tables, but who have no C in the Grade_report table. The point about "no C in the Grade_report table" can only be answered true by looking at all the rows in the inner query.

SQL Universal and Existential Qualifiers

In SQL, "for all" and "for each" are the universal qualifiers, whereas "there exists" is the existential qualifier. As mentioned in the preceding section, SQL does not have a "for all" predicate; however, logically, the following relationship exists:

For all x, WHERE P(x) is true

This is logically the same as the following:

There does not exist an x, WHERE P(x) is not true.

A "for all" type SQL query is less straightforward than the other queries we have used, because it involves a double-nested, correlated subquery using the NOT EXISTS predicate. The next section shows an example.

Example 1

To show a "for all" type SQL query, we will use another table in our student.mdb database—a table called Cap (for "capability"). This table has names of students who have multiple foreign-language capabilities. We begin by looking at the table by typing the following query:

```
SELECT   *
FROM     Cap
ORDER BY name;
```

This produces the following output (18 rows):

name	langu
Brenda	Bengali
Brenda	Hindi
Brenda	French
Joe	Bengali
Kent	Bengali
Lujack	Hindi
Lujack	French
Lujack	German
Lujack	Bengali
Mary Jo	Bengali
Mary Jo	French
Mary Jo	German
Melanie	French
Melanie	Bengali
Richard	German
Richard	Hindi
Richard	Bengali
Richard	French

Suppose we want to find out which languages are spoken by all students (for which we would ask the question, "For each language, does it occur with all students?"). Although this manual exercise would be very difficult for a large table, for our practice table, we can answer the question by following these steps:

1. Display and study the table ordered by name (as in the preceding output).

2. Display and study the table ordered by language.

To see how to answer a question of the type—"Which languages are spoken by all students?"—for a much larger table where sorting and examining the result would be tedious, we will construct a query. After showing the query, we will dissect the result. Following is the query to answer our question:

```
SELECT  name, langu
FROM    Cap x
WHERE NOT EXISTS
        (SELECT 'X'
        FROM Cap   y
        WHERE NOT EXISTS
              (SELECT 'X'
              FROM Cap z
              WHERE x.langu = z.langu
              AND y.name = z.name));
```

This produces the following output (7 rows):

name	langu
Brenda	Bengali
Joe	Bengali
Kent	Bengali
Mary Jo	Bengali
Melanie	Bengali
Richard	Bengali
Lujack	Bengali

> As you will see, all the for all/for each questions follow this double-nested, correlated NOT EXISTS pattern.

The Way the Query Works

To SELECT a "language" spoken by all students, the query proceeds as follows:

1. SELECT a row in Cap (x) (outer query).

2. For that row, begin SELECTing each row again in Cap (y) (middle query).

3. For each of the middle query rows, we want the inner query (Cap z) to be true for all cases of the middle query (remember that true is translated to false by the NOT EXISTS). As each inner query is satisfied (it is true), it forces the middle query to continue looking for a match—to look at all cases and eventually conclude false (evaluate to false overall). If the middle query is false, the outer query sees true because of its NOT EXISTS.

To make the middle query (y) find false, all the inner query (z) occurrences must be true (that is, the languages from the outer query must exist with all names from the middle one [y] in the inner one [z]). For an eventual "match," every row in the middle query for an outer query row must be false (that is, every row in the inner query is true).

These steps are explained in further detail in the next example, in which we use a smaller table so that the explanation is easier to understand.

Example 2

Suppose we have the following, simpler table, Cap1, when attempting to answer the question "Which languages are spoken by all students?":

Name	Language
Joe	Hindi
Mary	Hindi
Mary	French

> The table, Cap1, does not exist. You will have to create it. Keep the attribute names and types similar to the table, Cap.

The query will be similar to the one used in Example 1:

```
SELECT  name, language
FROM    Cap1 x
WHERE NOT EXISTS
       (SELECT 'X'
        FROM Cap1 y
        WHERE NOT EXISTS
        (SELECT 'X'
```

```
              FROM   Cap1 z
              WHERE  x.language = z. language
              AND    y.name = z.name))
      ORDER BY language;
```

This produces the following output:

name	language
Joe	Hindi
Mary	Hindi

The Way This Query Works

The following is a step-by-step explanation of how this query would work in the Cap1 table:

1. The row <Joe, Hindi> is SELECTed by the outer query (x).

2. The row <Joe, Hindi> is SELECTed by the middle query (y).

3. The row <Joe, Hindi> is SELECTed by the inner query (z).

4. The inner query is true:

```
      X.LANGUAGE = Hindi
      Z.LANGUAGE = Hindi
      Y.NAME = Joe
      Z.NAME = Joe
```

5. Since the inner query is true, the NOT EXISTS of the middle query translates this to false and continues with the next row in the middle query. The middle query SELECTs <Mary, Hindi> and the inner query begins again with <Joe, Hindi> seeing:

```
      X.LANGUAGE = Hindi
      Z.LANGUAGE = Hindi
      Y.NAME = Mary
      Z.NAME = Joe
```

This is false, so the inner query SELECTs a second row <Mary, Hindi>:

```
      X.LANGUAGE = Hindi
      Z.LANGUAGE = Hindi
      Y.NAME = Mary
      Z.NAME = Mary
```

This is true, so the inner query is true. (Notice that the X.LANGUAGE has not changed yet; the outer query [X] is still on the first row.)

6. Since the inner query is true, the NOT EXISTS of the middle query translates this to false and continues with the next row in the middle query.

The middle query now SELECTs <Mary, French> and the inner query begins again with <Joe, Hindi> seeing:

```
X.LANGUAGE = Hindi
Z.LANGUAGE = Hindi
Y.NAME = Mary
Z.NAME = Joe
```

This is false, so the inner query SELECTs a second row <Mary, Hindi>:

```
X.LANGUAGE = Hindi
Z.LANGUAGE = Hindi
Y.NAME = Mary
Z.NAME = Mary
```

This is true, so the inner query is true.

7. Since the inner query is true, the NOT EXISTS of the middle query again converts this true to false and wants to continue, but the middle query is out of rows. This means that the middle query is false.

8. Since the middle query is false, and since we are testing

```
SELECT distinct name, language
FROM Cap1 x
WHERE NOT EXISTS
    (SELECT 'X' FROM Cap1 y ...
```

the false from the middle query is translated to true for the outer query and the row <Joe, Hindi> is SELECTed for the result set. Note that "Hindi" occurs with both "Joe" and "Mary."

9. The second row in the outer query will repeat the steps from above for <Mary, Hindi>. The value "Hindi" will be seen to occur with both "Joe" and "Mary" as <Mary, Hindi> is added to the result set.

10. The third row in the outer query begins with <Mary, French>. The middle query SELECTs <Joe, Hindi> and the inner query SELECTs <Joe, Hindi>. The inner query sees the following:

```
X.LANGUAGE = French
Z.LANGUAGE = Hindi
Y.NAME = Joe
Z.NAME = Mary
```

This is false, so the inner query SELECTs a second row, <Mary, Hindi>:

```
X.LANGUAGE = French
Z.LANGUAGE = Hindi
Y.NAME = Joe
Z.NAME = Mary
```

This is false, so the inner query SELECTs a third row, <Mary, French>:

```
X.LANGUAGE = French
Z.LANGUAGE = French
Y.NAME = Joe
Z.NAME = Mary
```

This is also false. The inner query fails. The inner query evaluates to false, which causes the middle query to see true because of the NOT EXISTS. Since the middle query sees true, it is finished and evaluated to true. Since the middle query evaluates to true, the NOT EXISTS in the outer query changes this to false and "X.LANGUAGE = French" fails because X.LANGUAGE = French did not occur with all the values of NAME.

The "For All" Query as a Relational Division

Consider again the "for all" query presented in Example 2:

```
SELECT  name, language
FROM    Cap1 x
WHERE NOT EXISTS
        (SELECT 'X'
        FROM Cap1 y
        WHERE NOT EXISTS
        (SELECT  'X'
                FROM    Cap1 z
                WHERE   x.language = z. language
                AND        y.name = z.name))
ORDER BY language;
```

The tip-off of what a query of this kind means can be found in the inner query where the outer query is tested. In the phrase that says "WHERE x.language = z. language...," the x.language is where the query is testing which *language* occurs *for all* names.

This query is a SQL realization of a relational division exercise. Relational division is a "for all" operation just like that which we have illustrated above. In relational algebra, the query must be set up into a divisor, dividend, and quotient in this pattern:

Quotient (B) ← Dividend(A, B) divided by Divisor (A).

If the question is "What language occurs for *all* names?" then the Divisor, A, is names, and the Quotient, B, is language. It is most prudent to set up SQL like relational algebra with a two-column table (like Cap or Cap1) for the Dividend and then treat the Divisor and the Quotient appropriately. Our query will have the attribute for language, x.language, in the inner query, as language will be the quotient. We have chosen to also report name in the result set.

Example 3

Note that the preceding query is completely different from the following query, which asks, "Which *students* speak all languages?"

```
SELECT  DISTINCT name, language
FROM    Cap1 x
WHERE   NOT EXISTS
        (SELECT 'X'
        FROM Cap1 y
        WHERE NOT EXISTS
                (SELECT 'X'
                FROM    Cap1 z
                WHERE   y.language = z.language
                AND     x.name = z.name))
ORDER BY language;
```

This produces the following output:

name	language
Mary	French
Mary	Hindi

Note that the inner query contains x.name, which means the question was "Which names occur for *all* languages?" or, put another way, "Which students speak all languages?" The "all" goes with languages for x.name.

CHAPTER 10 REVIEW QUESTIONS

1. What is a non-correlated subquery?

2. Which type of subquery can be executed on its own?

3. Which part of a query is evaluated first, the query or the subquery?

4. What are correlated subqueries?

5. What does the EXISTS predicate do?

6. What are considered universal qualifiers?

7. Is correlation necessary when we use EXISTS? Why?

8. Explain how the "for all" type SQL query involves a double-nested correlated subquery using the NOT EXISTS predicate.

CHAPTER 10 EXERCISES

1. List the names of students who have received C's. Do this in three ways: as a join, as an uncorrelated subquery, and as a correlated subquery. Show both results and account for any differences.

2. In section "Existence Queries and Correlation," we were asked to find the names of students who have taken a computer science class and earned a grade of B. We noted that it could be done in several ways. One query could look like this:

```
SELECT  s.sname
FROM    Student s
WHERE   s.stno IN
   (SELECT  gr.student_number
    FROM    Grade_report gr, Section
    WHERE   Section.section_id = gr.section_id
    AND     Section.course_num LIKE 'COSC____'
    AND     gr.grade = 'B');
```

Redo this query, putting the finding of the COSC course in a correlated subquery. The query should be as follows:

The Student table uncorrelated subquery to the Grade_report table, correlated EXISTS to the Section table.

3.   In the section "SQL Universal and Existential Qualifiers," we illustrated both an existence query

```
SELECT   s.sname
FROM     Student s
WHERE    EXISTS
    (SELECT   'X'
     FROM     Grade_report gr
     WHERE    Student.stno = gr.student_number
     AND      gr.grade = 'C');
```

and a NOT EXISTS version:

```
SELECT       s.sname
FROM         Student s
WHERE NOT    EXISTS
    (SELECT   'X'
     FROM     Grade_report gr
     WHERE    Student.stno = gr.student_number
     AND      gr.grade = 'C');
```

Show that the EXISTS version is the complement of the NOT EXISTS version—count the rows in the EXISTS result, the rows in the NOT EXISTS result, and the rows in the Student table. Also, devise a query to give the same result with IN and NOT..IN.

4.   a.   Discover whether or not all students take courses by counting the students, and then count those students whose student numbers are in the Grade_report table and those whose student numbers are not in the table. Use IN and then NOT..IN, and then use EXISTS and NOT EXISTS. How many students take courses and how many students do not?

     b.   Find out which students have taken courses but have not taken COSC courses. Create a set of student names and courses from the Student, Grade_report and Section tables (use the prefix COSC to indicate computer science courses). Then, use NOT..IN to "subtract" from that set another set of student names of students (who take courses) who have taken COSC courses. For this set difference, use NOT..IN.

     c.   Change NOT..IN to NOT EXISTS (with other appropriate changes) and explain the result. The "other appropriate changes" include adding the correlation and the change of the result attribute in the subquery set.

5.   There exists a table called Plants. List the table and then find out what company or companies have plants in all cities. Verify your

result manually. Note: if you are having trouble finding Plants, ask yourself who owns the table, Plants?

6.   a.   Run the following query and print the result:

```
SELECT  distinct name, langu
FROM    Cap x
WHERE NOT EXISTS
        (SELECT 'X'
        FROM Cap y
        WHERE NOT EXISTS
                (SELECT 'X'
                FROM Cap z
                WHERE X.langu=Z.langu
                AND Y.name=Z.name));
```

Save the query (e.g., save forall) and hand in the result.

   b.   Re-create the Cap table under your account number (e.g., call it some other name, such as LANG1). To do this, first create the table and then use the INSERT statement with the subselect option (INSERT INTO LANG1 AS SELECT * FROM Cap;).

   c.   Add a new person to your table who speaks only Bengali.

   d.   Recall your SELECT from above (get forall).

   e.   CHANGE the table from Cap to LANG1 (for all occurrences, use CHANGE/Cap/lang1/ repeatedly, assuming that you called your table LANG1).

   f.   Start the new query (the one you just created with LANG1 in it).

   g.   How is this result different from the situation in which Newperson was not in LANG1? Provide an explanation of why the query did what it did.

7.   The Department_to_major table is a list of four-letter department codes with the department names. In Chapter 8, Exercise 7 (hereafter referred to as Exercise 8-7), you created a table called Secretary, which should now have data like this:

Secretary	
dCode	name
ACCT	Beryl
COSC	Kaitlyn
ENGL	David
HIST	Christina
BENG	Fred
HINDI	Chloe
Null	Brenda

In Exercise 8-7, you did the following:

a. Create a query that lists the names of departments that have secretaries (use IN and the Secretary table in a subquery). Save this query as q87a.

b. Create a query that lists the names of departments that do not have secretaries (use NOT..IN). Save this query as q87b.

c. Add one more row to the Secretary table that contains <null,'Brenda'>. (This could be a situation in which you have hired Brenda but have not yet assigned her to a department.)

d. Recall q87a and rerun it.

e. Recall q87b and rerun it.

We remarked in Exercise 8-7 that the NOT..IN predicate has problems with nulls: The behavior of NOT..IN when nulls exist may surprise you. If nulls may exist in the subquery, then NOT..IN should not be used. If you use NOT..IN in a subquery, you must ensure that nulls will not occur in the subquery or you must use some other predicate, such as NOT EXISTS. Perhaps the best advice is to avoid NOT..IN.

8. Here, we repeat Exercise 8-7 using NOT EXISTS:

a. Reword query q87a to use EXISTS. You will have to correlate the inner and outer queries. Save this query as q8_7aa.

b. Reword query q87b to use NOT EXISTS. You will have to correlate the inner and outer queries. Save this query as q8_7bb. You should *not* have a phrase "IS NOT NULL" in your NOT EXISTS query.

c. Rerun q87a with and without <null, Brenda>.

d. Rerun q87b with and without <null, Brenda>.

Note the difference in behavior versus the original question. List the names of those departments that have/do not have secretaries. The point here is to encourage you to use NOT EXISTS in a correlated sub-query rather than NOT..IN.

Indexes and Constraints on Tables

Topics covered in this chapter

In previous chapters, we concentrated primarily on retrieving information from existing tables. This chapter revisits the creation of tables, but now focuses on how indexes and constraints can be added to tables to make the tables more efficient and to increase the integrity of the data in the tables (and hence in the database).

An ***index*** speeds up queries and searches on the indexed fields and facilitates sorting and grouping operations. However, an index slows down updates on indexed fields, because the index may have to be rebuilt. A ***constraint*** is similar to an index, but a constraint can also be used to establish relationships with other tables. The CONSTRAINT clause can be used with the CREATE TABLE and the ALTER TABLE statements to create or delete constraints, respectively.

The "Simple" CREATE TABLE

You have seen a "simple" CREATE TABLE statement in earlier chapters. To refresh your memory, here is an example:

```
CREATE TABLE Test1
   (name          VARCHAR(20),
    ssn           CHAR(9),
    dept_number   INTEGER,
    acct_balance  CURRENCY);
```

In this example, we created a table called `Test1`. The following are the elements of the query:

• `name` is a variable-length character string with maximum length of 20.

• `ssn` (social security number) is a fixed-length character string of length 9.

• `dept_number` is an integer (which in Access simply means no decimals allowed.)

• `acct_balance` is a currency field.

Beyond choosing data types for fields in tables, you may need to make other choices to create an effective database. You can create indexes on tables, which then can be used to enforce certain validation rules. You also can use other "add-ons" called CONSTRAINTs, which make you enter *good* data and hence maintain the integrity of a database. In the following sections, we will explore indexes and then constraints.

Indexes

Access allows you to create several indexes on one table, and each index can have up to 10 fields. All indexes will automatically get dropped (deleted) if the table is deleted. We will begin by introducing the "simple" CREATE INDEX statement.

The "Simple" CREATE INDEX

The CREATE INDEX statement is used to create a new index on some field in an existing table. The following is the general syntax for the CREATE INDEX statement:

```
CREATE INDEX index_name
ON Tablename (field [ASC | DESC]);
```

For example, if we wanted to create an index called `ssn_ndx` on `ssn` in descending order for the `Test1` table, we would type the following:

```
CREATE INDEX ssn_ndx
ON Test1 (ssn DESC);
```

Although the user has the option of setting the field in ascending (ASC) or descending (DESC) order, if DESC is not included, the index will be created in ascending order, because ASC is the default. The value of the **Indexed** option, shown in Figure 11.1, is **Yes**, showing that the field, `ssn`, is now indexed. The "(Duplicates OK)" following **Yes** means that duplicates will be allowed in this indexed field (the `ssn` field).

To prevent duplicate values in indexed fields, you must use the UNIQUE option in the CREATE INDEX statement, as follows:

```
CREATE UNIQUE INDEX ssn_ndx1
ON Test1 (ssn DESC);
```

If the UNIQUE keyword is added, the **Indexed** option will say "No Duplicates." Note in the preceding statement that we created a new index called `ssn_ndx1`, instead of using the previously created one, `ssn_ndx`. The reason is that we cannot modify a pre-existing index using SQL in Access. Later in this chapter, we will discuss how to modify an existing index, in the section "Viewing and Modifying Indexes." Indexes can only be modified through the graphical interface of Access.

The UNIQUE option can also be used on fields that will not be a primary key in a table. UNIQUE will disallow duplicate entries for an attribute even though the attribute is not a primary key in a table.

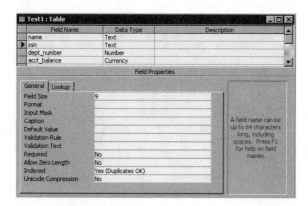

FIGURE 11.1 Indexing a Table

The CREATE INDEX with Options

Several other options are available with the CREATE INDEX command, including a WITH clause that can be used to enforce certain validation rules. The general format for the WITH clause in the CREATE INDEX is as follows:

```
CREATE [UNIQUE] INDEX index_name
ON Tablename (field ASC | DESC)
[WITH { DISALLOW NULL | IGNORE NULL | PRIMARY} ] ;
```

The DISALLOW NULL option prevents null entries in the indexed fields of newly inserted records. The IGNORE NULL option prevents records with null values in the indexed fields from being included in the index. The PRIMARY option designates the indexed field as the primary key.

`Test1` presently does not have a primary key. If we want to make `ssn` the primary key of `Test1` (which means that there will be no duplicates on the `ssn` field), we could type the following:

```
CREATE INDEX ssn_ndx2
ON Test1 (ssn DESC) WITH PRIMARY;
```

As shown in Figure 11.2, the **Indexed** option now indicates "No Duplicates," because `ssn` is now the primary key. Also note the primary key icon beside the `ssn` field, showing that `ssn` has become the primary key.

The UNIQUE property is implied in the creation of an index with a primary key, because the primary key field must always be unique.

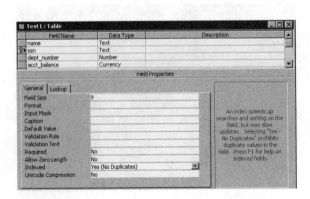

FIGURE 11.2 Index with Primary Key

If we want to create another index, ssn_ndx3, which will disallow nulls in the name field of Test1, we could type the following:

```
CREATE INDEX ssn_ndx3
ON Test1 (name ) WITH DISALLOW NULL;
```

The execution of this statement will create an index on name and disallow nulls in the name field of Test1, although the name field is not a primary key.

Viewing and Modifying Indexes

To view or modify indexes that you have created for a particular table, open the table in **Design** view (the view shown in Figure 11.2) and click the **Indexes** button, as shown in Figure 11.3. This shows all the indexes that have been created so far for the table Test1. You may now also modify the indexes on this screen as you wish.

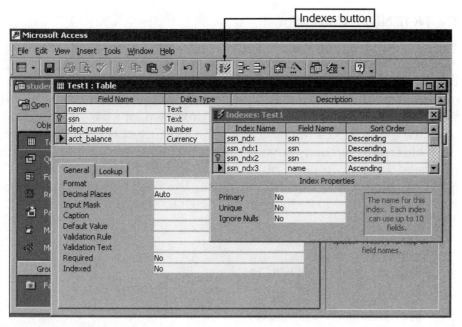

FIGURE 11.3 Viewing Indexes

DROP INDEX

Occasionally, you will want to delete an index and create a new one. You can use a DROP INDEX statement to delete an index. The general format of the DROP INDEX statement is as follows:

```
DROP INDEX index_name
ON Tablename;
```

For example, to delete the index, ssn_ndx1, created on Test1, you would type the following:

```
DROP INDEX ssn_ndx1
ON Test1;
```

Constraints

In addition to indexes, constraints can be added to tables to give them more integrity. In this section, we discuss the constraints available in SQL in Access: the NOT NULL constraint, PRIMARY KEY constraint, UNIQUE constraint, and a few referential constraints.

The NOT NULL Constraint

The NOT NULL option is an integrity constraint that allows the database creator to deny the creation of a row where an attribute would have a null value. Usually, a null signifies a missing data item. As discussed in previous chapters, nulls in databases present an interpretation problem—do they mean not applicable, not available, unknown, or what? If a situation in which a null is present could affect the integrity of the database, then the table creator can deny anyone the ability to insert nulls into the table for that attribute. To deny nulls, we can create a table with the NOT NULL constraint on an attribute(s) after the data type. The following example shows how to include the NOT NULL constraint using a CREATE TABLE statement:

```
CREATE TABLE Test2
  (name          VARCHAR(20),
   ssn           CHAR(9),
   dept_number   INTEGER NOT NULL,
   acct_balance  CURRENCY);
```

In this newly created table, Test2, the dept_number attribute now has a NOT NULL constraint included. As shown in Figure 11.4, the **Design** view of Test2 now has **Yes** for the **Required** option, which means that the dept_number field *cannot* be null (although the dept_number is not a primary key of the table).

The NOT NULL constraint can also be added to the attribute after the table has been created, by using the ALTER TABLE command. For example, suppose we create Test2 as follows:

```
CREATE TABLE Test2
   (name           VARCHAR(20),
    ssn            CHAR(9),
    dept_number    INTEGER,
    acct_balance   CURRENCY);
```

Now, we want to add a NOT NULL constraint after the table has been created. To do so, we must use the ALTER COLUMN option within the ALTER TABLE statement. The following is the general syntax for the ALTER COLUMN option within the ALTER TABLE statement:

```
ALTER TABLE Tablename
ALTER COLUMN column_name column_type(size) NOT NULL;
```

So, to set the dept_number field in Test2 to NOT NULL, we would type the following:

```
ALTER table Test2
ALTER COLUMN dept_number INTEGER NOT NULL;
```

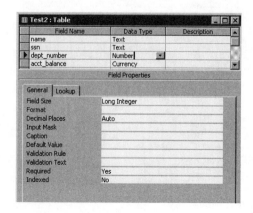

FIGURE 11.4 Design of Test2

You need to understand the following three things about the ALTER COLUMN extension of the ALTER TABLE statement:

• The column type and size must *always* be typed after the column name. For example, the following statement will cause Access to announce a syntax error, "Syntax error in field definition":

```
ALTER TABLE Test2
ALTER COLUMN name NOT NULL;
```

• If you type only the column type, without the column size, the column size will reset to the default maximum size. For example, if you type the following statement, the size of the name field will become 255 characters (as shown Figure 11.5), because the maximum size of a VARCHAR field is 255 characters:

```
ALTER TABLE Test2
ALTER COLUMN name TEXT NOT NULL;
```

> Oracle behaves a little differently here. Oracle will *not* allow a NOT NULL constraint on a column that already has a null value.

• If a null already exists in the column that you are trying to put a NOT NULL constraint on, Access (surprisingly) will not disallow the ALTER COLUMN command. After including the NOT NULL constraint with the ALTER TABLE command, Access will not allow you to include any new NULL values in this field, but it will not worry about the null values that have already been included in this field (prior to adding the NOT NULL constraint).

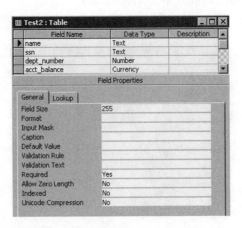

FIGURE 11.5 Field Size of name Field

The PRIMARY KEY Constraint

A PRIMARY KEY constraint will prevent duplicate attribute values for the attribute(s) defined as a primary key. Internally, the designation of a primary key also creates a primary key index. If the primary key for a table is a single field, Access will automatically set the **Indexed** property for that field (No Duplicates) to **Yes**.

Designation of a primary key will be necessary for the referential integrity constraints that follow. The designation of a primary key also automatically puts the NOT NULL constraint in the definition of the attribute(s). A fundamental rule of relational database is that primary keys cannot be null.

There are several ways to define a primary key. You have already seen how to define a primary key by defining an index. Another way to create a primary key is with the CREATE TABLE statement. Here, the PRIMARY KEY constraint is added to the attribute upon creation:

```
CREATE    TABLE xxx
   (ssn    CHAR(9)        CONSTRAINT ssn_pk PRIMARY KEY,
    name   VARCHAR2(20),  etc.
```

Here, `ssn_pk` is the name of the PRIMARY KEY constraint for `ssn`. It is conventional to name all constraints (although most people don't bother to name NOT NULL constraints). If you do not give the constraint a name, the system will define one; however, it is much better if you know what the name is (or should be) so that you can manipulate the constraint (for example, when using DROP).

A third way to create a primary key is called the "table format," in which the CREATE TABLE looks like the following:

```
CREATE TABLE xxx
   (ssn                CHAR(9),
    blah blah ... ,
    acct_balance       NUMBER,
    CONSTRAINT ssn_pk PRIMARY KEY (ssn))
```

A fourth way to create a primary key is to add the stipulation of the PRIMARY KEY *post hoc* by using ALTER TABLE. The syntax for the PRIMARY KEY in the ALTER TABLE command would be as follows:

```
ALTER TABLE Tablename
ADD CONSTRAINT constraint_name PRIMARY KEY (field_name(s));
```

So, to make `ssn` a primary key field in `Test2`, we could type the following:

```
ALTER TABLE Test2
ADD CONSTRAINT ssn_pk PRIMARY KEY (ssn);
```

As shown in Figure 11.6, we now see the icon of the primary key in the Design view of `Test2`.

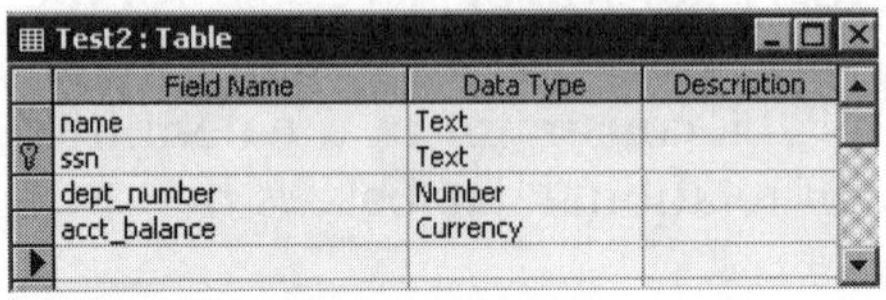

FIGURE 11.6 Primary Key Icon on `ssn` Field

> When more than one attribute makes up a primary key, it is called a *con-catenated* primary key.

The third and fourth ways of adding a primary key are preferable, because you *cannot* directly designate a concatenated primary key with a statement like the following:

```
CREATE TABLE xxx
   (ssn CHAR(9)     PRIMARY KEY,
    salary NUMBER   PRIMARY KEY);
```

However, you can add the primary key in the following way:

```
CREATE TABLE xxx
   (ssn CHAR(9),
    salary NUMBER,
    CONSTRAINT ssn_salary_pk  PRIMARY KEY  (ssn, salary));
```

Or, you can add the primary key in two separate statements, first with a CREATE TABLE

```
CREATE TABLE xxx
   (ssn CHAR(9),
    salary NUMBER);
```

then, with an ALTER TABLE:

```
ALTER TABLE xxx
ADD CONSTRAINT ssn_salary_pk PRIMARY KEY (ssn, salary);
```

This creates two primary keys, as shown in Figure 11.7 by the icons beside both the `ssn` and `salary` fields.

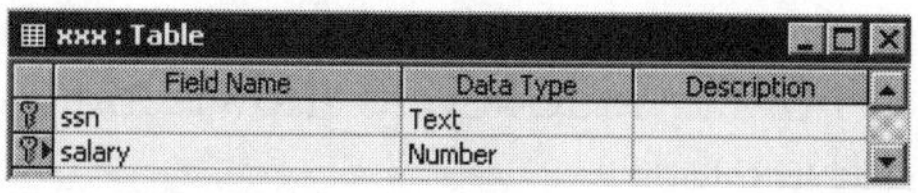

FIGURE 11.7 Two Primary Keys

If, for example, in a new table, Grade1, a grade cannot be determined by either the student_number field or the section_id field alone, and both attributes are required to uniquely identify a grade. The CREATE TABLE and ALTER TABLE sequence for Grade1 is shown next. First we create the Grade1 table:

```
CREATE TABLE Grade1
   (student_number    CHAR(9),
    section_id        CHAR(9),
    grade             CHAR(1));
```

Then we add the primary key as follows:

```
ALTER TABLE Grade1 ADD CONSTRAINT snum_section_pk
      PRIMARY KEY (student_number, section_id);
```

The UNIQUE Constraint

Like PRIMARY KEY, UNIQUE is another attribute integrity constraint. UNIQUE is different from PRIMARY KEY in three ways:

• UNIQUE keys can exist in addition to (or without) the PRIMARY KEY.

• UNIQUE does *not* necessitate NOT NULL, whereas PRIMARY KEY does.

• There can be more than one UNIQUE key, but only one PRIMARY KEY.

As an example of using the UNIQUE constraint, suppose that we created a table of names and occupational titles in which everyone was supposed to have a unique title. Suppose further that the table had an employee number as a primary key. The statement to create the table might look like the following:

```
CREATE TABLE Emp
   (empno      NUMBER,
    name       VARCHAR(20),
    title      VARCHAR(20),
    CONSTRAINT empno_pk   PRIMARY KEY (empno),
    CONSTRAINT title_uk   UNIQUE (title));
```

When a UNIQUE constraint is added, an index will be built for those attributes included in the unique key, as shown in Figure 11.8 (note that the title field is indexed).

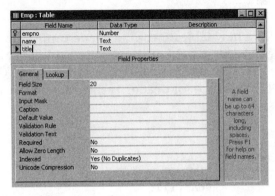

FIGURE 11.8 Using the UNIQUE Constraint

Deleting a Constraint

The following is the general syntax to delete any named constraint:

```
ALTER TABLE Tablename
DROP CONSTRAINT constraint_name;
```

For example, in the xxx table (refer to the earlier section, "The Primary Key Constraint"), we created a constraint called ssn_salary_pk, which made both the ssn and salary fields of the xxx table primary keys. If we want to delete this constraint, which means making both the ssn and salary fields just regular fields (and not primary keys), we would type the following:

```
ALTER TABLE xxx
DROP CONSTRAINT ssn_salary_pk;
```

Now the design of the xxx table would appear as shown in Figure 11.9 (note that the ssn and salary fields do not have the primary key icons next to them any longer).

Referential Integrity Constraints

To define two interrelated tables correctly, we can enforce a referential integrity CONSTRAINT, a foreign key–primary key constraint. A relational database consists of relations (tables) and relationships (foreign

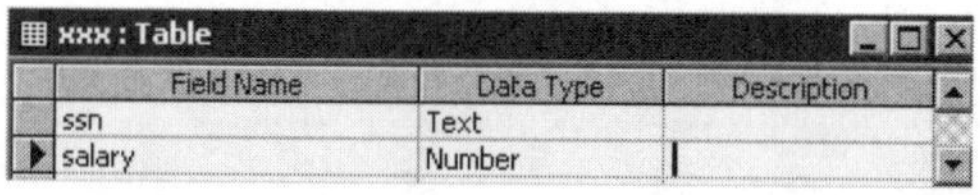

FIGURE 11.9 Primary Keys Deleted

key–primary key constraints). A referential integrity constraint is one in which a row in one table (the foreign key) cannot exist if a value in that table refers to a value in another table (the primary key) that does not exist. For example, suppose we have the following two tables:

Department	
deptno	deptname
1	Accounting
2	Personnel
3	Development

Employee		
empno	empname	dept
100	Jones	2
101	Smith	1
102	Adams	1
104	Harris	3

> A foreign key is an attribute in one table that is used to link that table to another table in which that attribute is a primary key. Relationships are implemented in relational databases through the foreign keys.

To maintain referential integrity, it would be inappropriate to enter a row (tuple) in the Employee table that did not have an existing department number already defined in the Department table. To try to insert the following row into the Employee table would be a violation of the integrity of the database, because department number 4 does not exist (that is, it has no integrity):

<105,'Walsh',4>

Likewise, it would be invalid to try to change a value in an existing row (that is, perform an UPDATE) to make it equal to a value that does not exist. If, for example, we tried to change

<100,'Jones',2>

to

<100,'Jones',5>

it would be an operation that violates database integrity because there is no department 5.

Finally, it would be invalid to delete a row in the Department table that contains a value for a department number that is already in the Employee table. For example, if

<2,'Personnel'>

were deleted from the Department table, then the row

<100,'Jones',2>

would refer to a nonexistent department. It would be a reference or relationship with no integrity.

In each case (INSERT, UPDATE, and DELETE), we say that there needs to be a referential integrity constraint on the dept attribute in the Employee table referencing deptno in the Department table. When this primary key (deptno in the Department table)–foreign key (dept in the Employee table) is defined, we have defined the relationship of the Employee table to the Department table.

> The DELETE CASCADE option is not available in Access.

In the INSERT and UPDATE cases from earlier, you would expect (correctly) that the usual action of the system would be to deny the action. In the case of the DELETE, there are options available in other versions of SQL (for example, Oracle) that will allow us to disallow (RESTRICT) the DELETE.

Defining the Referential Integrity Constraint

To enable a referential integrity constraint, it is necessary for the attribute that is being referenced to be first defined as a primary key. In the preceding Employee-Department example, we have to first create the Department table with a primary key. The CREATE TABLE statement for the Department table (the *referenced* table) could look like this:

```
CREATE TABLE  Department
  (deptno      NUMBER,
   deptname    VARCHAR(20),
   CONSTRAINT  deptno_pk    PRIMARY KEY (deptno));
```

The Employee table (the *referencing* table containing the foreign key) would then be created using this statement:

```
CREATE TABLE Employee
  (empno      NUMBER       CONSTRAINT  empno_pk PRIMARY KEY,
   empname    VARCHAR(20),
   dept       NUMBER       CONSTRAINT  dept_fk
                          REFERENCES  Department(deptno));
```

The CREATE TABLE Employee ... statement defines an attribute, dept, to be of type NUMBER, but the statement goes further in defining dept to be a *foreign* key that references another table, Department. Again, within the Department table, the referenced attribute, deptno, has to be an already defined primary key.

Also note that the Department table has to be created first. If we tried to create the Employee table before the Department table with the referential constraint, we would be trying to reference a nonexistent table and this would also cause an error.

Adding the Foreign Key After Tables Are Created

As we have seen with other constraints, the foreign key can be added after tables are created. To do so, we must first have set up the primary key of the referenced table. The syntax of the ALTER TABLE command would look like this:

```
ALTER TABLE xxx
  ADD CONSTRAINT dept_fk
  FOREIGN KEY (dept)
  REFERENCES Department(deptno);
```

The (optional) name of the constraint is dept_fk. Note that the column names have to match exactly.

CHAPTER 11 REVIEW QUESTIONS

1. What is an index?

2. Why does an index slow down updates on indexed fields?

3. What is a constraint?

4. How many indexes does Access allow you to have on a table?

5. What command would you use to create an index?

6. What is the default ordering that will be created by an index (ascending or descending)?

7. When can the UNIQUE option be used?

8. What does the IGNORE NULL option do?

9. How do you delete an index?

10. What does the NOT NULL constraint do?

11. What command must you use to include the NOT NULL constraint after a table has already been created?

12. When a PRIMARY KEY constraint is included in a table, what other constraints does this imply?

13. What is a concatenated primary key?

14. How are the UNIQUE and PRIMARY KEY constraints different?

15. What is a referential integrity constraint? What two keys does the referential integrity constraint usually include?

16. What is a foreign key?

CHAPTER 11 EXERCISES

Note: Unless otherwise directed, name all constraints except NOT NULL.

1. To test choices of data types, create a table with various types like this:

```
CREATE TABLE Test3
  (name          VARCHAR(20),
   ssn           CHAR(9),
   dept_number   INTEGER,
   acct_balance  NUMBER);
```

Then, insert values into the table to see what will and will not be accepted. The following data may or may not be acceptable. You are welcome to try other choices.

'xx','yy',2,5
'xx','yyy',2000000000,5
'xx','yyyy',2,1234567.89

2. a. Create an index of ssn in ascending order of ssn. Try to insert some new data in the ssn field. Does your ssn field take nulls?

    b. Does your ssn field take duplicates? If so, how can you prevent this field from taking duplicates?

c. Include the DISALLOW NULL option in your index by modifying your index (by going to the screen shown in Figure 11.3). Now try to insert some new data in the ssn field with nulls in the ssn field. What happens?

d. Create a new index using the `ssn` field (in ascending order) using the IGNORE NULL option. Now try to insert some new data in the `ssn` field with nulls. What happens?

e. In the index that has DISALLOW NULL (created in part 2c), is it necessary to include the PRIMARY KEY option? Why or why not? Now include the PRIMARY KEY option to this index and see if there is any difference in the types of values it accepts.

f. Include some data with null values in the `dept_number` and `acct_balance` fields. Now create an index with the option of DISALLOW NULL in the `dept_number` field. What happens?

g. Create another index with the option of IGNORE NULL in the `acct_balance` field. What happens?

Delete your indexes and delete `Test3`.

3. To test the errors generated when NOT NULL is used, create a table called `Test4`, which looks like this:

```
CREATE TABLE Test4
  (a  CHAR(2)   NOT NULL,
   b  CHAR(3));
```

Input some data and try to enter a null value for A. Acceptable input data for a null is "null."

4. a. Create or re-create, if necessary, `Test3`, which does not specify a primary key. Populate the table with at least one duplicate `ssn`. Then, try to impose the PRIMARY KEY constraint with an ALTER TABLE command. What happens?

b. Re-create the `Test3` table, but this time add a primary key of `ssn`. If you still have the `Test3` table from Exercise 4a, you may be able to delete *offending* rows and add the PRIMARY KEY constraint. Enter two more rows to your table—one containing a new `ssn` and one with a duplicate `ssn`. What happens?

5. Create the `Department` and `Employee` tables, as per the examples earlier in the chapter, with all the constraints (PRIMARY KEYs, referential and UNIQUE constraints). You can add the constraints at create time or you can use ALTER TABLE to add the constraints. Populate the `Department` table first with departments 1, 2, and 3. Then populate the `Employee` table.

Note: Before doing the next few exercises, it is prudent to create two tables, called Deptbak and Empbak, to contain the data you loaded, because you will be deleting, inserting, dropping, re-creating, and so on. You can create Deptbak and Empbak tables with the data we have been using with a command like the following:

```
CREATE TABLE Deptbak AS
SELECT *
FROM Dept;
```

Then, when you have added, deleted, updated, and so on, and you want the original table from the start of this problem, you simply run the following commands:

```
DROP TABLE Dept;
CREATE TABLE Dept AS
SELECT *
FROM  Deptbak;
```

    a. Create a violation of insertion integrity by adding an employee to a nonexistent department. What happens?

    b. Create an UPDATE violation by trying to change an existing employee to a nonexistent department, and then by trying to change a referenced department number.

    c. Try to delete a department for which there is an employee. What happens? What happens if you try to DELETE a department to which no employee has yet been assigned?

6. Create a table (your choice) with a PRIMARY KEY and a UNIQUE constraint. Insert data into the table and, as you enter data, enter a *good* row and a *bad* row (the *bad* row violates a constraint). Demonstrate a violation of each of your constraints one at a time. Show the successes and the errors as you receive them.

The Student Database and Other Tables Used in This Book

The Student Database

```
Student
    stno   NOT NULL     NUMBER(3)     PRIMARY KEY NOT NULL
    sname               VARCHAR2(20)
    major               CHAR(4)
    class               NUMBER(1)
    bdate               DATE

Grade_report
    student_number      NOT NULL      NUMBER(3)
    section_id          NOT NULL      NUMBER(6)
    grade               CHAR(1)
    PRIMARY KEY(student_number, section_id)

Section
    section_id   NOT NULL     NUMBER(6)  PRIMARY KEY NOT NULL
    course_num                CHAR(8)
    semester                  VARCHAR2(6)
    year                      CHAR(2)
    instructor                CHAR(10)
    bldg                      NUMBER(3)
    room                      NUMBER(3)

Department_to_major
    dcode  NOT NULL     CHAR(4)              PRIMARY KEY NOT NULL
    dname               CHAR(20)
```

```
Course
    course_name                        CHAR(20)
    course_number     NOT NULL         CHAR(8)        PRIMARY KEY NOT NULL
    credit_hours                       NUMBER(2)
    offering_dept                      CHAR(4)

Room
    bldg           NOT NULL            NUMBER(3)
    room           NOT NULL            NUMBER(3)
    capacity                           NUMBER(4)
    ohead                              CHAR(1)
    PRIMARY KEY(bldg, room)

Prereq
    course_number              CHAR(8)
    prerequ                    CHAR(8)
    PRIMARY KEY (course_number, prereq)
```

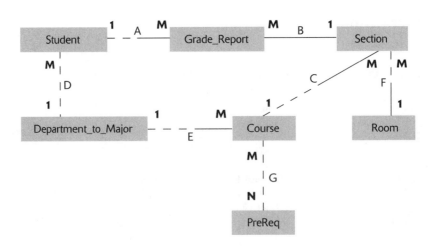

A.   A Student MAY be registered in one or more (M) `Grade_Reports`
     (Grade_report is for a specific course).

     A `Grade_Report` MUST relate to one and only one (1) `Student`.

     (Students may be in the database and not registered for any courses,
     but if a course is recorded in the `Grade_report` table, it must be
     related to one and only one student).

B.   A `Section` MUST have one or more (M) `Grade_Reports` (Sections
     only exist if they have students in them).

     A `Grade_Report` MUST relate to one and only one (1) `Section`.

C.   A Section MUST relate to one and only one (1) Course.

A Course MAY be offered as one or more (M) Sections.

(Courses may exist where they are not offered in a section, but a section, if offered, must relate to one and only one course).

D.   A Student MAY be related to one and only one (1) Department_to_major (A student may or may not have declared a major).

A Department_to_major may have one or more (M) Students (A department may or may not have student-majors).

E.   A Course MUST be related to one and only one (1) Department_to_major.

A Department_to_major MAY offer one or more (M) Courses.

F.   A Section MUST be offered in one and only one (1) Room.

A Room MAY host one or more (M) Sections.

G.   A Course MAY have one or more (M) Prereq (A course may have one or more prerequisites).

A Prereq MAY be a prerequisite for one or more (M) Courses.

Other Tables That Have Been Used in This Book

```
Plants
    company      VARCHAR2(20)
    plantlo      VARCHAR2(15)
    PRIMARY KEY(company, plantlo)

Cap
    name   VARCHAR2(9)
    langu  VARCHAR2(7)
    primary KEY(name, langu)
```

Glossary of Terms

Aggregate Function A function that returns a result based on multiple rows.

Alias A temporary substitute for a name. There can be table aliases and column aliases.

Alphanumeric A data type that will accept a combination of characters and numbers.

Anomaly An undesirable consequence of a data modification.

Attribute Column in a table or relation.

Binary Intersection A set operation on two sets that generates unique values in common between the two sets.

Binary Set Difference A set operation on two sets that generates values in one set less those contained in another.

Binary Union A set operation on two sets that generates all unique elements of both sets.

Candidate Key An attribute (or group of attributes) that identifies a unique row in a relation. One of the candidate keys is chosen to be the primary key.

Cardinality In a binary relationship, cardinality specifies the minimum and maximum number of relationship instances that an entity can participate in.

Cartesian Product A relational operation on two relations, R and S, producing a third relation T, with T containing the combination of every row in R with every row in S.

CHAR(*size*) Data type that gives fixed-length character data, *size* characters long.

Columns Attributes of a table. Columns hold the same kind of values.

Column Alias A temporary column name.

Correlated Subquery A subquery in which the information in the subquery is referenced by the outer, main query. A correlated subquery cannot stand alone; it depends on the outer query.

Data Facts concerning entities such as people, objects, or events.

Database A shared collection of logically associated or related data.

Database Administrator (DBA) *See* DBA.

DATE Data type that is used for date and time data.

DBA (Database Administrator) Person who has all system privileges and the ability to grant all privileges to other users. The DBA creates and drops users and space.

DDL (Data Definition Language) Used by the DBA and database designers to define the internal schema and conceptual schema.

DML (Data Manipulation Language) Enables users to manipulate (INSERT, UPDATE, and DELETE) data.

Domain The set of all possible values that an attribute can have.

Entity "Something" in the real world that is of importance to a user and that needs to be represented in a database. An entity may have physical existence (such as a student or building) or conceptual existence (such as a course).

Entity Integrity Constraint A constraint that states that no key value can be null.

Entity Set The collection of all entities of a particular entity type in a database.

Entity Type A collection of entities that have the same attributes.

Equi-join A join condition with equality comparisons only.

File A collection of logically related records.

First Normal Form (1NF) Where the domain of an attribute must include only atomic (simple, indivisible) values and the value of any attribute in a row (or tuple) must be a single value from the domain of that attribute.

Foreign Account An account that you do not own.

Foreign Key An attribute that is a primary key of another relation (table). A foreign key is how relationships are implemented in relational databases.

Float A data type that accepts numbers with decimals (this data type is rarely used).

Full Outer Join Used to designate the union of the left and right outer joins.

Functionally Dependent A relationship between two attributes in a relation. Attribute Y is functionally dependent on attribute X if attribute X identifies attribute Y.

Group Function A function that returns a result based on multiple rows. Also known as an aggregate function.

Hierarchical Database A data model that represents all relationships using hierarchical trees, where a record represents a node of a tree and all relationships in the tree are represented by a parent-child relationship type. Each record in a hierarchical model may have several offspring but only one parent record.

Hierarchical Model A data model in which all the data is logically arranged in a hierarchical fashion (also known as a parent-child relationship).

Inline View A view that exists only during the execution of a query.

Integer A data type that accepts only whole numbers and no decimals.

Internal Schema Describes the physical storage structure of the database.

Join Operation used to combine related tuples (rows) from two relations into single tuples (rows) based on a logical comparison of column values.

Key An attribute or data item that uniquely identifies a record instance or tuple in a relation.

Large Object Data Type (LOB) LOBs can store large amounts (up to four gigabytes) of raw data, binary data (such as images), or character text data.

Logical Model Conceptualizing how data will be organized. It can be considered as the mapping of the conceptual model into a processible data model.

Many-to-Many (M:N) Relationship Where many tuples (rows) of one relation can be related to many tuples (rows) in another relation.

Meta-data Data concerning the structure of data in a database is stored in the data dictionary. Meta-data is used to describe tables, columns, constraints, indexes, and so on.

Natural Join An equi-join without the duplicate columns.

Network Database Represents data as record types, where each record type may have relationships of any cardinality with any other record type in that network.

Network Model A data model in which you are not restricted to having one parent per child. Many-to-one (M:1) and many-to-many (M:N) relationships are acceptable.

Noncorrelated Subquery A subquery that is independent of the outer query.

Normal Forms The process of decomposing complex data structures into simple relations according to a set of dependency rules.

One-to-Many (1:M) Relationship Where one tuple (or row) of one relation can be related to more than one tuple (or row) in another relation.

One-to-One (1:1) Relationship Where one tuple (or row) of one relation can be related to only one tuple (row) in another relation.

Optionality A constraint that specifies whether the existence of an entity depends on its being related to another entity via a relationship type (also known as participation).

Outer Join A join condition where all the rows from one table (for example, the first table) are kept in the result set even though those rows do not have matching rows in the other table (the second table).

Physical Model A representation of the form and details of how data is stored in the computer.

Primary Key A candidate key selected to be the key of a relation. The primary key will uniquely identify a row or tuple in a relation or table.

Qualifier A prefix used to identify the owner of a table or a particular attribute of a table. For example, in `rearp.Student`, `rearp` is the qualifier for the table `Student`.

Query A SQL instruction to retrieve data from one or more tables or views. Queries begin with the SQL keyword SELECT.

Record A named collection of data items. In a relational model, a record is a physical realization of a row and tuple.

Recursive Relationship Relationship among entities in the same class.

Redundancy Storing the same data multiple times.

Referential Integrity The property that guarantees that values from one column that depend on values from another column are present in the "other column."

Relation A two-dimensional array containing single-value entries and no duplicate rows. The meaning of the columns is the same in every row, and the order of the rows and columns is immaterial. Often a relation is defined as a populated table. *See also* Table.

Relational Algebra A data manipulation language that provides a set of operators for manipulating relations.

Relational Database A database consisting of relations. A relational database is structured according to the principles of normalization.

Relational Model A logical data model in which all data is represented as a collection of normalized relations.

Relational Select A conditional relational algebra operation performed on a relation, R, producing a relation, S, with S containing only the rows in R that meet the restrictions specified in the condition.

Relationship An association between two entities.

Result Set Output of a SQL statement.

Row A group of columns in a table. All the columns in a row pertain to the same entity. A row is the same as a tuple.

Row Filter A command that is used to select rows based on certain criteria.

Row Function A function that is performed on every single row of a table.

Second Normal Form (2NF) A relation that is in first normal form and in which each nonkey attribute is fully functionally dependent on the primary key.

Self Join A join condition where a table is joined with itself.

Set A data structure that represents a collection of values with no order and no duplicate values.

Set Compatibility For two sets (or tables) to be set compatible, both sets must match in number of items and must have compatible data types. Set compatibility is also referred to as union compatibility.

Software Engineering A discipline that aims at production of fault-free software that satisfies the user's needs.

Spool Copying information from one place to another.

Spurious Tuples Tuples (rows) generated as a result of a join of tables that were decomposed incorrectly.

SQL (Structured Query Language) A language for defining the structure and processing of a relational database.

SQL statements Used to issue commands to a database.

String A mixture of letters, numbers, spaces, and other symbols.

String Function A function used to manipulate string data.

Structural Constraint Indicates how many of one type of a record are related to another of record and whether the record must have such a relationship. The cardinality ratio and participation constraints taken together form the structural constraints.

Subquery The inner query within the outer (main) query; usually one SELECT query within another SELECT query.

Subset Some group of objects taken from a set.

System Privileges Privileges that allow the user to execute specific sets of commands.

Table Consists of one or more rows of information, each of which contains the same kind of values (columns). It is also referred to as a relation in the relational model.

Table Alias A temporary name given to a table.

Table Qualifiers A table qualifier precedes a field name whenever two fields have the same name in two different tables and both fields are being used in the same query.

Temporary Table A derived structure or table in which the result of a SELECT can be intermediarily saved and then used in another SELECT.

Theta Join A join with one of the following comparison operators: =, <, <=, >, >=, and not =.

Third Normal Form (3NF) A relation that is in second normal form and in which no nonkey attribute is functionally dependent on another nonkey attribute (that is, there are no transitive dependencies in the relation).

Tuple Rows in a table or relation.

Union Compatibility When working with sets (tables), for two sets to have union compatibility, both sets must match in number of items and must have compatible data types.

View A query that is stored in the data dictionary and is resolved when accessed by a user or some other process.

Waterfall Model A series of steps that software undergoes, from concept exploration through final retirement.

Glossary of Important Commands and Functions

ABS SQL function for absolute value.

ALPHANUMERIC Data type; synonym for CHAR data type.

ALTER COLUMN SQL command that allows a user to change a column's size or type in a table.

ALTER TABLE SQL command that allows a user to add to or modify a table.

AND A logical operator used in SQL statements.

ASC SQL function that is used to put a SQL result set into ascending order.

AVG SQL function that averages a group of attributes.

BETWEEN An operator that allows for an optional way to combine comparisons in a WHERE clause.

BINARY Data type that can store data of any type.

BIT Data type used for fields that store only one of two values.

BOOLEAN Data type; synonym for BIT data type.

BYTE Data type; synonym for TINYINT data type.

CHAR(*size*) Data type used to store text and numbers.

CHARACTER Data type; synonym for CHAR data type.

CHARACTER VARYING Data type; synonym for CHAR data type.

CONSTRAINTS Restrictions that can be placed when creating database objects such as tables and views.

COSC Row-level SQL function used to find the cosine of a number.

COUNT(*) SQL function that counts the total number of rows in a table.

COUNT(*attribute*) SQL group function that counts the number of rows where *attribute* is not NULL.

CREATE INDEX SQL command that creates an index.

CREATE TABLE SQL command that creates a table.

CURRENCY Data type; synonym for MONEY data type.

DATE Data type; synonym for DATETIME data type.

DATETIME Data type used to include data and time values between the years A.D. 100 and A.D. 9999.

DAY Date function that extracts a day from a date.

DEC Data type; synonym for DECIMAL data type.

DECIMAL Data type that is an exact numeric data type.

DELETE SQL command that deletes all rows in a table that satisfy a particular condition.

DESC SQL function that is used to put a SQL result set into descending order.

DISTINCT SQL function that shows unique values that are selected with the DISTINCT(*attribute_name*). DISTINCT also makes group functions summarize unique values.

DISTINCTROW SQL function that omits rows based on entire duplicate records, not just duplicate fields.

DOUBLE Data type; synonym for FLOAT data type.

DROP column_name SQL command that deletes a column in a table.

DROP INDEX SQL command that deletes an index.

DROP TABLE SQL command that deletes a table.

EXISTS SQL operator that returns true in a WHERE clause if the subquery following it returns at least one row.

FIRST SQL function that returns a field value from the first row (tuple) in the result set returned by a query.

FLOAT Data type used for double-precision floating-point values.

FLOAT4 Data type; synonym for REAL data type.

FLOAT8 Data type; synonym for FLOAT data type.

GENERAL Data type; synonym for IMAGE data type.

GROUP BY SQL clause that produces one summary row for all selected rows that have identical values for the attributes specified in the GROUP BY.

HAVING SQL clause used to determine which groups the GROUP BY will include in the result set.

IEEEDOUBLE Data type; synonym for FLOAT data type.

IEEESINGLE Data type; synonym for REAL data type.

IMAGE Data type that is used with OLE objects.

IN A logical operator for a WHERE clause, which tests for inclusion in a named set.

INDEX BY SQL feature that creates an index on a table. The index will be created by the attribute specified in the INDEX BY.

INNER JOIN SQL command used to join two tables.

INSERT INTO..SELECT One way to put values into *one* row of a table.

INSERT INTO..VALUES A way to insert *many* rows into a table at one time.

INSERT SQL command that allows for the addition of new rows to a table or view.

INSTR SQL function that returns the location of a pattern in a given string.

INTEGER Data type that holds numbers.

INTEGER1 Data type; synonym for TINYINT data type.

INTEGER2 Data type; synonym for SMALLINT data type.

INTEGER4 Data type; synonym for INTEGER data type.

LAST SQL function that returns a field value from the last row (tuple) in the result set returned by a query.

LCASE SQL function used to turn output into lowercase.

LEFT SQL row-level function that returns the left portion of a string.

LEFT JOIN A join where all the rows from the first (left) relation are kept.

LEN SQL function that returns the length of a desired string.

LIKE SQL command that matches a particular pattern.

LOGICAL Data type; synonym for BIT data type.

LONG Data type; synonym for INTEGER data type.

LONGBINARY Data type that is equivalent to Oracle's LOB type.

LONGCHAR Data type; synonym for TEXT data type.

LONGTEXT Data type; synonym for TEXT data type.

LTRIM SQL function that stands for "left trim." LTRIM trims (removes) a certain set of characters from the left side of a string.

MAX SQL function that gives the highest of all values from an attribute in a set of rows.

MEMO Data type; synonym for TEXT data type.

MID SQL function that returns the middle portion of a string.

MIN SQL function that gives the lowest of all values from an attribute in a set of rows.

MINUS SQL function that returns only those rows from the result of the first query that are not in the result of the second query.

MONEY Data type used when working with currency data.

MONTH SQL function that extracts the month from a date.

NATIONAL CHARACTER Data type; synonym for CHAR data type.

NCHAR Data type; synonym for CHAR data type.

NOT SQL operator that comes before and reverses the effect of any logical operator like IN, LIKE, and EXISTS.

NOT EXISTS SQL operator that returns false in a WHERE clause if the subquery following it returns at least one row.

NOT NULL SQL operator that is true if an attribute has a non-null value.

NOTE Data type; synonym for TEXT data type.

NOW SQL function that gives the present date and time.

NTEXT Data type; synonym for TEXT data type.

NULL SQL command for value that is unknown.

NUMBER Data type; synonym for FLOAT data type.

NUMERIC Data type; synonym for DECIMAL data type.

NZ SQL function that allows something to be substituted in place of a NULL value.

OLEOBJECT Data type; synonym for IMAGE data type.

OR Logical SQL operator that returns a true value if either one of the expressions is true.

ORDER BY SQL clause that sorts the results of a query before they are displayed.

PERCENT SQL function that is used to return a certain percentage of records that fall at the top of a range specified.

PRIMARY KEY SQL command; a constraint used to create a primary key in a table.

REAL Data type be used for single-precision floating-point values.

REFERENCES A constraint that defines the table name and key used to reference another table.

RIGHT SQL row-level function that returns the right portion of a string.

ROLLBACK SQL command that reverses changes made to tables.

ROUND SQL function used to round numbers off to a certain number of decimal places.

RTRIM SQL function that stands for "right trim." RTRIM trims (removes) a certain set of characters from the right side of a string.

SELECT SQL command that allows you to retrieve rows from tables (or views or snapshots) in a database.

SHORT Data type; synonym for SMALLINT data type.

SIN SQL function that returns the sine of a number.

SINGLE Data type; synonym for REAL data type.

SMALLINT Data type that holds an integer between –32,768 and 32,767.

STDEV SQL function that returns the standard deviation of a number.

STRING Data type; synonym for CHAR data type.

SUM SQL group function that adds up all the values for an attribute in a set of rows.

TAN SQL function that returns the tangent of a number.

TEXT Data type used to store text and numbers.

TIME Data type; synonym for DATETIME data type.

TINYINT Data type used to store integer values between 0 and 255.

TOP SQL function that returns a certain number of records.

UCASE SQL function used to turn output into uppercase letters.

UNION SQL function that combines two queries such that it returns all distinct rows for the result of both queries.

UNION ALL SQL function that combines two queries and returns all rows from both the SELECT statements (queries). A UNION ALL also includes duplicate rows.

UNIQUE Another attribute integrity constraint. UNIQUE disallows duplicate entries for an attribute even though the attribute is not a primary key. UNIQUE does not necessitate NOT NULL like the primary key.

UNIQUEIDENTIFIER Data type that is a unique identification number used with remote procedure calls.

UPDATE SQL command that changes values in specified columns in specified tables.

VARCHAR Data type; synonym for CHAR data type.

WEEKDAY SQL function that extracts the day of a week from a date.

WHERE SQL clause that allows you to specify qualifiers on columns for rows that are being selected from a table. It is a row filter.

YEAR SQL function that extracts the year from a date.

Index of Important Commands and Functions

Index of Important Commands and Functions

Index

A

Access, 22. *See also* databases
accessing views, 171
aggregation, 221
  attributes, 224
  functions, 110–15, 230–34
  GROUP BY clause, 221–27
  HAVING clause, 228–30
  mismatch of, 231
  null values, 238–41
  ORDER BY clause, 225–27
aliases, 49–52
  columns, 173
  table qualifiers, 52–53
  views, 162–63
ALPHANUMERIC command, 59
ALTER TABLE command, 74–76

analysts, 18
AND clause, 44
AND operator, 42
anomaly, 11–12
applying
  inline views, 173–74
  views, 160–61
ascending (ASC) order, 39–40, 277
attributes, 2, 6–7
  aggregation, 224
  class
    GROUP BY clause, 230
    temporary tables, 232–33
  COUNT function, 47–48
  equi-joins, 10
  LIKE function, 137–42
  ohead, 224
auditing
  queries, 216
  subqueries, 234–38
AVG function, 113–14

B

BETWEEN operator, 42, 45–47
binary intersection, 180
binary set difference, 180
BINARY type, 61
binary unions, 180
BIT type, 61
blanks, deleting, 134
Boyce Codd Normal Form (BCNF), 15–17

C

calculations
  AVG function, 113–14
  DATETIME type, 60–61
  FLOAT type, 60
calendars, DATETIME type, 60–61
candidate key, 16
cardinality, 3
Cartesian product, 91–94